Consulting

FOR

DUMMIES®

Consulting FOR DUMMIES®

by Bob Nelson, Peter Economy, and Philip Albon

A John Wiley and Sons, Ltd, Publication

Consulting For Dummies®

Published by John Wiley & Sons, Ltd
The Atrium
Southern Gate
Chichester
West Sussex PO19 8SQ
England

E-mail (for orders and customer service enquires): cs-books@wiley.co.uk

Visit our Home Page on www.wiley.com

For general information on our other products and services, please contact our Customer Care Department within the U.S. at 800-762-2974, outside the U.S. at 317-572-3993, or fax 317-572-4002.

For technical support, please visit www.wiley.com/techsupport. Wiley also publishes its books in a variety of electronic formats. Some content that appears in print may not be available in electronic books.

British Library Cataloguing in Publication Data: A catalogue record for this book is available from the British Library

ISBN: 978-0-470-71382-2

Printed and bound in Great Britain by Bell and Bain

10 9 8 7 6 5 4 3 2 1

With thanks to the Institute of Business Consulting for their kind permission to reproduce an extract from their Code of Ethics.

WILEY

Consulting For Dummies®

Cheat Sheet

Ten Consulting Success Secrets

There are many different ways to become a more effective consultant; however, some work better than others. We've found that if you make the following ten techniques a part of the way you do business, you'll be *way* ahead of your competition:

- **Listen to your clients.** To determine the best solutions for your clients, you must listen to them and understand what they want. Make a point of listening to your clients more than you talk.

- **Quickly establish rapport with your clients.** Consulting is very much a one-to-one, person-to-person kind of business. Establishing rapport with your clients builds a bridge that enables trust to grow.

- **Be direct and honest**. Your clients are employing you because they need help – sometimes a lot of help. You're doing them no favours by sugar-coating any bad news you might have for them. Give them your best assessments and advice at all times.

- **Be flexible and responsive.** Flexibility is one of the main reasons why people hire consultants. You'll have a tremendous advantage over the competition if you can quickly respond to customer needs as they present themselves.

- **Don't overprice your services.** The higher your price, the less demand there will be for your services. That might be fine if you can survive with a relatively few, high-paying jobs. However, if your prices are significantly higher than the competition, be prepared to explain the additional value you bring to the table.

- **Don't underprice your services.** If your price is too low, you may find it difficult to make a profit. Don't be a 'busy fool' and remember – no client will ever tell you that you should charge a higher rate!

- **Have more than one primary client.** It's never a good idea to trust the success of your business to just one or two clients. Secure a number of clients in a variety of fields instead of just one or two.

- **Accept as much work as you can without compromising quality.** Small jobs may lead to big jobs. Avoid turning down new work unless doing so will cause the quality of your current work to suffer.

- **Treat your current clients like gold.** Not only do your current clients pay your bills, but they're your best source for referrals to new clients. Don't forget that your most important clients are your *current* clients.

- **Constantly market to bring in future business.** Although your current clients are most important, you need a constant stream of future clients to keep your consulting business afloat. Set aside about one-third of your time prospecting for new clients.

Doing the Right Thing

Every consultant relies on relationships with clients, and these relationships are built on a strong foundation of trust. Building trust with your clients means doing the right thing, including:

- Account for your time accurately and honestly.
- Don't make promises that you can't keep.
- Don't recommend products or services that your clients don't need.
- Be candid and give your honest opinion.
- Protect your clients' confidentiality.
- Follow through on your promises.
- Disclose conflicts of interest.
- Don't use inside information to your advantage.
- Don't break the law.

Head to Chapter 5 for more detailed information about ethics and you.

For Dummies: Bestselling Book Series for Beginners

Consulting For Dummies®

Cheat Sheet

Tips for Building an Effective Website

It's the rare consulting business (or business of any sort, for that matter) that doesn't have a website. The problem is, if your website isn't attractive, professional, up to date, and able to be easily navigated by your prospective clients, then you're wasting both time and money – and losing business. Here are seven tried-and-true tips for building a website that will keep your clients coming back for more:

- **Consider hiring a pro.** Remember that first impressions are important. Your website may be the first impression a potential client has of your business. By hiring a pro to design and build it, you'll have a better chance of making the first impression a good one.

- **Be easy to find.** Make sure your website address (URL) closely matches the name of your business or is linked to it in some way.

- **Get out the word.** Be sure to include your website address wherever you can, including on your letterhead and business cards, marketing brochures, within your email signature, on the side of your car – anywhere a potential client might see it.

- **Capture contact information.** Encourage visitors to leave their contact information so you can open up a dialogue with them. Provide them with a free subscription to a useful monthly newsletter in exchange for their email address.

- **Give clients a reason to visit.** Your website needs to contain information that will be of value to clients and that will entice them to visit your site on a regular basis. This information might include articles, links to other websites, and blogs,

- **Visit your site regularly and check web stats.** Check your site regularly to make sure it's running smoothly, and that all links and interactive elements are working the way they should. And be sure to monitor your web stats so you know who's visiting, and what pages they find of greatest interest.

- **Consider blogging.** Think about setting up a current and interactive blog as well as your static website. Blogs are easy to set up and maintain. Before you set up a web presence, research what other consultants in your field are doing, and be sure to take your findings into account.

Building Business with Your Current Clients

It's easy to throw a *lot* of money at marketing your business while forgetting your best and most reliable source of new business: your current clients. An effective marketing campaign starts with making sure that your current clients are your biggest fans and supporters. Here are some proven techniques for doing so:

- Be on time and within budget.
- Anticipate your clients' needs (and be ready with suggestions to address them).
- Be easy to work with.
- Keep in touch with your clients.
- Be honest and ethical.
- Give a little more than you promise.
- Ask your clients for testimonials and referrals.
- Offer financial incentives for continuing to do business with you.
- Educate your clients about all the services that you offer.
- Do great work.

Chapter 14 has lots more detailed tips about boosting business with current clients.

For Dummies: Bestselling Book Series for Beginners

About the Authors

Bob Nelson is founder and president of Nelson Motivation, Inc., a management training and consulting firm based in San Diego, California. As a manager and a best-selling author, he is an internationally recognised expert in the areas of employee recognition, rewards, motivation, morale, retention, productivity and management. He is author of the bestselling book *1001 Ways to Reward Employees* (Workman), which has sold over 1.5 million copies worldwide, and coauthor of the best-selling book *Managing For Dummies,* with Richard Pettinger and Peter Economy (Wiley), as well as 18 other books on management and motivation. You can visit Bob's website at www.nelson motivation.com.

Peter Economy is a freelance business writer and publishing consultant who is associate editor of the Apex award-winning magazine *Leader to Leader,* and coauthor of the best-selling book *Managing For Dummies* with Richard Pettinger and Bob Nelson (Wiley), as well as the author or coauthor of more than 30 other books on a wide variety of business and other topics. You can visit Peter's website at www.petereconomy.com.

Philip Albon is founder of Techniques for Change, a change and management training consultancy based at London Gatwick Airport. Techniques for Change has worked with people from seven out of the world's top ten companies, over 50 of the FTSE 100 companies and a wide range of public sector clients. In conjunction with the Institute of Business Consulting, Techniques for Change offers both a Certificate and a postgraduate level Diploma in Management Consultancy.

Philip has served on the General Council of the UK Institute of Business Consulting, is a Chartered Fellow of the Chartered Institute of Personnel and Development and holds a Master of Arts in Management Learning from Lancaster University. A highly experienced management consultant, he has delivered practical solutions around the globe for over 20 years.

To find out about the award-winning services of Techniques for Change call 01293 568817 or visit his website www.techniquesforchange.co.uk. Philip's email is Philip@techniquesforchange.co.uk.

Publisher's Acknowledgements

We're proud of this book; please send us your comments through our Dummies online registration form located at www.dummies.com/register/.

Some of the people who helped bring this book to market include the following:

Acquisitions, Editorial, and Media Development

Project Editor: Rachael Chilvers

Content Editor: Jo Theedom

Copy Editor: David Price

Commissioning Editor: Sam Spickernell

Executive Project Editor: Daniel Mersey

Cover Photos: © altrendo images/Getty Images

Cartoons: Ed McLachlan

Composition Services

Project Coordinator: Lynsey Stanford

Layout and Graphics: Reuben W. Davis, Melissa K. Jester, Sarah Philippart, Ronald Terry

Proofreader: Amanda Graham

Indexer: Rebecca Salerno

Contents at a Glance

Table of Contents

xiv Consulting For Dummies _____

The ABCs of Contract Negotiation 228
    Anticipating the negotiation...229
    Basic rules of the negotiation road 230
    Closing a deal 233

Chapter 17: Keeping Track of Your Time and Money 235

Keeping Track of Your Time 235
    The daily client activity log 236
    Client time sheets 238
Invoicing Your Clients and Collecting Your Money 240
    Invoicing for your services 240
    Collecting overdue accounts...242
Building Better Budgets...244
    Budgeting for different parts of the business 245
    Creating a budget...246
    Staying on budget 247

Chapter 18: Communicating Your Way to Success 249

Putting It in Writing...250
    What to put in writing 250
    Two basic consulting reports..251
    Seven steps to better writing 254
Harnessing the Power of the Spoken Word................................256
    Understanding the power of the personal touch...............256
    Asking the right questions at the right time......................258
    Making in-person meetings efficient: Five tips.................260

Chapter 19: Troubleshooting Issues and Problems 263

Poor Cash Flow 263
    Require immediate payment (Or sooner!)...........................264
    Don't pay sooner than you have to 264
    Make sure your invoices are right 265
    Invoice upon delivery..265
    Invoice more often...265
    Manage your expenses...266
Clients Who Want Free Advice 266
Can't Get That First Sale 268
Clients Who Are Slow (Or Refuse) to Pay.................................270
Can't Get Clients to Pay You What You're Worth 272

Introduction

· ·

*A*nyone can become a consultant. Becoming a *successful* consultant, however, is a different story. Prospering as a consultant requires you to have expertise that others are willing to pay you to provide, and it requires having good business skills. Oh. And it requires some amount of motivation on your part to *want* to consult for others.

Writing this book was a labour of love for us. We are all consultants and have been for many years. If we don't do a good job, we don't get paid. And if we don't get paid, we don't eat. Our goal is to provide you with the skills you need to become a successful consultant, whether you're a beginner who is just getting his business off the ground, or an experienced consultant who wants to fine-tune her already successful practice.

As you may have already discovered or suspected, consulting can be an exciting and rewarding profession – and not just in a financial sense. Working with people to help solve problems can be an immensely satisfying thing to do. Of course, in the real world, consulting involves much more than tapping your client's head with a magic wand and watching all the problems go away.

Consulting For Dummies is specifically written to address the unique needs of both new and experienced consultants as well as aspiring consultants. If you're new to the business, you can find everything you need to know to be successful and in demand. If you're an experienced consultant, we challenge you to shift your perspective and take a fresh look at your philosophies and techniques – what's working for you and what's not. We offer some new approaches and techniques to help you take your business to a higher level.

About This Book

Consulting For Dummies is full of useful information, tips, and checklists that any consultant aspiring consultant can use right away. Whether you're just thinking about becoming a consultant or you're already a seasoned professional, you can find everything you need to make consulting fun and profitable for you and your clients.

The good news is that the information you find within the covers of this book is firmly grounded in the real world. This book isn't an abstract collection of theoretical mumbo-jumbo that sounds good but doesn't work when you put it to the test. We've culled the best information, the best strategies, and the best techniques for consulting from people who already do it for a living – including us. This book is a toolbox full of road-tested solutions to your every question and problem.

Consulting For Dummies is *fun*, which reflects our strong belief and experience that consulting can be both profitable and fun. Nobody said that you can't get your work done while making sure that you and your clients enjoy yourselves in the process. We even help you to maintain a sense of humour in the face of upcoming deadlines and seemingly insurmountable challenges that all consultants have to deal with from time to time. Some days, you will be challenged to your limit or beyond. However, on many more days, the satisfaction of resolving a production bottleneck, recommending a new accounting system, or installing a new client-server computer network will bring you a sense of fulfilment that you never could have imagined possible.

The material in this book is easy to access. What good is all the information in the world if you can't get to it quickly and easily? Have no fear; we have designed this book with you, the reader, in mind. Here's how to find the precise information you seek:

- ✔ If you want to find out about a specific area, such as gathering data or setting up a home office, you can flip to that chapter and get your answers quickly – faster than you can say, 'The cheque's in the post'. Let the table of contents and index be your guides.

- ✔ If you want a crash course in consulting, read this book from cover to cover. Forget learning by trial and error. Everything you need to know about consulting is right here. You'll avoid pitfalls and all kinds of mistakes if you follow our advice.

We know from personal experience that consulting can be an intimidating job. Consultants – especially those who are just learning the ropes – are often at a loss as to what they need to do and when they need to do it. Don't worry. Help is at your fingertips.

Conventions Used in This Book

When writing this book, we included some general conventions that all *For Dummies* books use. We use the following:

- ✔ **Italics:** We *italicise* any words you may not be familiar with and provide definitions.

 ✔ **Boldface type:** We add **bold** to all keywords in bulleted lists and the actual steps in numbered lists.
 ✔ **Monofont:** All websites and email addresses appear in `monofont`.

Also, we should note that, in this book, we use the term consultant quite loosely. We define a *consultant* simply as someone who sells his or her unique expertise to someone else, often on an hourly basis. There are many different kinds of consultants, from those who advise businesses on how to become more effective to those who advise people on which colours they should wear to be successful to those who can help you set up your home computer's wireless network.

Foolish Assumptions

While we were writing this book, we made a few assumptions about you. For example, we assume that you have at least a passing interest in starting your own business that specialises in helping others solve their problems or capitalise on opportunities. Maybe you're already a consultant, or perhaps consulting is something that you might like to try. We also assume that you have a skill or expertise for which your friends, relatives, or clients will be willing to pay. This expertise may be providing your advice on anything from postage stamp collections to Internet consulting to aerospace engineering services. One more thing: We assume that you don't already know everything there is to know about consulting and that you're eager to acquire some new perspectives on the topic.

How This Book Is Organised

Consulting For Dummies is organised into seven parts. Each part addresses a major area of the how, what, or why of becoming a consultant – and growing your business. Because of this organisation, finding the topic that you're looking for is simple. Whatever the topic, you can bet that we cover it somepwhere! Here's a quick overview of what you can find in each part.

Part 1: So You Want to Be a Consultant

Consultants are many things to many people. In this part, we provide an overview of the entire book, and then consider how to determine whether or not consulting is for you, before diving into the topic of starting your own consulting business.

Part II: Getting Your Consulting Business Off the Ground

Consulting is just like any other business – you need to do certain things to get it off the ground and running smoothly. This part focuses on starting up a successful consulting business as well as the financial, legal, and ethical considerations that you'll encounter along the way. Finally, we take a look at how to set your fees.

Part III: The Consulting Process

Consulting can be done one of two ways: the right way or the wrong way. In this part, we discuss the right way. We explain how to clearly diagnose the client's problem (and write a winning proposal), collect data effectively, and analyse it quickly and efficiently. Finally, we talk about how to give feedback to your clients and ensure that your advice gets implemented.

Part IV: Selling and Marketing Your Consulting Services

To be a successful consultant, you have to learn how to sell your services (and yourself) effectively. This part considers the selling process and how to spread the word about your business. We consider how to build business through current clients, as well as how to build business with new ones.

Part V: Taking Care of Business

In this part, we dig a bit deeper into the business side of consulting, taking a close look at contracts and negotiating deals, keeping track of time and money, communicating with clients, and troubleshooting the kinds of issues and problems that every businessperson has to face from time to time.

Part VI: Taking Your Consulting Business to the Next Level

Once your consulting business is well established, you'll want to take it to the next level to make it even more successful than it already is. In this part, we consider different approaches to build on your success, including the use of pricing strategies and enhancing your image and reputation.

Part VII: The Part of Tens

Here, in a concise and lively set of short chapters, you find tips that can really launch your consulting practice into orbit. In these chapters, we address using the Internet and other publicity tools to market your services, avoiding consulting mistakes, writing proposals, negotiating contracts, and building business with existing clients.

Icons Used in This Book

To guide you along the way and point out the information you really need to know about consulting, this book uses icons along its left margins. You see the following icons in this book:

Remember these important points of information, and you'll be a much better consultant.

This icon points you to tips and tricks to make consulting easier.

These real-life anecdotes from yours truly and other consultants show you the right – and occasionally wrong – way to be a consultant.

Watch out! If you don't heed the advice next to these icons, the entire situation may blow up in your face.

Where to Go from Here

If you're a new or aspiring consultant, you may want to start at the beginning of this book and work your way through to the end. A wealth of information and practical advice awaits you. Simply turn the page and you're on your way!

If you're already a consultant and you're short of time (and what consultant isn't?), you may want to turn to a particular topic to address a specific need or question. If that's the case, the Table of Contents gives a chapter-by-chapter description of all the topics in this book, and the thorough index can help you find exactly what you're looking for.

Regardless of how you find your way around *Consulting For Dummies*, we're sure that you'll enjoy getting there. If you have specific questions or comments, please feel free to visit our websites at www.techniquesfor change.co.uk (Philip), www.nelson-motivation.com (Bob) or www. petereconomy.com (Peter). We would love to hear your personal anecdotes and suggestions for improving future revisions of this book, and we promise to take every one of them to heart.

Here's to your success!

Part I
So You Want to Be a Consultant

'How about a pint of my blood every month as an ncentive to use our company as your consultants?

Part I
So You Want to Be
a Consultant

In this part . . .

Although the term *consultant* can mean different things to different people, if you've decided to become one, then you need to decide exactly what it means to you. In this part, we give you an overview of the topic, and then dig in a bit deeper by exploring whether or not consulting is right for you. We show you how to assess your own skills and preferences, and how to prepare to make the move to consulting. Finally, we consider exactly what you need to do to take the plunge into starting your own consulting business as painlessly (and profitably) as possible.

Chapter 1

Introducing the Wonderful World of Consulting

In This Chapter

▶ Understanding what a consultant is and why people become consultants

▶ Exploring the contents of this book

▶ Taking the consulting challenge quiz

Consulting has taken the world of business by storm, and today it seems that you can find a consultant to do almost anything that you could ever want done. A consultant can be a partner in a large management consulting firm or a freelance writer; a self-employed website designer or a part-time cosmetics salesperson; an architect who works out of his or her home, an expert witness hired to testify at the latest big court case, or a virtual share trader who provides investment advice to clients around the globe over the Internet.

In this book, we use the term consultant quite loosely. We define a *consultant* as someone who sells his or her special expertise to someone else. This expertise can be anything from showing someone how to lay out, plant, and fertilise an organic vegetable garden, to analysing and recommending changes to a complex aerospace manufacturing operation.

So, while many people think of consultants only in terms of the narrow field of professional management consulting – firms like KPMG, McKinsey & Co., PricewaterhouseCoopers, and others – the world of consulting is much bigger than that. Whenever someone pays you for your special expertise or advice – whether in creating a snazzy website for a friend's business or estimating the drainage requirements of a new home or providing coaching support to slimmers over the phone – you're acting as a consultant.

In this chapter, we consider the many reasons why energised and talented people like you are becoming consultants, and we then embark on a broad overview of the contents of this book. we briefly cover the topics of starting up your own consulting firm, understanding the consulting process, selling your services, and taking your business to the next level. Finally, we invite you to complete the nifty Consulting Challenge Quiz.

Considering the Reasons for Consulting

Men and women from all walks of life with all manner of experience and expectations have reasons for becoming consultants. Some exploit their knowledge to help their clients, and enjoy the variety of assignments that consulting can bring. Some prefer working for large, diversified consulting firms – with offices scattered around the globe – and some are simply tired of working for someone else and are ready to start their own consulting firms in a spare bedroom of their house. Others are just looking for a way to make some extra money.

Whatever your reason for becoming a consultant, businesses of all sorts – and individuals and organisations – are using consultants more than ever. According to the Management Consultancies Association, the UK management consultancy market alone has annual revenues of over £8 billion – that's more than the amount the British spend on chilled food. One key reason for this is that skilled consultants can be brought into an organisation at short notice, fix a problem, and then move on to another organisation in need. So it's not necessary to recruit someone, pay him or her a salary, and provide benefits and a pension plan.

And although some think that money is the main reason people choose to become consultants, that's not really what it's all about. Sure, a lot of people earn good money as consultants – make no mistake about it. But to many people, the benefits of being a consultant go far beyond the size of their bank accounts. This section talks about some of the most compelling non-financial reasons why people enter the consulting field.

Exploiting your talent

Everyone is especially knowledgeable about at least one thing. For example, you may have worked for 20 years as a building loan specialist for a large bank. When it comes to building loans, saying that you're an expert is probably an understatement. And because of the huge network of contacts that you've developed over the years, many other organisations could benefit from your particular experience.

Or you may enjoy exploring the Internet in your spare time. You've built many websites for yourself and your friends, and you always keep up with the latest in design tools and other developments. Although you work on the supermarket tills ten hours a day, five days a week, you always manage to find time to pursue your favourite hobby. Would it surprise you to find out that many businesses would hire you and pay you good money to build and maintain websites for them? It shouldn't – that's what consultants do.

Being tired of working for someone else

Most people have dreams of what they want to do with their lives. Some dream of buying a larger home. Some dream of furthering their career or family. Others dream of winning the lottery and moving to Monaco. However, in our experience, one of the most common dreams – the one that most people who work in an organisation have at least once or twice a day – is that of being their own boss.

It's not that all bosses are bad. We authors have had great bosses over the years, and we hope that we've been good bosses to those who have worked for us. Most people, however, are born with a strong desire to be independent and to make their own decisions rather than have others make their decisions for them. And when, as time goes on, you begin to know more about what you do than your supervisors or managers, working for someone else can become especially difficult.

Getting made redundant

The days of having a job for life are long gone. Today's economy is one of rapid change and movement. As companies continue to search for ways to cut costs, they increasingly turn to hiring temporary workers or contracting work out to consultants. Having a job today is no guarantee of having one tomorrow. When you work for a company – no matter how large – you can be declared redundant at any time, with little notice. If you're lucky, you get a good redundancy package. If you're not so lucky, your last day is just that, and you're on your own.

Becoming a consultant is a good way to assure your financial future in the face of economic uncertainty. Why?

  ✔ One: Because you control the number of jobs you take on and how much or how little extra work you want to keep in reserve.

  ✔ Two: Because you can often make more money consulting for a firm than you can as an employee of that same firm. Many companies are more than willing to pay a premium to hire an expert consultant to do the same job that an employee could do for much less money.

Having a flexible second source of income

If you want a flexible second source of income, then consulting is just what the doctor ordered. When you're a self-employed consultant, you set your own schedule. If you want to work only at the weekend, you can decide to work only at the weekend. If you want to do your work late at night, that's fine, too. And because you decide exactly how much work you take on, you can work for one client at a time or many clients at once. Decisions about your schedule and your workload are all up to you.

And another thing: If you conduct your business from your home, this second source of income may mean a significant deduction from your income tax. The government allows owners of home-based businesses to take a variety of tax deductions that are not available to most other individuals. Look into this carefully though – there may be implications for your council tax as well as capital gains tax when you come to sell your property. Even if you don't work out of your home, you can write off the majority of your business-related expenses. Check out Chapter 5 for some basic information about the tax benefits of becoming a self-employed consultant. For more detailed advice speak to an accountant.

Putting something back in

Many organisations benefit greatly from the services of good consultants because they generally bring an independent and objective outside perspective along with them. Unfortunately, non-commercial organisations can't afford to pay for a consultant's expertise like most larger, well-established businesses can. Schools, churches, charities, and other community-based organisations rely on members of the community to provide expertise and assistance. Many consultants make a regular practice of providing their expertise to community organisations at no charge as a way of giving back. If you're one of these people, you may already be consulting without even realising it!

Why would anyone want to do this?

- If you really believe in something – whether it's the goals of a particular political candidate or your child's primary school, then the psychological benefits are much greater than any financial benefits.

- The work you do for your favourite charity or community group may get you noticed, resulting in fee-paying work. Most community organisations are supported by a variety of people from all walks of life. The network that you establish with these individuals can be invaluable to you in your working life as well as your social life. Although establishing a network of contacts may not be the main reason that you decide to offer your services to the group of your choice, it's not the worst thing that could happen to you, is it?

Philip Albon consults!

In this interview Philip describes how and why he got into consulting and what he thinks of it as a career.

Consulting for Dummies: How did you find out consulting was right for you?

Albon: My own career began in 1979 at BT just after Margaret Thatcher was elected. My early work was in HR but later I moved to roles involving management training, internal consultancy and implementing change programmes. When I first got involved in this internal consultancy work I knew I'd found my niche. I really enjoyed the research and analysis work and working with clients to develop and implement the changes.

CFD: So you can consult internally or externally?

Albon: Management consultants can work for themselves or for consultancy firms but many consultants work in-house for large organisations. As such there's always movement both ways between consulting firms small and large and organisations in industry or the public sector. The skills of a consultant are extremely valuable not only to the consultancy industry but also to a wide range of organisations. This makes it an excellent career choice.

CFD: So how was it working for a big consulting firm?

Albon: I joined Coopers & Lybrand in London (a precursor firm to PWC) in 1986. Coopers served as the launch pad to my career in consultancy and is one of the reasons I am where I am now. Within the first year I'd worked for clients in sectors new to me including automotive, IT and government and in countries I hadn't previously worked in including America, Germany and Sweden. I also started to work in different fields including cost reduction, procurement and IT implementations. Quite simply my years at Coopers constituted the most intensive period of on-the-job training of my life. In addition to new sectors, cultures and consulting fields I also learnt how to write compelling reports, deliver professional presentations, facilitate workshops and how to sell to and influence board members. If you have the right attitude, working in consultancy can really help you to develop. Quite quickly you find yourself working with very senior clients.

CFD: What else has helped you along?

Albon: Research and keeping up to date with your own area of expertise is an important part of consultancy. While at BT I started a part time MA in Management Learning at Lancaster University and finished it whilst at Coopers & Lybrand. The course was based on self-directed and experiential learning which meant I could use my experience and work in consultancy to compliment my studies and vice versa.

CFD: So did you start your own firm while you were at Coopers?

Albon: No. In 1992 I joined a small consultancy firm. I wanted to start my own firm but before taking the plunge I was keen to learn how a small firm ran. There I sharpened my sales skills selling work around the globe. I started Techniques for Change in 1994 with the following mission: 'We are committed to enabling organisations to drive successful change internally through the provision of consultancy skills and practical techniques.' Since that time we've worked with people from seven of the world's top ten companies, over 50 of the FTSE 100 companies, one in four of the European top 100 companies and over 60 NHS trusts.

CFD: Was it easy to get it off the ground?

(continued)

(continued)

Albon: No, but I think it was a great help to know what consultancy I was trying to sell and exactly who I was selling it to. That focus helps us to this day.

CFD: You help other consultants don't you?

Albon: Yes. We've always been involved with training consultancy professionals and recently we launched two great qualifications from the Institute of Business Consulting: the Certificate in Management Consulting Essentials and the Diploma in Management Consultancy. They both help people develop their career in consultancy, be it internal or external or both.

CFD: So you're a top consultant to consultants?

Albon: Yes. My firm won an award at the Institute of Business Consulting Annual Awards, 2007. This was to recognise the valuable contribution to the profession by Techniques for Change for providing training and development opportunities for people to become consultants as well as those already working within the profession.

CFD: Do you still consult or do you just run the business?

Albon: I still consult personally and enjoy it massively. In recent years I've helped to redesign and restructure a major UK energy company, run a culture change programme in a major European company and worked on many change programmes around the world.

CFD: What's the attraction for you?

Albon: The fact that you're charging high fees for your time, advice and input means that you're constantly challenged to perform well and I like that. As a consultant I don't believe you could ever find the work stale because there are just so many opportunities to develop. Even last week I was still learning while working in Brazil for the first time.

CFD: Sounds great! Are there any downsides?

Albon: In common with many careers, consultancy can impact your personal life. Pressure peaks due to deadlines and periods spent working away from home are common. Also, when you run your own business you always have to work hard at networking and winning new business. It's no good being a good consultant without clients – you need to sell to stay in business.

CFD: Sounds like a lot of pressure.

Albon: It's all about focusing on what's important. I believe it's possible to manage your work/life balance but it's up to you to do it. I learnt early that managing how much I take on and how long it takes me to do it was up to me. As such, I've had the opportunity to spend quality time with my wife and two children. When my children were younger, my family would often travel with me on consulting trips away. The project-based nature of consulting means that, with careful management, you can work flexibly and spend time with family and friends.

CFD: To any of our readers out there considering becoming a consultant, is it worth it?

Albon: For a good consultant the rewards socially, intellectually and financially are fantastic. Consulting doesn't suit everyone, but it certainly suits me.

So You Want to Be a Consultant

While many consultants work for someone else – in all sorts of companies, in all sorts of industries – for many others, a major attraction of becoming a consultant is starting their own consulting firm. The good news is that many millions of consultants have successfully made the transition to being their own bosses – and are enjoying the financial, professional, and lifestyle benefits that result. The bad news is that starting up your own consulting firm – and keeping it on an even keel – is a lot of hard work.

Before you can start – and build up – your own successful consulting firm, you first need to be certain what kind of consulting you want to do. For some of you, the answer is obvious – 'I want to help small, engineering firms learn how to use computer-aided design software better for their benefit', or 'I want to help people design the gardens of their dreams'. However, some of you may not be quite so sure. If so, you need to assess your skills and your own personal preferences to help you decide. But whether or not you already know what kind of consulting firm you want to start, you need to be sure a market exists for what you want to do.

Finally, once you've decided that you do indeed want to start your own consulting business – and you know what kind of consulting it is that you want to do – you need to decide when the time is right and exactly how you can make the transition from your current employer to the new world of self-employment. This requires assessing your professional, financial, and personal considerations, and creating a step-by-step plan for making the transition. While some self-employed consultants simply walk into their boss's office one day and hand in their notice, starting their own business that very moment, others make the transition over a period of weeks, months, or even years.

Starting up your own consulting firm

The first thing to keep in mind when starting up your own consulting firm is that you're starting your own *business*. According to Business Link, the UK Government advice body for new businesses, the following are the most common mistakes business start-ups make:

- Carrying out poor or inadequate market research and financial planning
- Setting sights too high
- Neglecting to keep an eye on the competition
- Insufficiently controlling suppliers and customers
- Failing to properly manage stock and assets
- Hiring the wrong people

However, Business Link also says: 'with hard work and an awareness of the issues, a new business can be a great success'. To start a new business, you also need:

- Sound management practices, including an ability to manage projects, handle finances, and communicate effectively with customers

> ✔ Industry experience, including the number of years you've worked in the same kind of business as the one you intend to start, and familiarity with suppliers and potential customers
>
> ✔ Technical support, including your ability to seek out and find help in the technical aspects of your business
>
> ✔ Planning ability, including an ability to set appropriate business goals and targets and then create plans and strategies for achieving them

You need to attend to a variety of matters when starting up your own consulting firm – from getting your business set up (including finding a space in your home for it, and getting office equipment and supplies) to securing the services of a good accountant, banker, and perhaps even a solicitor. You need to consider legal issues, such as deciding what form of business to adopt, deciding on a name for your business, and dealing with any planning or regulatory issues (head to Chapter 5). And, of course, you need to set up a bookkeeping system and be prepared to pay your taxes, buy insurance, and perhaps secure your own health insurance and other benefits.

And you need to address one more thing when starting up your own consulting firm: the fees you'll charge your clients to do work for them. You can choose from many different approaches for setting your fees – ultimately, you need to adopt one that's appropriate for your industry, that creates value for your clients, and that provides you with enough profit to make a good living. If your fees are too high, you may not get enough business to keep your business afloat. However, set your fees too low, and you may find yourself swamped with business, but not really making any money – a 'busy fool'. Ideally, you'll find a win-win approach where both you and your clients are happy with the results. Chapter 6 can help you out.

Understanding the consulting process

People have been consulting for hundreds – maybe thousands – of years. Over these many years, a five-step approach to consulting has emerged that is the standard approach for many consultants today – whether self-employed, or working for someone else. This five-step consulting process includes:

1. Defining the problem

2. Collecting data

3. Problem solving

4. Presenting recommendations

5. Implementing recommendations

Selling your services

Like any other kind of business, consultants have to sell themselves – their expertise, their experience, their ability to get the job done – and convince someone to pay the kind of fee that will make consulting worth their while. In a way, every consultant – at least, every *successful* consultant – is also a salesperson. And the better salesperson you become, the better able you'll be to land the clients and projects you need to become profitable and to grow your business.

Selling your services involves many different parts of an equation that results in a client signing a contract with your firm. These parts include such things as identifying the real decision-maker in your client's company, making a sales pitch, promoting your business, building business and referrals through your current clients, and building business with new clients. The success you find as a consultant is often directly proportional to the time and expertise you apply to the selling process.

Taking care of business

Consulting is a business and as such you need to plan to attend to its unique needs. Every consultant relies on contracts to formalise agreements with clients: How long will an engagement take? What work will be accomplished? How much will your client pay you for your services – and when? Negotiating agreements with your clients is a vital skill for consultants. Also of great importance is the tracking of your time (the hours you put into a particular project) and your money (the fees that are attributable to a particular project). This may involve setting up and maintaining client activity logs or time sheets, and keeping to budgets.

You also need to be sure that you become an expert communicator – in writing, over the telephone, and via email and other technology-enabled modes of communication. Finally, your business *will* run into problems and challenges from time to time – every business does. Whether the challenge is poor cash flow, getting clients to pay, or finding the right client for your kind of business, identifying a problem – and then correctly diagnosing and solving it – is a critical skill that you need to master if you want to help ensure your long-term success as a consultant.

Taking it to the next level

Building – and growing – a consulting business that will be successful over a long period of time involves more than merely the basics of setting up your office, finding good clients, working through the consulting process, becoming an effective salesperson, negotiating contracts, and keeping track of your time and money. You also need to understand how to tune up your firm's growth engine, how to integrate advanced pricing strategies into the way your do business, and create a top-rank image and reputation in your particular industry. Many consultants are happy building a certain level of business, and then simply maintaining it. If that's the situation you're in and you're happy with it, then that's perfectly fine. However, if you dream of building a consulting business that will expand to employ others, and serve customers in a variety of markets – outside of your region, or even internationally, then you want to do what it takes to move your business to the next level.

The Consulting Challenge Quiz

Maybe you're thinking that this consulting thing may not be such a bad idea. Now the big question is: Do you have what it takes to become a consultant? Do you want to find out? Then simply take the Consulting Challenge Quiz. It's quick, it's easy, and it's guaranteed to help you sort fantasy from reality. Don't forget to total your score at the end of the test to see where you fit.

Answering the questions

Here are the questions. Read each one and circle the answer that comes closest to your personal feelings. If you're not sure how to answer a question on your first attempt, move on to the next question and come back to the tricky one later.

1. Do you like to solve problems?

    A. Yes, solving problems is my sole reason for being.

    B. Yes, I like solving certain kinds of problems.

    C. Can I trade one of my problems for one of yours?

    D. Is there someone else who can solve them?

    E. No. Yuck. Never.

2. Can you set your own goals and then follow them to completion?

    A. I don't know what I would do if I didn't always have goals to pursue.

    B. Yes, I set my own goals, but I don't always follow up on them.

    C. I haven't tried before, but if you show me how, I will.

    D. I don't set my own goals; they set themselves.

    E. Sorry, I don't have any goals.

3. Are you an independent self-starter?

A. I don't need anyone to tell me what to do – let's get going!

B. I'm independent, but I sometimes have a hard time getting motivated to do things on my own.

C. No one has ever let me make my own decisions before. I kind of like the idea of doing things on my own, though.

D. Hum a few bars, and maybe I can sing it.

E. Do I have to be?

4. Are you confident about your ability to get the job done?

A. Without a doubt.

B. I'm fairly certain.

C. I'm not sure.

D. Can we discuss this some other time?

E. Absolutely, unequivocally not.

5. Do you enjoy pursuing tasks to completion, despite the obstacles in your path?

A. I am very persistent.

B. Usually, although I sometimes avoid tackling problems directly.

C. As long as we understand up front that no one is perfect.

D. Is any task ever truly complete?

E. Some things were just never meant to be done.

6. Can you adapt to rapid changes?

A. My middle name is change.

B. It's easier for me to adapt to good changes than to adapt to bad changes.

C. If you've seen one change, you've seen them all.

D. As long as it's you who changes and not me.

E. I just don't do change

7. Are you creative?

A. Just give me a pencil and a piece of paper, and you'll have your solution in five minutes.

B. Usually, but it depends on what mood I'm in.

C. Let me think about that for a while.

D. Why waste a lot of effort creating something that someone else has probably already figured out the answer to?

E. I like things the way they are.

8. Do you like to work with people?

A. Working with people is what makes work fun.

B. Definitely – some people more than others, however.

C. Yes – it definitely beats working with trained seals.

D. I really prefer my computer.

E. I want to be alone!

9. Are you trustworthy, loyal, honest, and brave?

A. All of the above and more!

B. Well, three out of four isn't bad, is it?

C. How about two out of four?

D. I'd like to believe that there are other, more important human qualities.

E. Next question, please.

10. Are you interested in making a decent living?

A. My opportunities are unlimited.

B. Sure, as long as I don't have to work too hard at it.

C. I don't know; I'm pretty comfortable the way things are now.

D. Just how do you define 'decent'?

E. I'm going to win that lottery one of these days!

Analysing your score

Now add up your results. Give yourself 5 points for every A answer, 3 points for every B, 0 points for every C, –3 points for every D, and –5 for every E.

We've divided the possible scores into six separate categories. By comparing your total points to the points contained in each category, you can find out whether consulting is in your future.

25 to 50 points: You're a born consultant. If you're not already working for yourself as a consultant, we strongly suggest that you consider quitting your job right now and start passing out your business card to all your friends, acquaintances, and prospective clients. Read this book for tips on how to sharpen your already well-developed skills.

1 to 24 points: You definitely have potential to be a great consultant. Consider starting your own consulting practice in the very near future, but make sure that you keep your day job until you've got enough clients to keep you afloat. Read this book to understand the basics of consulting and find out how to grow your new business.

0 points: You could go either way. Why don't you try taking this test again in another month or two? Read this book to ensure that you pass next time.

–1 to –24 points: We're sorry to tell you, but consulting is currently not your cup of tea. We strongly recommend that you read this book and then take this test again. If you don't do better the second time, then maybe working for someone else isn't the worst thing that could happen to you.

–25 to –50 points: Forget it. Your DNA just doesn't have the consulting gene built into it. Sell this book to one of your colleagues right now. Maybe he or she will score higher on this test than you did.

More than 50 or less than –50 points: Mental arithmetic is not your forté – try again!

Chapter 2

Determining if Consulting Is Right for You

*I*f you're already a consultant, then this chapter is probably not for you. You've already stepped onto the consulting path, and you're most likely looking for new ways to improve your practice – topics we cover in great detail elsewhere in this book. But if you're considering becoming a consultant, but not sure whether or not starting your own consulting business is the right choice for you, then you've come to the right place.

How do you decide whether starting a consulting business is the right thing for you? Many of us have arrived at this decision point in our lives because we feel we have more to contribute if we own and operate our own consulting firms. Others believe that having their own a consulting business is a much more lucrative proposition than working for someone else (and, in many cases, it can be). But perhaps the attraction is simply the idea of calling the shots, and not having to answer to a boss.

John, a friend of Philip's, worked for years for a major UK insurance company. He worked on quality and service improvement projects. The work was challenging but arduous; the senior managers often moved the goalposts at a late stage and this required working for very long hours to deliver projects on time. However John wanted more control over his work/life balance. An element of his job had involved running training courses and facilitating workshops and he started to form a vision of working as a freelance management-training consultant.

After testing the water on a part-time basis, John left the insurance company. Now instead of toiling away, burning the midnight oil at senior managers' whims, he works approximately half the hours needed in his previous role, makes more money and spends valuable time with his loved ones.

Can we let you in on a little secret? Your work can be your love. You don't have to spend the rest of your life working in a job that brings you little or no joy or satisfaction. All three authors jumped off the 9-to-5 career merry-go-round to start their own companies – each more than 10 years ago. And they would never go back. Becoming an independent consultant can be the key that unlocks the door to the rest of your future if you just take a small step forward and give it a try. And you don't have to do it all at once. You can (and, indeed, our advice is that maybe you *should*) keep your current day job while you try out consulting in your spare time.

In this chapter, we help you determine what you really want to do with your life and what skills you have that can get you where you want to go. We also help you determine whether what you want to do is marketable enough to allow you to make a living. (Making a living at whatever you decide to do is always a plus!) Finally, we tell you how to do some simple test-marketing of your business ideas to see which ones will fly and which ones may be better suited to lining your budgie cage.

Assessing Your Preferences

Undoubtedly, you like to do certain kinds of work more than others. Take a moment right now to think about the things you most like to do as part of your job. Perhaps your great love in life is to create massive computer spreadsheets. Maybe you really like to read and analyse procurement contracts. Or is your number-one favourite activity making travel reservations for your organisation's salespeople?

One problem with a career in most organisations is that you may very well be promoted right out of the things that you enjoy doing the most, into new roles that you may find much less enjoyable. If you're talented in a particular area of technical expertise, you're inevitably recognised for your skill and eventually promoted into a supervisory or management position. When this happens, suddenly your job changes from, say, creating advertising campaigns yourself to coaching a team of employees to create advertising campaigns. And although you may still do some creative work, suddenly your day is chock-full of management activities, such as budgeting department resources, controlling expenditures, counselling employees, building teamwork, attending endless meetings and filling out forms for anything and everything you can imagine. Before you know it, you're doing tasks that have nothing to do with what you really enjoy doing.

In this section, your task is to decide exactly what you enjoy doing the most – at work and otherwise. Your goal is to identify new work opportunities that allow you to do what you enjoy doing. Think in terms of a new career where you – and not others – decide the things you do. Don't worry now about whether you can make money at it. Making money is indeed an important consideration (that is, if you want to be able to afford to eat, or not live in a cardboard box on the street) and we look into that in the section 'Can your business become profitable?'

What do you really like doing?

Start this exercise by considering what things you really like to do. Our logic is that if you like to do it – really like to do it, you can do it well. And doing the things you like to do well generates success. For the moment, forget about the things you just sort of like to do or the things you feel ambivalent about. Be honest with yourself – don't put on your list things that someone else thinks you should like to do. Instead, look deep within yourself to tap into your own feelings. Use the space below each question to write in your ideas. Or photocopy the pages so that you can go through the exercise again in a few months or a few years.

What would your ideal day look like ten years hence? Divide it into 30-minute segments and describe what you'd be doing in each part of your day.

_____

_____

_____

_____

What would your perfect job be? Visualise it. Hear it. Feel it. Taste it. (Okay – don't taste it.) What would you do every day? How would you spend your time? With whom would you work?

_____

_____

_____

_____

List your most positive and enjoyable work experiences. What was it about these experiences that made them so enjoyable? Exactly what skills were you applying?

_____

_____

_____

_____

What are your five favourite things to do at work? Why do you like each of these five things?

1.

2.

3.

4.

5.

What are your five favourite things to do away from work? Why do you like each of these five things?

1.

2.

3.

4.

5.

What strengths would you bring to your dream job? What gaps in knowledge or experience do you need to fill so that you can start work in your dream job today?

_____

_____

_____

_____

What do you really dislike doing?

Just as you have things that you really like to do – both at work and away from it, you invariably have things that you really can't stand. The next step in this exercise is to focus on the things that you really don't like to do. Again, be honest with yourself – now's the time to get it all out on the table. (Don't worry – we're not going to show this to your boss.)

> *What would your worst job be? What would this job entail doing every day? With whom would you be working? How would you be spending your time?*
>
> *List your most negative and unenjoyable work experiences. What about these experiences made them so unenjoyable? Exactly what skills were you applying?*
>
> *What are your five least favourite things to do at work? Why are these your least favourite things?*

1.

2.

3.

4.

5.

> *What are your five least favourite things to do away from work? Why are these your least favourite things?*

1.

2.

3.

4.

5.

Assessing Your Skills

It's one thing to want to do something – to be in tune with your likes and dislikes – but it's another thing altogether to have the skills and expertise needed to carry out your selected endeavour successfully. To get a sense of whether a particular brand of consulting is really in your future (or in your present, for that matter), you've got to first take the time to assess the skills that you bring to the task. In the sections that follow, we help you do just that.

A visualisation exercise

As you work on getting in touch with the things that you like and the things that you dislike, you can amplify the effectiveness of this process by participating in a visualisation exercise. First, find a nice, cosy chair where you can relax – away from the phones or the hustle and bustle of your home or office. Turn down the lights and let your mind wander. No, don't go to sleep – you need to be awake for this one. Visualise your ideal life. What is a typical day like in your ideal life? Start at the very beginning of your day when you wake up and work through it until you go to bed at night. Ask yourself the following questions:

Where are you living?

How do you wake up?

What time do you wake up?

What clothes do you put on?

What do you eat for breakfast?

With whom do you eat breakfast?

Where do you go to work?

How do you get there?

Whom do you see at work?

What does your work environment look like?

What does it feel like?

What do you do at work?

Whom do you talk to?

What do you talk about?

Continue to work through your typical day in your ideal life – the rest of the morning, lunch, afternoon, the commute home in the evening (if you have one), dinner, after dinner and bedtime. Ask detailed questions about what you're doing, where you're doing it, when, and with whom. Use the results of this exercise to help guide you in your answers to what you really want to do with your life.

What are you really good at?

In your years of experience in the business world, you undoubtedly excel in certain tasks. Perhaps you're the world's greatest budget forecaster, or maybe you have an incredible eye for displaying products in department store windows to increase sales. Whatever skills you excel in, now's the time to get in touch with them.

What are your most outstanding job skills (for example, accounting or nego-tiating), and what makes you so skilled in those particular areas?

What things have other people told you that you do well?

What personal qualities (for example, analytical ability or persistence) do you possess that support your most outstanding job skills?

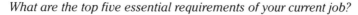

What are the top five essential requirements of your current job?

1.

2.

3.

4.

5.

What special training or courses have you taken to improve your job skills?

What special certificates, licences, or registrations do you possess for your current job (for example, a Chartered Accountant qualification or a certificate in psychometric test administration)?

What aren't you so good at?

Figuring out what you're not good at is just as important as figuring out what you're good at – in fact, it can save you a lot of time and heartbreak. However, deciding what you're not good at is often easier said than done. Why? Because many people have an idealised vision of what they think they ought to be good at, whether they are or not. For example, you don't admit that you're hopeless at figures and discard that option from your list of possibilities. Instead, you say, 'One of these days I'm going to concentrate on getting better at working with numbers,' leaving open the possibility. The implicit assumption is that you should hang on to every possible avenue to the future, regardless of the probability that you'll ever travel along it. Truth be told, that is not the best approach. Although the motive behind doing this type of thinking is noble, it only diffuses your focus and concentration on the things that you do best.

What job skills (for example, accounting, negotiating, and so on) are you least comfortable with, and why are you uncomfortable with them?

What personality traits (for example, decisiveness or persistence) would you work on to enhance your job skills and why?

What tasks do you avoid and why?

Matching Your Skills with Your Preferences

After you assess your likes and dislikes, your skills, and the areas that you're less skilled in, put together all this information to create a coherent picture of who you are and what kind of consultancy is the best choice for you. You may be surprised to find that the perfect job for you bears little resemblance to your current job. On the other hand, you may be surprised to find out that you're not cut out to be a consultant. Whatever the result, you need to know one way or the other.

To begin this exercise, review all the comments that you wrote under the section titled 'What do you really like to do?' The point of this section is to allow you to unleash your imagination and consider what kind of work you really want to do. For a moment, forget that you've been a bank cashier in Leicester your entire working life or a call centre manager in Crawley for the last ten years. As you read through your responses, take time to step back, close your eyes, and visualise your answer to each question.

Think about what kinds of consulting businesses you could start that would allow you to apply your life's preferences. Don't be shy – now's the time to let your imagination go wild. Try to list at least five or more possible consulting businesses. Jot them down here:

Next, review your responses under the section titled 'What are you really good at?' Your responses to the questions in this section don't necessarily indicate that you want to do something, only that you're good at it. And if you need some additional training to get the credentials you need, weigh the amount of time and money that you need to get them. Step back and, based on your answers, visualise the kinds of consulting businesses that you could start. Again, think of five or more business possibilities and list them here:

_____

_____

_____

_____

Now compare your lists. Do you have any possibilities in common? Yes? Great! Circle them right now with a red marker pen. You don't have any in common? Go through the exercise again and really let yourself go – dive deep within and find your true self. When you start your new consulting business, pick something that lets you do what you want to do with your life, but also choose something that you're already good at or that you could become good at within a reasonable amount of time.

_____

_____

_____

_____

Finally, review your responses to 'What do you really dislike doing?' and 'What aren't you so good at?'. Would any of your responses to the questions in these sections cause you to delete any of the consulting possibilities that you circled with that red marker pen? Yes? Then take that red marker pen and put a big X through them. No? Good. Enter the surviving items of this exercise in the space below:

Now complete the following sentences:

I am in the _____ consulting business.

I help my clients _____.

Congratulations! You've identified the consulting businesses that best match your desires and your talents. You have the best chance for success if you pursue one or more of the opportunities revealed by this synergy. Of course, success takes more than a great idea. You have to have clients who are willing to pay you for your services, and your idea has to be profitable. The next section addresses these issues and a host of related issues.

Deciding Whether Your Idea is Marketable

Should you or shouldn't you? Only you can make the decision whether to become an independent consultant.

Unfortunately, trying to predict whether your consulting business will fly high or go down in flames is a difficult task. Many new businesses succeed each year, but many fail. How will yours fare? Only time will tell. Many factors add up to potential success or disaster when running your own business – most importantly, your drive to succeed, the availability of clients who are willing to pay enough for your services so that you can make a profit, and your ability to keep your current clients satisfied while attracting new clients.

In this section, we address some of the most important issues surrounding your decision whether to make the move. Before you leave your day job, give serious consideration to these issues.

Who are your clients and what are their needs?

You may have a great idea, but unless you also have clients who need your services and are willing to pay for them, all you have is an idea. Ideas don't pay your bills; clients do. Identifying your clients and their needs – defining and describing them – is an important step in determining whether you have a viable idea.

So who are your clients, and what do they need? You need to be able to list real names and phone numbers, not just stuff like 'anyone who needs an online presence for their business' or 'a large number of investors who aren't being served adequately by big brokers'.

As you consider exactly who your clients are and what they need, ask yourself the following questions:

- ✔ **Who are your most likely clients?** Make a list. Name names and list phone numbers and addresses. You can find clients by looking in the Yellow Pages or in industry trade magazines, by networking, or by researching possible firms of interest on the Internet. Vague, ambiguous, pie-in-the-sky entries do not cut it on this list, so don't even waste your time with them!

- ✔ **Exactly what do your clients need?** As you develop your list of likely clients, also note what each client needs. For example, your targeted clients may need someone to offer training in skills for new managers. The best way to find out what your clients need is by talking to them one-to-one. Will you provide exactly what they need, or are you going to try to sell them something they don't need?

- ✔ **What advantages do you offer over your competitors?** Although you may have a great idea, other consultants can probably offer much the same services to your potential clients (yes – it's true!). Determine why your clients would pick you over your competitors, and then concentrate on those advantages. If you're not sure what advantages your competitors have over *your* consulting business, ask your clients. They'll probably be happy to point out the pluses and minuses of you and your competition.

Can your business become profitable?

Doing what you want to do with your life instead of being just another cog in the wheels of some humungous bureaucratic maze of an organisation is a great goal. Consulting is, above all, about freedom – the freedom to decide what you want to do and then to pursue it. However, don't forget one minor detail. Unless you recently won the lottery, found undiscovered oil reserves in your back garden, or inherited the McLaren F1 racing team, you have to make a profit if your consulting business is to live long and prosper.

To determine whether your business can be profitable, do your maths and take the following items into account:

- ✔ **What are your anticipated revenues?** Consider potential clients and decide the level of revenues that you can reasonably anticipate bringing in for several different periods – a month, a quarter, and a year. Be prudent and conservative; this is not the time to get overexcited or kid yourself. Do some outside research to discover what your competitors charge and the volume of business that they bring in each year.

- ✔ **What are your anticipated expenses?** List all of your potential expenses for several different periods – a month, a quarter, a year. Think hard. You don't want to forget anything. Do a reality check by examining your bank and credit card statements. Typical expenses for a consulting firm include:

    - Rent

    - Utilities (electricity, gas, water)

    - Computer equipment

    - Furniture

    - Office supplies (paper, staples, pens)

    - Travel (train and air fares, petrol, hotels)

    - Postage, overnight courier fees

    - Subcontractors (work outsourced to other firms)

    Here's a tip: It's always best to underestimate revenues and overestimate expenses.

- ✔ **Do your anticipated revenues exceed expenses or vice versa?** As they say in the US, this is the $64,000 question. When your revenues exceed your expenses, the leftovers are called profit. Profit is good. When your expenses exceed your revenues, especially for a prolonged period of time, this is called a 'going-out-of-business plan'. This kind of plan is definitely not good. Although you must expect your consulting business to need several months to a year or more to become profitable, the sooner you can make more money than you spend, the better! Remember – Rover needs to be fed!

Is the timing right?

In business, as in life, timing can be everything. Although hard work and persistence can overcome almost any obstacle, having the right product for the right client at the right time is also important. For example, if you had started a website consulting firm in 1990, you might have starved. In 1990, few people or companies had yet heard of the Internet, much less established a presence on it. However, if you had started the same business in 1996, you'd have had more than enough to do up to the present day and probably for a long time to come.

Consider the following when you try to determine whether your timing is right:

- ✔ **Does what you want to do provide a necessary service?** You may have the greatest idea since sliced bread, but you may find that no one wants or needs your product. This is why all the big FTSE 100 companies spend tons of money on marketing studies, focus groups, and product opinion surveys. You don't want to spend a great deal of time and money chasing a market that just isn't there. Before you start your consulting practice, survey the market you want to enter and establish whether real clients will spend real money for what you have to sell. You can find out if people need your service by making phone calls to potential clients, conducting focus groups, or using a variety of other market research methods.

- ✔ **Are you too far ahead of your time?** You may have an idea that is so great, but so far ahead of its time that your clients aren't even aware that they need it. When you're too far ahead of your clients, convincing them that they need your services can take a great deal of time and effort. If you're on the cutting edge of the kinds of services you offer, don't get so far out on the edge that your clients can't catch up with you!

- ✔ **Are you too far behind the times?** On the other hand, jumping into a booming field only to find that your potential clients' attention has already moved on to the next big thing is even easier. For example, total quality management (TQM) was a booming field for almost a decade and attracted loads of attention from a wide array of clients and consultants. Now, however, organisations that once embraced TQM have left it far behind and moved to the next business fad. If you were to start a firm specialising in TQM today, you'd be hard-pressed to line up enough business to pay your electricity bill, much less make a profit. As you decide on a consulting speciality, look towards the future – where your customers are heading – instead of to the past, where they've already been.

Considering Whether You Have What It Takes

This question goes way beyond the nuts and bolts of starting and running a successful business. It goes to your personality, your motivation, your personal support systems, your whole existence. If you prefer the security of working for a large corporation and the thought of being out on your own makes you break into a sweat, maybe full-time consulting isn't for you. Take it slowly and work your way into it.

Don't forget that you may be able to consult on a part-time basis while you continue to hold down a conventional full-time job. In fact, if at all possible, this is exactly what we recommend. A good idea is to work into it gradually, building your business as you go, until you're ready to progress to a full-time consulting business of your own. You may have the option of increasing the amount of time you devote to your consulting business and decreasing the amount of time you devote to your other job. If you become a victim of a downsizing, rightsizing, or re-engineering, you're ready for it. However, heed one word of caution: Before consulting part-time, check out your current employment contract terms. Some employers place restrictions on what jobs you can do in your spare time – some require you simply to seek permission, while some even disallow it completely.

Consider these things when you're trying to decide whether you're cut out to be a consultant:

- **Do you dream of being your own boss?** Perhaps that's not quite the right question. Maybe it should be: 'How often do you dream of being your own boss?' Being in control of one's life can be a very strong motivator for a consultant – a motivator strong enough to bring your enterprise great success through the sheer force of your desire to succeed.

- **Are you independent and a self-starter?** When you're an independent consultant, you don't have anyone to hold your hand. No one is there to make sure that you get out of bed in the morning, to tell you that you're not working hard enough, or to praise you for doing a great job. You probably won't run into anyone at the coffee machine to socialise with, except maybe your cat or your seven-year-old daughter. It's all up to you. Are you up to the challenge? If you need to be jump-started on Mondays, then maybe consulting just isn't for you.

✔ **Can you support yourself as you establish your practice?** Although supporting yourself financially is important (for some reason, the people from whom you buy the things you need to run your business expect you to pay them for their trouble), supporting yourself emotionally is just as important – perhaps even more so. Are you mentally ready to make the move to consulting? Do you have the support of your friends, relatives, and significant others? Are you ready to answer the inevitable question: 'Why would you leave that great job you have?' When you're comfortable with your answer to that question, you're truly ready to become an independent consultant.

Believe us: No one said that starting your own consulting business was going to be an easy proposition. Or, if they did, then they were stretching the truth more than just a bit. Starting any business is a risky proposition – official statistics reveal that the majority of new businesses fail within five years after they start up. That's one of the potential downsides to starting your own consulting business, but the upsides can be very rewarding – not just financially, but also in terms of the personal satisfaction that comes from being in control of your own work and your own destiny. Once you've left the corporate 9-to-5 behind for good, you'll ask yourself why you didn't make the move sooner – and you'll never want to go back to the world you've left behind.

Chapter 3

Taking the Plunge with Your Own Consulting Business

In This Chapter

▶ Understanding when the time is right

▶ Easing into consulting

▶ Starting up: first things first

*T*aking the plunge into consulting is a big step for most people – especially those who have worked for traditional, established organisations for most or all of their working lives. For many, letting go of a traditional 9-to-5 job can be a time for deep soul-searching, introspection, and worry. *Am I disciplined enough to be my own boss? Will people be willing to pay for my knowledge and services, and how much will they pay? What will my family think if I decide to leave my regular job to start my own business? Am I ready to leave my job? Can I survive without getting a salary every month? How will I obtain benefits like health insurance and a pension plan?* All of these questions – and many others like them – must be answered and dealt with before you can take the plunge. Listen carefully to the answers you give because they'll ultimately determine whether you're ready to make the transition to independent consulting and whether you'll succeed in your new endeavour.

So how do you make the transition to starting your own consulting business? And, perhaps more importantly, how do you know whether you're ready to make the transition? Is there a way to find out the answer to this question before you put your career (and potentially the welfare of both you and your significant others) on the line? Can you make the transition a little at a time, or does it have to happen all at once? And exactly how do you make your first moves towards becoming a consultant? Funny you should ask. Those just happen to be the very questions that we address in this chapter.

Deciding When the Time Is Right

Congratulations! If you've found your way to this particular section of this particular chapter, we can guess that either you've decided to join the growing ranks of men and women who are taking control of their lives and their financial futures by becoming consultants, or you're seriously thinking about it. When considering some of the factors that determine exactly when the timing is best for you, don't be surprised if your answers differ from those of your family, friends, or colleagues – everyone has a unique schedule.

In this section, we examine some of the key issues that help determine exactly when you might make your move into consulting. This list is by no means exhaustive – feel free to add any considerations that affect you directly.

Professional considerations

Before you can become a successful independent consultant, you have to attain a certain level of professional expertise. For example, if you expect someone to hire you to set up a new manufacturing quality system, you need to have a strong base of experience in the area of manufacturing quality systems. If you spent your 20 years of experience on the checkout in Tesco, you may have a tough time selling yourself as an expert in manufacturing.

If you're thinking about making a living as an independent consultant, be sure to keep the following professional considerations in mind:

- ✔ **Subject matter expertise:** Most people hire a consultant because they want the benefit of a consultant's extensive expertise. They know that hiring a competent consultant isn't an inexpensive proposition, but they also know that the overall price is less than if they specifically hire or train an employee to do the same task. Before you become a full-time consultant, become an expert (or pretty damn close) in your field. If you can ease into consulting by working on a part-time basis, you gain the benefit of learning while being supported by your full-time job.

- ✔ **Certifications and licences:** In some cases, you may need to obtain special credentials before you can pursue your chosen vocation. For example, if you plan to become an independent financial adviser, you must give serious consideration to earning your IFA qualification before you jump into the fray. Many other professions require extensive certifications or licensing before you can practise them. If you work for an organisation that pays for your required training and testing, by all means take advantage of these resources. Getting a regular salary while earning your certification is better than trying to earn a living on your own while you pursue the necessary paperwork.

✔ **References:** The ability to point to a long list of satisfied clients is a critical selling point for any consultant. Try to do as many jobs as you can with as many customers as possible before you go out on your own. Not only can you take your current clients with you when you make the move to independent consulting, but you also create a valuable network of associates that you can tap to locate new clients.

✔ **Organisational ability:** Making a business work takes more than printing up a set of business cards. You have to be organised, you have to have a plan, and you have to know (or learn) how to run a business. Running a consulting business is no different than any other business in that you have deadlines to meet, bills to pay, office facilities to secure, and associates and clients to coordinate with. Before you launch your new consulting business, take the time necessary to plan ahead and get organised. The time you invest before you get started pays for itself many times over once you're under way.

Financial considerations

Certainly, financial considerations weigh heavily in deciding when to become a consultant. Becoming complacent is easy when you're earning a decent wage and you're getting an attractive package of benefits. However, what's here today can easily be gone tomorrow – none of us owns a working crystal ball so we just don't know for sure what's going to happen in the future. We have far too many acquaintances who have been pushed out of organisations that are desperate to cut costs in any way possible. Businesses often don't care how many years you've worked there or how talented you are. When the budget axe falls, the results can be devastating if you're not ready with your own plan. So when you hear 'Breaking Up Is Hard to Do' on the music system, grab a box and get ready to pack your personal things.

Before you go out on your own, however, you must be able to support yourself and any significant others who depend on you. Consider the following financial issues before you launch a consulting practice:

✔ **Weigh your income against your expenses:** It's a simple rule of business and of life in general. To survive, your income has to be more than your costs. If it's not, you go into debt. And if you go far enough into debt, eventually you're forced out of business when you apply for bankruptcy. Remember Mr Micawber in *David Copperfield*? 'Annual income twenty pounds, annual expenditure nineteen, nineteen and six, result happiness. Annual income twenty pounds, annual expenditure twenty pounds, nought and six, result misery.' As you plan your consulting business, review all your projected sources of income and expenditure. If your income exceeds your costs, no problem – you can go forward confidently. However, if your costs exceed your projected income as a consultant, figure out how to put yourself in a more favourable position before launching into full-time consulting. How? Consider the following approaches first, and then turn to Chapter 6 for detailed information on how to set your fees to optimise the amount of money you can make as an independent consultant:

- Increase the amount of work that you do.

- Increase the rates that you charge your clients.

- Decrease your costs.

- Upgrade the type of clients you pursue to those who focus on the value you bring to the table rather than your rates.

✔ **Assess how much you have in savings:** It's been said that most people are only a few pay cheques away from bankruptcy. That's just one reason why having money squirreled away in a savings account or other highly liquid asset, such as a money market account, is important. You need to have some money saved whether you're working for an established organisation or working for yourself. Do you have enough money saved to get you through times when your business is down and your clients aren't paying your invoices as quickly as you'd like? You need at least three months' worth of living expenses – preferably more – to survive on your own. Assess your savings account and, if you find it lacking, direct as much money to it as you possibly can before you go out on your own. Believe us – when you need the funds to get through a particularly rough patch, you'll be glad you took this precaution.

✔ **Plan for the inevitable surprises:** Life is full of surprises, which can be both good and bad. A good surprise in business is an early payment from a client or a large, unexpected contract from a client you had just about written off. A bad surprise is finding out that a client has decided to go bankrupt before paying your bill or receiving a notice that Her Majesty's Revenue and Customs wants a much larger chunk of your income than you planned to contribute this year. Again, you have to be financially prepared for surprises – especially bad ones. Make sure that your income is sufficient and that you have adequate savings to get you safely past bad surprises.

Personal considerations

You have other considerations besides professional and financial when you decide to become an independent consultant:

✔ **Friends and family:** What will your friends and family think about your choice to become a consultant? In some cases, everyone may be incredibly supportive of your move. In other cases – especially when you already have a well-paid career, and will be giving up a steady salary and benefits – your friends and family may question your sanity in deciding to become an independent consultant. Have you lost your marbles? Why would you want to do that? You may have to counsel your family about your reasons for consulting and about your new role. Before you make the move to consulting, make sure that you're clear about why you want to make the change. Explaining your decision to others is easier when you can first explain it to yourself!

✔ **Lifestyle:** Becoming a self-employed consultant can mean quite a change in your lifestyle. For example, when you work for an organisation, you're almost always given a long list of tasks and assignments to complete. However, when you're working for yourself, suddenly you have to direct and motivate yourself to get things done. Self-motivation can be a liberating but frightening prospect for someone who has been told what to do and when to do it for years. Self-employment requires lots of self-discipline. You still have to get up each morning and go to work, even when your office is only a few steps across the landing – or at a coffee shop down the street – rather than 40 minutes on the motorway.

✔ **Personal goals:** Do you have personal goals? If so, how does becoming a consultant affect them? Becoming a self-employed consultant isn't something that you do on the spur of the moment. It requires serious planning and preparation. Whatever your personal goals, be they financial, professional, or whatever, make sure that consulting does not conflict with them.

Only you can decide when the time is right to leave your day job and step into a new world of unlimited opportunity – a world where you control the reins of your destiny. If the prospect of consulting seems too overwhelming right now, don't forget that you can make the transition from your current job to a career in consulting at your own pace – one small step at a time or one great leap forward. The choice is yours.

Preparing for Stops Along the Way

Becoming a self-employed consultant isn't something that just happens to you one day. It's something that deserves and requires significant planning to make it a successful reality in your life. Yes, some people do walk into their offices one day and resign, starting their own businesses before they've developed an adequate client base, and others are sacked or made redundant before they've had the chance to prepare. Most independent consultants, however, build successful businesses by making a stop or two along the way.

Big organisation, to consulting firm, to self-employment

Many self-employed consultants have found a very natural transition from a full-time regular job to independent consulting by making a stop along the way as an employee for a consulting firm. For example, Philip has a friend who worked for a large company for 10 years – all the while gaining valuable experience and company-paid education and training. He was lured away by a large international consulting firm and was put to work doing consulting jobs for firms in a wide range of industry sectors and around the world. Eventually, after he had sharpened his consulting skills and established a huge network of industry contacts, he started his own successful independent consulting business in London.

Moving from a big organisation to an established consulting firm and then to your own independent consulting business offers numerous advantages:

- ✔ If you stay with your big-organisation position long enough, you can collect retirement or a pension after you leave.

- ✔ While working for an established consulting firm, you develop and hone strong consulting and client skills while you learn the ins and outs of the consulting industry. Plus, working for a recognised consulting firm represents a seal of approval of your expertise.

- ✔ An established consulting firm also gives you the opportunity to develop a valuable network of contacts that may become the client base of your own consulting business (but watch out for any restrictive covenants in your employment contract).

- ✔ Once you've set up business independently, your former employer might retain you as a consultant. Because you already know the company, its customers, and its competitors, you can contribute immediately with no additional training or orientation.

Part-time work

Easing into your consulting business on a part-time basis can be one of the safest and least painful ways to make the transition. For most prospective self-employed consultants, this is the best approach. On the plus side, you can keep your regular job as long as you like while you maintain your consulting business on a part-time basis. On the minus side, doing both jobs can create occasional diary headaches. For example, imagine what you would do if an emergency at your regular job required you to fly to Manchester on the same day that you were supposed to present your final recommendations to an important consulting client in Canterbury.

Both jobs can peacefully coexist, however, with careful planning and extra work on your part. For example, you can keep one master calendar to ensure that you don't have surprise diary conflicts. And, if you need to take a day's leave from your regular job to do some work for a consulting client, you can request permission for the leave far enough in advance to minimise the negative impact of your absence on your current organisation. You also need to set up regular 'office hours' – time when you're not at your regular job – so your consulting clients can contact you. You can hire a phone answering service relatively cheaply so that clients can contact you almost anytime. Who knows – you may build up such a successful business that you have no choice but to quit your regular job sooner than you had anticipated and go into independent consulting on a full-time basis.

Here are some of the positive outcomes of doing your consulting on a part-time basis:

✔ You can try various consulting alternatives and build a strong client base while maintaining the security of your regular full-time job.

✔ You retain your health insurance and other important job benefits (a monthly salary, for one!) as long as you remain in your regular job.

✔ If your foray into the wonderful world of consulting doesn't work out, you can keep your regular job and try consulting again some other time.

Full-time work

Pursuing a regular full-time job while running a full-time consulting business can be very demanding on your schedule and on your sense of reality ('Where am I?' 'Who am I working for today?'), and it may be one of the least preferred options. Yet holding two full-time jobs is an option for many people as they make the transition from their regular jobs to careers as independent consultants. On the plus side, not only can you fully immerse yourself in the wonderful world of consulting, but you can start developing a solid client base and generating significant consulting revenues – greatly accelerating your transition – all within the safety and security of your regular job. On the minus side, you could possibly quite literally work yourself to death. (This is probably not what you had in mind when you decided to become an independent consultant.)

We can't with a clear conscience recommend taking on full-time consulting business on top of a full-time job. However, if you do decide to go that way, moving from a regular job to independent consulting by pursuing your new business on a full-time basis can work to your benefit in the following ways:

✔ You get the best of both worlds – a regular salary and benefits from your current job and full immersion in your new consulting endeavour.

> ✔ By building a base of consulting clients and income more quickly than you can by consulting on a part-time basis, you can greatly accelerate your transition to full-time independent consultant.
>
> ✔ You'll sleep well at night because you're so tired from working two full-time jobs.

Check out your employment contract thoroughly before working and consulting at the same time.

A big contract

For some people, starting an independent consulting business is an all-or-nothing kind of thing. Bob has a business acquaintance who submitted proposals to a variety of potential clients while working in a full-time position as an employee of an organisation. When Bob's acquaintance was selected as the successful bidder on a million-dollar contract, she had all the motivation and reason she needed to leave her job and dive into independent consulting on a full-time basis. If you consider this route, have an adequate base of consulting contracts lined up before you make the move to full-time consulting, and don't, we repeat, don't, submit your resignation before you have a signed contract in your hands! We discuss the ins and outs of writing winning proposals in Chapter 7.

Starting up your independent consulting practice by landing a big contract offers these advantages and many more:

> ✔ You don't have to leave the security of your full-time job until you win a big contract.
>
> ✔ Producing and submitting contract proposals to potential clients in your after-work hours is easy. You must limit such work to after hours to prevent conflicts of interest and future legal wrangles with your current employer.
>
> ✔ If you don't land a big contract, all you've lost is some of your time and the cost of copying your proposals and posting them out.

Total immersion

Finally, you have another way of shifting to independent consulting: total immersion. You may go to work one day and, because of a reorganisation, be notified that you have been selected for redundancy. Here's your cheque, please clear out your desk, thank you very much for all your fine work, don't call us, we'll call you. Or you may reach the end of a long career of service to your organisation and decide to retire. Or maybe you just can't stand the idea of spending one more day in your office doing the job you do or answering to a boss you no longer respect, and you resign.

Although total immersion isn't always the best way to start an independent consulting business – you may not be able to keep your personal financial boat afloat very long without a regular salary, for example, it does offer the following benefits:

- ✔ You can focus all your work energy on establishing a successful consulting business.

- ✔ The prospect of being out of work has a special way of focusing your attention on the real necessities in life: paying your rent or mortgage, buying food, and making your car repayments. In the words of Samuel Johnson, 'Depend upon it, sir, when a man knows he is to be hanged in a fortnight, it concentrates his mind wonderfully'.

- ✔ If your former employer established a pension plan for you, you may be able to tap into those funds to help get your business off the ground and buy yourself time as you establish a client base.

Taking the First Steps

Assume for the moment that you've decided that you're ready to take the consulting plunge. Whether you decide just to stick your toe in first or to give it all you've got, testing the water before you jump in is always a good idea. Testing the water is simple when you're at home in your bath, but when you're starting a new business – your new business – you have to do more than just check the temperature to make sure that you don't get burnt!

Here are a few tips that can help you take those first steps as you get your consulting business going.

Talk to people who do what you want to do

You don't need to reinvent the wheel. Many people before you made the transition to independent consulting – including some, no doubt, who are doing exactly what you want to do. Some have succeeded beyond their wildest dreams, and others haven't. You can really learn from someone who is already doing what you want to do.

Before you start your new business, find people who do what you want to do and talk to them – as often and for as long as you can. Arrange an appointment to meet them at work, or invite them to an informal get-together after work. Find out what things worked for them and what things didn't. Ask them about the good times and the bad times, and what you can do to bring about more of the former. You may find the flames of your desire to start your own independent consulting firm fanned to new heights by your acquaintances' enthusiasm. Or the embers may die when you learn that what you thought you wanted to do really isn't what you want to do. Either way, you learn important lessons that can make you and your business much stronger. Besides, you're building an informed network of consultants who one day could help you expand your business.

Start small

Given a choice, you're better off to start small and work your way up to larger projects as you hone your consulting skills. Why? One reason is that you can devote more of your time and attention to a small project than you can to a large one. If you're still working full-time in a traditional job, you have to fit the project into your schedule whenever you can – most likely at nights or during weekends. We can guarantee from our personal experience that finding extra time to work on a small project is easier than finding time to work on a large project. Not only that, but you can learn the ropes of your chosen field at a pace that is comfortable to you, and you have a lot more time available to refine and polish your work.

Evaluate the results

How do you know whether your tentative first steps at consulting are taking you in the right direction? The way to find out is to evaluate your results:

✓ **Is consulting what you expected?** Many people have a glorified view of how wonderful consulting must be. Consulting is wonderful – but for many, the reality of consulting doesn't quite match up with the fantasy. Is consulting what you expected, or is it something less or more? If it's something less, then reconsider the kind of consulting that you've decided to take on or your approach to doing it. Don't worry: you may need several tries before you get it right!

✓ **Do you like what you're doing?** Don't forget: You're supposed to be having fun doing what you're doing. If you enjoy the consulting work that you're doing, great! If not, why not? Is your view likely to change as you get more involved in consulting and devote more of your life to doing it? Don't forget that the first few months (perhaps even the first few years) of transition to your own consulting business may be an emotional roller coaster for you and your loved ones. These highs and lows are a natural part of making a major life change. If you hang in there and keep trying, things will probably soon get better. If, however, you've been trying for some time and things aren't getting better, then maybe becoming a self-employed consultant isn't your cup of tea.

✔ **Do your clients like what you're doing?** Liking what you do is a great feeling. But knowing that your clients like what you do is equally important (at least if you want to pay the bills). If you plan to consult on a part-time basis only to supplement your current income, you don't need a lot of clients to keep your enterprise afloat. However, if you plan to pursue consulting on a full-time basis, you'll need lots of very satisfied clients to keep you fully employed. How do you find out whether they're satisfied? Ask them. You can do so in the form of a direct interview, a casual conversation, a feedback form, or a questionnaire. If you do good work at a fair price and are dependable, don't worry: they will come.

So are you ready to take the plunge? If your current job still has the advantage, don't feel that you need to make your move right away – the opportunity will always be there waiting for you. However, if consulting has the edge, now may be the time to make the switch. If you do, we wish you the very best and offer this advice: Don't look back.

Part II
Getting Your Consulting Business Off the Ground

'Well now we've hired you as our consultant perhaps you can advise us on a better way to test the strength capacity of our chairs.'

Part II

Getting Your

Consulting Business

Off the Ground

In this part . . .

*E*very self-employed consultant started somewhere –
at the beginning.

In this part, we take a close look at exactly what it takes to
start a successful consulting business, including the legal
and financial ins and outs, taxes, and a topic of particular
importance to consultants: ethics. We also delve deeply
into the critical topic of determining what you're worth to
your clients, and setting fees that reflect your value while
helping you develop a profitable consulting business
that's built to last.

Chapter 4

Starting a Successful Consulting Business

. . . .

In This Chapter

▶ Deciding whether to establish a home office

▶ Setting up your home office

▶ Reviewing your home office checklist

▶ Determining when to move your home office out of your home

. . . .

*A*s you may imagine, when you become a self-employed consultant, you need to find a new place to work. For most of us, this means creating an office in our homes, or perhaps finding a small office outside the home. Regardless of where you decide to plant yourself and your new business, you need to set it up, and you need to find the kind of support services – accounting, banking, legal – that you probably took for granted when you were working for an established company.

As you get set up, remember: You're the boss. You get to decide when and where you do business. If you want to rent a city centre office or one in a business park, you can do so if you like. Many consultants (especially those who have employees) do rent office space, and they are very happy with that arrangement. However, you now have a chance to take a different path – one that offers an array of opportunities and benefits that you just don't get by working in a traditional office.

In this chapter, we focus on establishing a home office. We look into the space and furnishings you need to get started, and we review some of the financial incentives to establishing a home office and explain how you can take advantage of them. Finally, we talk about finding and using support services to your advantage.

Getting Set Up

Setting up your office is probably the most fun part of running a business from your home. Remember all the dingy offices that you were crammed into in your past jobs? Remember the too-small desks, the uncomfortable chairs, the barely adequate computers and the stuffy air? This is your big chance to make up for all your previous employers' transgressions against your sensibilities and to design an office that meets your needs.

One more thing: This is also your big chance to take advantage of the financial benefits that setting up a home-based consulting business can offer to you. In the UK, if you play your cards right, Her Majesty's Revenue and Customs can help you pay for your home office by making all your business expenses – as well as the portion of your housing expenses that is attributable to your home office – tax-deductible.

This tax deduction can be a real financial benefit to you and your business; however, the government is very particular about exactly who is eligible to take the home-office deduction and under what circumstances. Writing off a part of your home as a business can raise a red flag for tax inspectors, and can create council tax issues and result in capital gains tax being applied to a portion of your house value when you sell it, so be sure that you know what you're doing. Consult your accountant for more details on the home-office tax rules.

In this section, we explore the essentials of setting up your own home office – from the space to the equipment in it. Don't forget that you'll be spending a great deal of time in your office. Make it as nice a place to work in as possible.

Your space

The total amount of space that you're going to need in which to set up a functioning home office depends on the nature of your consulting business. For most consultants, the ideal situation is to take over an existing bedroom or study and convert it into an office. Not only do you get plenty of space for all your furniture, equipment, and supplies, but a bedroom or study with a door also offers privacy – an important ingredient in any home office. In addition, a room that is 100 per cent dedicated to your business is easier for you to use.

Here are some key things you need to do to set up an inviting and productive workspace in your home:

 ✔ **Find an out-of-the-way place.** For example, you don't want your home office to be in the middle of your family's traffic flow during the morning get-the-kids-ready-for-school rush, nor do you want it to be in a garage that fills with smelly fumes every time someone starts up the car. Ideally, your office is a private sanctuary where you can focus on your work, not on everything else *but* your work. On the other hand, if you find yourself working late into the night, make sure your activities don't bother your spouse or partner. If you've selected your own bedroom as your home office, this can lead to problems.

✔ **Make the space inviting.** You're going to be spending a lot of time in your home office, so you want it to be comfortable and inviting. It must have adequate heating when you need it but also plenty of cool air on a hot day. Decorate the walls in a neutral colour, and put up blinds on the windows that enable you to control the amount of outside light that enters your office.

✔ **Provide for easy access.** Make sure that your office is easy to access without disturbing the other members of your household. You don't, for example, want the only entrance to your office to be through the baby's nursery.

✔ **Have good lighting and plenty of it.** Good lighting is critical to your productivity. Ideally, your office will have both plenty of natural light from windows (most bedrooms are already well catered for in this department) and from artificial light sources, such as overhead lighting and desk lamps.

✔ **Ventilate the space early and often.** Make sure that your home office has access to plenty of fresh air. This is especially necessary if you have computers, printers, copiers, and other office equipment that generate ozone, dust, and heat.

✔ **Get wired.** Your home office needs plenty of earthed (three-prong) electrical sockets to plug in all your office equipment. Not only do you need sockets for your computer, but you also need sockets for your printers, your fax machine, your scanner, your battery charger for your mobile phone, your desk lamps, a radio, and anything else that you may need to plug in. In addition to electricity, you need at least one phone line – maybe more – as well as a modem or router to connect to the Internet.

✔ **Make sure it's secure.** What would happen if someone stole your computer, along with all your disks and backup media? For some consultants, this incident would be an unmitigated please-shoot-me-now-to-put-me-out-of-my-misery, disaster. If you don't have a home security system connected to an alarm or monitoring service, consider getting one. While you're at it, buy a small fireproof safe to store your backup disks – and make sure that you use it!

Your furniture

Your home office can be nothing more than a desk and a chair, or it can be a fully equipped suite with everything found in any commercial office, including fax machines, computers, copiers, and much more. When you decide to furnish your home office, get good-quality furnishings that are both comfortable and built to last. You're going to be spending a lot of time in your office, so make it a joy – not an ordeal – to work there.

If you're watching your budget (and who isn't?), consider buying your furniture used instead of new. Keep an eye on eBay for deals in your area. You may also want to consider renting or leasing your office furniture, although doing so may not be a great idea in the long run because you'll probably pay far more than if you just bought it to start with.

With that advice in mind, here are some key items that you need to consider when shopping for office furniture:

- ✔ **Your chair:** If you're looking for somewhere to invest a little extra money for your office setup, then spend it on the chair. Spend the extra money to get a high-quality, ergonomically correct task chair. If you've used an ergonomic chair at work, you already know the importance of being in the correct working position – especially when you spend most of your time at your desk. Using a quality chair reduces fatigue and helps to prevent back pain and other ills that can occur when your posture is incorrect for long periods of time. Remember also that if you buy a big chair, although it makes you feel like Alan Sugar, it may completely dominate or even not fit into your small study at home.

  If you expect clients to visit, make sure that you have comfortable chairs available for them, too.

- ✔ **Your desk:** When shopping for your desk, think big! No matter how large your desk, by the time you load it up with a computer, a printer, a phone, a calculator, and a personal planner or two, you have precious little space left over on which to do your work. Get a sturdy desk – you don't want it to be rocking to and fro as you type up proposals. Also be sure that your desk has more than enough room to accommodate whatever you intend to put on it whilst leaving you enough clear space to spread out your work. A large traditional office desk or even a sturdy work-table will do just fine. However, don't buy a desk so big that you have to go on a diet to get around it.

  While you're shopping, make sure that you look for a desk that is at the proper height so that working on your computer is an ergonomic dream rather than a nightmare. According to experts, a computer workstation needs to be at a height of about 70 centimetres (28 inches) off the floor.

Ideally, your keyboard will be on an adjustable tray so you can find the most comfortable setting (which will probably be closer to a height of 63 to 66 centimetres (25 or 26 inches).

✔ **Work-tables:** A couple of work-tables can give you the extra room you need to get your work done more efficiently and to stay organised. You don't need anything fancy here – a simple table with folding legs or a sturdy dining-room table works fine.

✔ **Filing cabinets:** You may be able to make do with a file drawer in your desk. If you deal with volumes of paperwork as a part of your consulting practice, however, you need additional filing space. An organised filing system is critical to your efficiency, so spend some serious time designing and implementing a filing system before you jump into your consulting business. Plenty of choices are available, and your ultimate decision depends on the amount of paperwork that you need to keep at hand. At the very least, get a freestanding, four-drawer filing cabinet. You can easily add more cabinets as the need arises. For long-term storage, pull the documents from your filing cabinets and place them in the cardboard storage boxes commonly known as archive boxes. You can then stick the storage boxes in a loft or in the garage. Reserve the space in your filing cabinets for documents that you actively use and need to access regularly.

✔ **Bookshelves:** What would an office be without bookshelves? In addition to holding books, bookshelves are handy for a variety of other purposes. Philip's bookshelves – which are actually dark wood storage shelves that he bought at IKEA – are filled with books, his laptop computer and related accessories, stacks and stacks of magazines for research, laser printer paper, envelopes, postal supplies, and his cherished CD player and radio. No matter how many bookshelves you get, we can guarantee that you'll fill them up.

✔ **Supply storage:** Make sure to set aside a drawer or shelf to hold your office supplies. Pens, pencils, paper clips, staples, marker pens, and all the other fruits of your office-supply shopping spree need a place safe from your dog, cat, or children.

Your equipment

As with any office, your home office requires certain pieces of equipment and supplies for you to conduct business. For example, doing an in-depth automated spreadsheet analysis without a computer is pretty hard. And contacting your clients is particularly difficult if you don't have a phone.

This section discusses obtaining the basic equipment you need to get your business up and running.

- **Telephones:** You definitely need at least one telephone – maybe more. If you have only one phone, get a basic telephone with a hold button and 'hands-free' facility. If you're like 99.9 per cent of the rest of us, you also need a reliable mobile phone. Be sure to get one that will work wherever you may be travelling for your consulting services and carefully research for the right tariff. And don't forget to get an answering machine or voicemail service so that your callers can leave a message if you're not around.

- **Computer:** Your computer is the nerve centre of your home office and an essential element in your consulting business. Get the best you can afford, and make sure that it has the kinds of software that you need to get your work done. If you'll do most of your work at your home office, get a standard desktop computer. If you'll be on the road frequently or plan to spend much time with clients, consider getting a laptop computer. Bob's laptop is powerful enough to be used as his desktop computer simply by plugging in a monitor and keyboard. For software, a complete office suite, such as Microsoft Office, is a smart way to go. Microsoft Office contains word processing, spreadsheet, presentation graphics, and email programs, all in one package. Also consider some of the latest Internet-based offerings such as the Google Office suite (`http://docs.google.com`), which can be accessed anywhere you can get an Internet connection.

- **Internet access:** Having access to the Internet is absolutely essential these days, and you've got lots of options for getting it. You can access the Internet with a telephone modem using a broadband service such as BT Broadband, or you can add broadband from your cable or satellite service, such as those provided by Sky Broadband or Virgin Media. If you don't already have one, get a broadband connection (the fastest that you can) so that you can run your computer as well as your fax and phone all on one line.

- **Fax machine:** If your computer has a data/fax modem, you can use it as your fax machine. However, if you don't want to leave your computer turned on all day long, buy a dedicated fax machine. Be sure to get one that uses plain paper – not the old 'toilet rolls' of thermal paper. New fax machines have added benefits: You can use most of them as copiers, printers, and scanners.

- **Network:** If you've got more than one computer in your home office, or if you want to hook up all the computers and other computer-based devices (such as your Playstation, Wii, and so on) in your home, then you probably need to set up a computer network. You can choose to go with either a wired (generally using a router and Ethernet cables) or a wireless setup (using a wireless router). If you go with a wireless system, be sure to turn on password protection so your neighbours aren't tempted to avail themselves of your service!

✔ **Copier/scanner:** If you need to make only a few copies of documents on an irregular basis, you can use your fax machine or scanner as a copier or rely on a local copying service, such as KopyKwik. However, if you make lots of copies on a regular basis, buy or lease a decent office copier. To save yourself grief and headaches down the road, get one that at a minimum has an automatic document feeder and can handle A4-size paper. Also get a service contract that guarantees service within one business day after you make your service call.

Other business essentials

The big stuff is out of the way. Now it's time to get down to the little things that really make an office an office. Remember those awful pens that head-quarters produced to save money? Or those tacky desk calendars? Or how about those flimsy A4 pads that fell apart more often than they held together? You'll never have to use any of those again. Now you decide what kinds of pens, pencils, paper, calendars, and other office supplies that you keep in your office.

When you set up your home office, stock up on plenty of office supplies. Visit your local office supplier store like Staples or shop online. Here are a few essentials for any well-equipped home office:

✔ **Writing utensils:** Get plenty of your favourite pens and pencils – now's your big chance to really let yourself go. In addition, buy an assortment of colour marker pens in sizes ranging from fine to broad. If you have a whiteboard in your office, you need special marker pens for that. And don't forget to stock up on those handy yellow highlighters, too.

✔ **Paper:** If you use your computer printer frequently or have an office copier, consider buying your standard copier paper by the box. Be sure to buy paper that is designed for the use that you intend; for example, laser printer or plain paper fax. Also get some more substantial, heavier paper such as 100gsm for sending out letters to your favourite clients. Depending on your personal preferences, you may also want to buy some ruled pads of A4-sized paper, some notepaper, and index cards. In these days of environmental responsibility, print drafts both sides and consider buying recycled paper. Some clients may expect this, but be prepared to fork out a higher price to help save the planet.

✔ **Fasteners:** If your office doesn't have a stapler, it is not truly an office. Pick up a stapler and some matching staples to go with it. Buy plenty of paper clips (we like the jumbo size best), bulldog clips (get an assortment of all the different sizes), and rubber bands. A roll of Sellotape is a definite must, and a large roll of parcel tape can be a real lifesaver from time to time.

✔ **Envelopes:** Stock up on DL (110x220mm) envelopes – these are the standard business size. If you plan to run them through your printer, make sure that the box says that they are made for that purpose. Also get some C4 (229x324mm) envelopes so that you can post A4 documents without folding them.

✔ **Folders:** If you have a filing cabinet, you need file folders to go in it. You can choose from a wide variety of sizes, colours, and types – including hanging and non-hanging folders. Try out several different kinds of folders until you find the ones that work best for you.

Home office checklist

Here's a quick and easy checklist to use for setting up your home office that summarises all the items listed in the section 'Getting Set Up'. Now you don't have an excuse for not setting up an office right away!

✔ **Space:** Pick out a space in your home that is out of the way, quiet, and inviting. Make sure that it has adequate lighting and that it is sufficiently wired for electricity, phones, and data communications. If you don't have a home alarm and a fireproof data safe, consider getting them.

✔ **Furniture:** Get a comfortable, ergonomic task chair, as well as some comfortable chairs for your clients if you'll be meeting them in your home office. Invest in a desk that is sturdy and large enough to accommodate your computer, peripherals, and your work. Buy work-tables, filing cabinets, and bookshelves, too. Buy big but not so big that you make the room cramped.

✔ **Equipment:** Buy a telephone for your office (and one for the road!). Get connected to the fastest Broadband service that you can. Get the best computer you can afford and consider buying a plain-paper fax machine, unless you plan to use your computer to receive and send faxes. As well as Broadband access for your email and web surfing, and you may need a network – wired or wireless – and an office copier as well.

✔ **Office supplies:** Go to your nearest office supply warehouse, grab a shopping trolley, fill your boots! Pens, pencils, staplers, tape, and much more are all waiting for the opportunity to serve you.

Making Use of Support Services

Whether your business is small or large, there are certain things that only you can do – the things that bring you and your practice the greatest financial return. Similarly, always delegate certain things to others because doing them yourself takes you *away* from doing the things that bring you the greatest return. As an independent, self-employed consultant, you may find yourself constantly balancing the temptation to do everything yourself against the very real need to free up as much of your time as possible so that you can focus on the things you do best.

Your job is to use your time and resources in the most cost-effective way while maximising their return. Our humble belief – developed over years of experience in business and consulting – is that the best way to accomplish this goal is to make effective use of support services. Support services are the full range of business services available to you – anything from clerical support to photocopying to legal and financial advice to a fully equipped rented office – that enable you to spend less time doing the things that have a low return to your business and spend more time doing the things that have a high return.

In this chapter, we address the importance of making use of your experience and focusing your efforts on making your business a success, and we consider the variety of different staffing options available to you. We also take a look at the virtual office and explain how it can help make you a more efficient and effective consultant.

Recruiting a good secretary

Getting a secretary or personal assistant is one of the quickest and most cost-effective ways to free up your time to focus on the things that you need to do and that bring your practice the greatest financial benefit. You don't have to make a major commitment to start out. Your secretary may be your spouse or partner working on a part-time basis. Or perhaps a college student or a temporary employee who works for you a couple hours a day or a few days a week. As your workload increases, you can gradually extend your secretary's work schedule to meet your needs and the needs of your clients, or recruit a full-time person or additional people as required.

Carefully chosen, a good secretary can deliver benefits far beyond taking care of clerical duties. Here are some of the benefits of recruiting an assistant:

✔ **You save time.** A secretary can take over your routine tasks – answering the phone, responding to client enquiries, sorting and prioritising mail, voicemail, and email messages – and thus free you to focus on client projects and securing new business.

✔ **You save money.** The financial value of your time probably far exceeds whatever you would pay a secretary. For example, you may make £50 or more an hour as a consultant, but your secretary may make a fraction of that – say, £10 to £13 an hour.

✔ **You make a more positive impression on your clients.** When clients are helped by a secretary, they're likely to be impressed and feel that they're receiving better service – and they probably are!

✔ **You create opportunities to get away from your office.** When you're a one-person business, it's easy to feel that you have to be in your office all the time to make sure that you don't miss important client calls. Recruiting a secretary enables you to get out of your office to visit clients and network with prospective clients.

✔ **You get another point of view.** No one has a monopoly on the truth. A secretary often can give you a second point of view or a second opinion. For a one-person operation, this can be a refreshing breath of fresh air.

As soon as you can afford to recruit a secretary (can you afford not to?), do it! You'll be amazed at what you can do with all the time that suddenly becomes available – and so will your clients.

Finding a good solicitor, accountant, and bank

Every business needs occasional support from outside professionals, including accountants, bank managers, solicitors, and others. Indeed, finding good professionals is one of the most important things you can do – besides finding lots of good clients – to ensure the success of your consulting business.

Before you sign on the dotted line, be sure to check your chosen professionals out thoroughly. The idea is to find someone who is not only talented and affordable, but who can grow with you and your company and become a long-term partner and trusted associate. Consider the following when selecting:

✔ **Qualifications:** Hire professionals who are as qualified and experienced as possible. Do not recruit someone who merely dabbles in an area of professional expertise, or who does it as a hobby. You need someone who is a pro and is fully committed to your success.

- ✔ **Accessibility:** Make sure that the professionals you recruit are available when you need them and aren't overcommitted with other clients.

- ✔ **Price:** While you must generally plan to pay more for more experience and skill, you mustn't pay more than you need to. Don't be afraid to shop around for the best combination of skill, experience, and price.

- ✔ **Ethics:** The accountants, bank managers, solicitors, and other professionals you work with need to have ethical standards that are just as high as your own. If you choose someone with flexible ethics you're asking for trouble.

- ✔ **Compatibility:** Ideally, you'll find someone who meets all of the above criteria and is also compatible with you and any business partners and associates you may have. Nothing is much worse than trying to work with someone you don't get along with.

Interview your prospective candidates (either in person or over the phone) and find out the following kinds of information:

- ✔ Does your candidate have specific experience working with home-based consulting businesses?

- ✔ Does your candidate show an active interest in the future growth of your business?

- ✔ Does he or she keep abreast of the latest changes in the field as it pertains to your industry?

- ✔ What do the candidate's references say about his or her performance and reliability?

- ✔ What is his or her fee structure?

- ✔ Does your candidate have a network of other potentially beneficial contacts within your community?

- ✔ Are you comfortable with him or her, and are your personal philosophies compatible?

In the sections that follow, we consider the key professionals that self-employed consultants most often turn to for help and support.

Solicitors

A solicitor's services are an important part of any business's – including an independent consultant's – support team. What can solicitors do for you?

Here are some of the most common tasks solicitors take on for their consultancy business clients:

- ✔ Choosing a form (legal structure) for your business
- ✔ Drafting terms of business for consultancy proposals
- ✔ Writing and reviewing, and negotiating business contracts
- ✔ Helping with credit problems and bankruptcy
- ✔ Addressing consumer issues and complaints
- ✔ Giving employment law advice
- ✔ Advising on your legal rights and obligations
- ✔ Representing you in court

Find a solicitor who specialises in working with small businesses and start-ups. To find a good one, ask around. Check with your friends and business associates – particularly those who own small businesses. One more thing: Make a point of asking your solicitor how much a particular task is going to cost *before* you engage his or her services, not after. You do not want your solicitor's bill for services to come as a nasty surprise.

Both the Institute of Directors (IOD) and The Federation of Small Businesses (FSB) operate legal support services as part of their membership and this can often suffice for day-to-day advice.

Accountants

If you're not an expert in accounting (few independent consultants are), getting a good accountant is a definite must. As the owner of your own business, you need to know exactly how much money is going in and out of your bank accounts, and for what purposes it is being used. This knowledge allows you to assess the financial health of your company, and it provides the basis for determining how much you owe the government in taxes and other fees.

Inadequate record keeping is a key contributor to the failure of small businesses – including consulting firms. A good accountant can be worth his or her weight in gold, and will usually become a long-term partner in the growth of your firm.

Here are some common tasks that accountants perform for their small-business customers:

- ✔ Small business start-up, business sale, or business purchase
- ✔ Accounting system design and implementation

✔ Preparation, review, and audit of financial statements

✔ Tax planning

✔ Preparation of income tax returns

✔ Tax appeals

Find and select an accountant in much the same way that you select any other professional adviser. Check with friends and business associates for recommendations and references. Interview several candidates to be sure that your personalities are compatible.

Qualified accountants usually have the words 'chartered' or 'certified' attached to their title. They also usually belong to one of accountancy's professional associations.

A number of professional associations can provide you with assistance relevant to you. You can:

✔ Find a chartered accountant at the website of the Institute of Chartered Accountants in England and Wales (ICAEW) (visit www.icaew.co.uk)

✔ Get advice on choosing an accountant at the website of the Association of Chartered Certified Accountants (ACCA) (visit www.accaglobal.com)

✔ Find an accountant at the website of the Chartered Institute of Management Accountants (CIMA) (visit www.cimaglobal.com)

✔ Find an accountant at the website of the Institute of Chartered Accountants of Scotland (visit www.icas.org.uk)

✔ Read advice on selecting a chartered accountant in Ireland at the website of the Institute of Chartered Accountants in Ireland (visit www.icai.ie)

Banks

As the old saying goes, money makes the world go round. Your bank will inevitably play a central role in your consulting business – from maintaining current and savings accounts, to providing tax services, to lending you money when you need it. These kinds of ongoing financial needs make finding and establishing a relationship with a good bank manager a must.

When Philip's bank lent him a large amount of money to buy out a major shareholder, that gave the bank a vested interest in making the business go well. Over the years the bank's advice has saved him money even though he pays for the bank services.

Okay, so what kind of financial institution is right for self-employed consultants? A number of different financial institutions are available to you, and each has its unique spin on the world of money and banking.

- ✔ **Banks and building societies** are the financial institution of first choice for many businesses. They traditionally make a wide variety of loans available, both commercial and consumer, and they are often the place to go for special small business loans offered in conjunction with a range of government-backed schemes. Visit www.businesslink.gov.uk to check out grants and support available in your area. Most also offer special accounts designed specifically for businesses, along with a wide array of business-oriented products and services.

- ✔ **Credit card companies** offer interest rates that are often significantly higher than the rates you would get on the same amount of money from a bank, yet countless entrepreneurs have financed their business start-up and growth using credit card loans. Keep in mind that even if the credit card has your company name on it, it's likely that you're personally responsible for the charges.

- ✔ **Commercial finance companies** specialise in working with businesses, usually in financing equipment leasing or purchases or the acquisition of inventory. The deals that commercial finance companies offer – particularly leasing – may have tax advantages and are worth checking out.

- ✔ **Consumer finance companies** are businesses that specialise in making loans to borrowers who have a hard time obtaining loans from their banks, perhaps because they've defaulted on loans in the past or because their credit is already overextended. Consumer finance companies generally charge higher rates than banks.

Outsourcing – You can do it, too!

After you establish your consulting business, you may find that you have far more clients who need your services than you have the time to do work. Unfortunately, one person can do only so much. When your workload exceeds the amount of time that you can devote to completing it, you have one of three choices:

- ✔ You can tell the client to find someone else to do the work.

- ✔ You can subcontract the work out to another firm.

- ✔ You can recruit new employees to help you complete your assignments.

The first choice – rejecting the work – is clearly not the best option. Not only do you lose the opportunity to grow your business, but you may be turning down a vital piece of business that you'll need if your other business goes away for some reason. And, believe us – you never know what business disaster may be waiting for you just around the corner.

Although you must turn away business that's not in your area of expertise or that's not profitable enough for you, few consultants have the luxury of turning away good, profitable work. If you repeatedly turn clients away, then after a while, they won't bother to offer you work.

The second choice – subcontracting the work out to another firm or independent consultant – can be a good idea, especially if the other firm occasionally sends work your way, too. This approach can be very successful, as long as the quality is up to your own high standards, and delivery times don't suffer. In most cases, your client doesn't even have to know that you're subcontracting out the work (be sure, however, to check your contract to see if you're legally required to notify your client if you subcontract work to another firm). However, no matter how accomplished and reliable your subcontractor may be, when you send work to another firm, you lose some control over the process – and you're still held responsible by your clients for the quality of the work done by your subcontractors, regardless of how good or bad it is.

This brings us to a third choice, one that gives you even more control over the work process: recruiting employees to help you complete your assignments. If your increased workload is long-term in nature, then you may want to recruit a 'permanent' employee, that is, one with no defined period of employment. But what if the assignment is relatively small or short-term in nature? You don't want to recruit an employee or two for a couple weeks and then have to lay them off. But through the modern miracle of temporary workers, you can expand and contract your staff as often as you like, without going through the trauma of recruiting employees only to lay them off a short time afterwards.

And 'temps' – the common term for temporary workers – aren't limited to just secretaries and receptionists anymore. Computer programmers, systems analysts, technical writers, communications engineers, accountants, editors, customer service specialists, managers, and more are available through temporary employment agencies. According to the people who keep track of such things, approximately 90 per cent of all businesses use temporary workers from time to time. Why not you? To get an idea of what's available locally, check out the Yellow Pages under 'Employment – Temporary,' or do an Internet search for temp agencies in your area.

Here are some of the advantages of using temporary workers to help you get through the inevitable surges in your workload:

- **They're as temporary as you want them to be.** You can use temporary workers for a day, a week, a month, or a year – it's up to you. And when you finish your assignment, you don't have to lay off your workers or give them two weeks' notice – the temporary employment agency merely reassigns your temps to another organisation.

- **There's no tedious recruiting process.** You don't have to put an advertisement in the newspaper, read a mountain of CVs, and spend days interviewing job candidates. All you need to do is pick up the phone, call a temporary employment agency, and help is on the way – quickly and easily.

- **Temps are there when you need them.** You can often have a temporary worker at your office ready to work within a few hours of your call – certainly by the next business day. When you need someone quickly and you can't afford to mess around, calling a temp agency is one of the best and most reliable ways to meet your needs.

- **The temp agency pays all employee-related expenses.** You don't have to worry about trying to understand the payments that you have to make to the government whenever you recruit an employee. In addition to an hourly wage, the temporary employment agency pays your worker's income tax and National Insurance.

- **Temporary employees can save you money.** You pay only for the time that your temporary worker is actually working for you. You don't have to worry about paying for sick leave, holidays, or other absences.

Considering a serviced office

How would you like to have all the benefits of a fully staffed and equipped office without recruiting any employees or buying any equipment? And not just any old office or one in the corner of your garage, nestled between the hedge trimmer and the geranium cuttings, but a real office with a desk, a door, and more. Don't get us wrong; Bob and Peter both have offices at home – and Bob has a traditional office as well – and they're very happy with them. Philip's company rents space on site at London Gatwick Airport (handy for his clients). But a home office or space in an office block may not be right for you.

Enter the 'serviced office'. What's a 'serviced office', you ask?

A serviced office is a business that rents offices – by the hour, day, week, or month – to busy consultants and businesspeople like you. Sometimes they are called business centres. Everyone shares a common receptionist, conference rooms, and kitchen. Not only do you get access to an office in exchange for your money, but you also have a wide variety of business tools and services at your disposal – for a price, of course.

Why would anyone want to rent a serviced office? Many good reasons exist:

- **Flexibility:** You can rent an serviced office for an hour, a few hours a week, a couple weeks a month, or on a full-time basis for as long as you like. You can work out almost any arrangement.

- **Minimal capital outlay:** You have the choice of bringing your own furniture and office equipment or renting these items from your landlord. According to serviced office providers, the cost of using a serviced office is approximately 40 to 50 per cent of the cost of setting up and staffing a comparable conventional office.

- **Turnkey operation:** When you rent a serviced office, you don't have to waste your time designing an office, installing electric and phone lines, recruiting staff, and taking care of all those other details. With a serviced office, you can make one call today and have a fully functional office tomorrow.

- **Convenience:** In most areas, a wide selection of serviced offices are available. You can therefore decide to locate your office near your home or close to your clients. And because you aren't tied to the long-term leases (typically three to five years) that are common in the commercial real estate market, you can quickly and easily pull up your roots and move to another serviced office or your own office if things don't work out.

- **Camaraderie:** One of the biggest complaints of consultants who work at home is that they miss the stimulation and company of being in a traditional office setting with other associates. Serviced offices solve this problem by placing you in the midst of a group of other motivated businesspeople who share many of your goals and interests.

Other office options

Another way to achieve the same goal as using a serviced office, and save some money at the same time, is to sublease an office or offices from a business such as a law firm or estate agent that has vacant space to fill. The setup is much the same as for a serviced office: You use a common receptionist and telephone service, and you share kitchen, post room, and other facilities – probably even the organisation's copying equipment and computer network. However, most likely you have to provide your own furniture, computer, and other equipment.

For those of you who spend more than a little time in the air, one of the best deals going for short-term office space is available in almost every major airport around the world. The big airlines – BA, American Airlines and others – have established clubs in these airports that offer a variety of facilities and services for the busy traveller. If you don't clock up enough miles, your airline may not let you in to their lounge. But don't despair – join Priority Pass and gain access to cool lounges all over the world. Check out www.prioritypass.com.

Chapter 5

The Legal, Financial, and Ethical Considerations of Your Business

In This Chapter

▶ Doing the (legally) right thing

▶ Looking into financial matters

▶ Keeping ethics at the forefront of your practice

*W*hether your consulting firm is a one-man or woman band or a vast global consultancy employing thousands, your firm is first and fore-most a business. As the owner of the business, there are many things for you to consider beyond simply providing consulting services to your clients. You need to make a profit. You need to ensure that you're following the law. You need to be able to track the financials of your business – quickly and accu-rately – and you need to pay the appropriate taxes when they are due. And, of course, you need to be an ethical business person setting an example for your employees.

In the pages that follow, we turn the spotlight on three key areas of building and maintaining your consulting business: legal, financial, and ethical. Get this consulting trio right, not only will you be able to sleep more easily at night, but you'll also find you've got more time to focus on doing what you do best: consulting.

Legal Do's and Don'ts

As anyone who has started a business knows, there are many do's and don'ts when it comes to the law. While you may be able to hobble along for some time ignoring the legalities of your consulting business, eventually they'll catch up with you. So if you're getting ready to start your own consulting business, our advice is to take care of the legal considerations now – as you establish your business and get it off the ground. And if you have an established consult-ing firm but have neglected the legalities of your business, our advice is to also take care of the legal considerations – now.

Understanding the legal structures of businesses

You've no doubt noticed that some businesses have little taglines after their names – things like Ltd, or plc. These taglines are there because of the form of business that these companies selected at some point in their founding or development.

While this alphabet soup of letters seems simple enough, the reality is much more complex. When you pick a legal form for your business, you're making an entire set of decisions that will have an impact on how your business can operate, how it is taxed, if it will be personally liable – or not – in the event of some catastrophic business occurrence, and many other matters. In this section, we give you enough basic information on the topic to help you decide which legal structure is right for your business. These are just the basics – you need to contact an accountant or solicitor to discern the specific advantages and disadvantages of each and to help you decide which is best for you. One thing to note: This discussion is applicable to businesses based in the United Kingdom – consulting firms in other countries are subject to different rules.

Self-employment

To work as a sole trader, a partner, or a member of a limited partnership you have to be self-employed and registered as such with Her Majesty's Revenue and Customs (HMRC). You can still work elsewhere as an employee but any work you do for your business must be done on a self-employed basis.

There are tax advantages in the UK associated with self-employment both for you and your clients. Because of this, our friends at the HMRC are quite picky about whether you consult for a company or in fact work for them. Here are some of the questions to ask yourself to see if you'll have true self-employed status:

- ✔ Do you carry out work for a number of clients?
- ✔ Do you invoice your clients for the work you do for them?
- ✔ Do you have control over what work is to be done, when, and where the work is done?
- ✔ Are you responsible for the losses of your business?
- ✔ Can you send other people employed by you or a partner to do the work?
- ✔ Do you have to correct unsatisfactory work in your own time and at your own expense?

✔ Have you invested your own money in the business?

✔ Have you provided any major items of equipment that are a fundamental requirement of the work?

If you answered yes to these questions:

✔ Do the consulting contracts reflect these points?

If you can already say yes to most of these questions you must let HMRC know quickly. Get the advice of an accountant because you can get fined £100 for failure to register within three months of becoming self-employed. You can download and complete form CWF1 to register as self-employed from the HMRC website at www.hmrc.gov.uk.

Sole Trader

Many small businesses – including consulting firms – are *sole traders*. This doesn't mean that you have to work alone but that you and you alone are completely responsible for the business. To put it bluntly you take all of the profits but you're personally liable for all of the debts to the full extent of your means. In other words, if you don't leave enough money in the business to pay your business debts then anything you owe may be taken in settlement – even your home! Table 5-1 lists the good news – and the bad – about being a sole trader.

Table 5-1	Sole Proprietorship
On the Plus Side	*On the Negative Side*
You as the owner have complete control over the business	Sole traders are generally seen as less prestigious than other forms of business
It's inexpensive to set up	Obtaining outside financing can be difficult
It's easy to start and to end	The business dies with the owner
You as the owner keep all of the profits	The owner is personally liable for the debts or in the event of a lawsuit

Partnership

In a *partnership* form of consulting business, each partner agrees to provide specific skills, expertise, and effort – while sharing the partnership's expenses – in return for an agreed-upon portion of the company's profits. The legal agreement spelling out these terms and conditions is called a *partnership agreement*.

A business partnership is an association of two or more people trading together as one firm and sharing the profits. The partnership itself and each partner must make annual self-assessment returns to HMRC.

There are benefits to working in a partnership – you're in it together and can support each other. The bad news is that if one partner absconds, the other partners have to pay all the outstanding tax including the absconder's share. All of the partners can be held liable for the whole of the firm's debts or any liability to the full extent of their means, yes, even their homes, just as if they were sole traders. Table 5-2 summarises the pros and cons.

Table 5-2	Partnership
On the Plus Side	*On the Negative Side*
Two or more heads can be better than one	Partners may not always agree on business decisions
Business risks are shared by the partners	Each partner is legally liable for actions of the other partners
The partners may provide moral support to one another	Partners often have disagreements and quarrels. When partnerships break up, things can get very messy
Expenses are shared by all partners	Profits are distributed to all partners

Limited liability partnership LLP

A limited liability partnership (LLP) is similar to an ordinary partnership: partners share in the costs, responsibilities, risks, and profits of the business. However, one big difference may help you sleep more easily: The partners' liability is limited to the amount of money they've invested in the business and any personal guarantees (PGs) they've given to help raise finance.

Each member of the partnership must register as self-employed and at least two of the members must be designated members and they'll have extra responsibilities under the law. Specifically, the designated partners are held liable for the correct filing and recording of the limited liability partnership affairs. They are subject to criminal penalties of any failure to comply. To find out more about this visit the Companies House website at www.companies house.gov.uk.

Limited companies

A limited company is a legal entity whose finances are separate from the personal finances of its owners (known as *shareholders*). Shareholders can be individuals or other companies and they cannot be held responsible for the company's debts unless they've given personal guarantees (PGs) for a loan for example. However the shareholders may lose the money they've invested in the company if it fails. Profits are distributed to shareholders via dividends, apart from those profits retained in the business to create capital or reserves.

Companies must be registered at Companies House and must have one Director (two if it's a public limited company, or plc) who is at least 16 years of age. The companies are governed by strict legislation which you can read about at the Companies House website (www.companieshouse.gov.uk) and the Department for Business, Enterprise and Regulatory Reform (BERR) website (www.berr.gov.uk). For more on the Director's responsibilities visit the Institute of Directors' (IOD) website at www.iod.com.

The two main types of limited companies are:

- ✓ **Private limited companies (Ltd),** which may have one or more shareholders but cannot offer shares to the public.

- ✓ **Public limited companies (plc),** which must have two or more shareholders and must have issued shares to the public to a value of a minimum of £50,000 before being able to trade.

Tables 5-3 and 5-4 show the pros and cons of private and public limited companies.

Table 5-3	Private Limited Companies
On the Plus Side	*On the Negative Side*
Limited liability for company's shareholders and treated as separate entities for taxes	Additional costs and work associated with filing accounts and returns
Costs less to set up and maintain than companies	Costs more to set up than sole traderships
The Ltd tag can give more prestige than sole traderships	More legal hoops and requirements to meet

Table 5-4	Public Limited Company
On the Positive Side	*On the Negative Side*
Higher prestige business image than other forms. (plc = big in clients minds)	Can be relatively expensive to start and operate
Limited personal liability of shareholders	Lots of paperwork

(continued)

Table 5-4 *(continued)*

On the Positive Side	On the Negative Side
Can survive their owners	Can sometimes be more difficult to sell. The majority of shareholders must agree to sell the company
Can raise money by selling shares	Suitable only for a large-scale company

Most consulting firms start out as either a sole tradership, a partnership, or a limited company. As time goes on, however, many consulting firms consider the advantages and disadvantages of other available forms of business, especially in terms of liability and taxes. Be sure you put a lot of thought into deciding what form of business is right for you. Get the advice of a good accountant.

Registering a name

Choosing the name of your company is one of the most critical decisions you make as you set up your business. While the right name can help pave the way to your success, the wrong name can have the completely opposite effect.

Here are some points to consider:

- Do you want the name to reflect what your business does (such as consulting) or would something more abstract be better?

- Would it be a good idea to include your name?

- Do you want a more traditional name to imply history or solidity or a modern name suggesting a new or innovative service?

- Have you chosen a name that may date quickly or is simply naff? Humorous puns don't usually work for consultancy firms.

- Will you trade overseas – if so, what does the name mean in other languages? (Remember the French soft drink called Pschitt?) Also, how easy will it be for people overseas to pronounce?

- Is the name overly long so that callers or customers may want to avoid saying or typing into search engines?

- Are you targeting a particular market sector such as retail, or a geographical area such as the South-East?

- Does the name meet with regulations (covered in the next section)?

Limited company names

If you're forming a limited company or limited liability partnership you must register the name with Companies House. Before you complete all of the forms be sure your proposal name doesn't break the rules:

- ✔ Your company name must end with Limited, plc, or Ltd for companies, or limited liability partnership, LLP (or the Welsh equivalent), and this must not be used anywhere other than at the end of the name

- ✔ The name must not be offensive

- ✔ The name mustn't be the same as or very similar to one already in the register

- ✔ The name mustn't include so-called sensitive words or expressions unless you've been granted permission to use them (read on).

Sole trader or partnership names

If you set up as a sole trader or partnership you can choose to trade under your own names or choose a business name.

Sole trader or partnership rules:

- ✔ The name must not be offensive.

- ✔ You may not include the words limited, plc, limited liability, LLP or equivalent.

- ✔ The name must not contain sensitive words or expressions (see the following list).

For example the following require permission from the Secretary of State because they may give a false impression:

- ✔ British, International, European

- ✔ Association, Authority, Institute

- ✔ Charity, Register, Trust

- ✔ Health Centre, Architect

- ✔ Royal, Government

To find out more, and see the complete list, visit Companies House website.

Passing off

Another entity or person can take action against you if they consider that your name is in effect an attempt to pretend you're associated with their good name. This may be under common law or trademark law if their name is protected by Trademark. For example, registering your consultancy as PWC Ltd or McKinsey would attract such action from those established global consulting firms.

This law is called *passing off*. The entity could be a company, trust, council, or even a person who thinks you're passing off.

Displaying your business name

There are requirements about displaying your business name so that your clients and suppliers know who they're dealing with. But don't spend money on this until you're sure you're able to use the name you've chosen. You must display your name and certain other details:

- ✔ Outside every place of business, even your home if that is where your business operates.
- ✔ On all business letters, emails, orders, payments invoices, receipts, and other business documents.
- ✔ On your website.

The rules for limited companies and limited liability partnerships are very precise, so read them all in the guidance notes or company information on the Companies House website.

Getting your name onto the web

To do business you're probably going to have to be on the web and for this you're going to need a domain name. The website address, for example, techniquesforchange.co.uk, is known as the domain name. To operate in the UK the ending .co.uk is suitable.

Names ending in .com can imply a more global preserve but many UK searchers may assume the company is American so may not click on your site. When Philip set up Techniques for Change he bought both the .co.uk and the .com domains to give him flexibility for the future. If your business meets certain criteria you can apply for a .eu domain ending. Find out more at European Registry Internet Domain Names' website at www.eurid.eu.

What's in a name?

Philip Albon founded Techniques for Change, a leading change and management training consultancy, in 1994. Here Philip explains how he chose the name for his business.

✔ **Firstly, I considered how a name could work as a memorable brand.** I wanted my name to spread by word of mouth, so it was important that my name was catchy and memorable but also conveyed what I did. I decided that what we were about was providing clients with techniques to enable them to implement change.

At the time few people might have recognised the name Albon but Techniques for Change took the 'it does exactly what it says on the tin' line from that irritating but memorable TV ad.

✔ **Next, I ensured the name was available on the Internet.** Back then it was easier to buy domain names outright so we bought techniquesforchange.com and .co.uk. The UK name was used first because we were starting in the UK but the .com might be handy for when we expanded. I looked at key words like 'change' but these were all either reserved or only on sale for silly money. Change.tv was available but co.uk sounded more solid.

✔ **I then linked the name to a simple and memorable logo and identity.** The orange dot (shown in the photo) in the box device was my idea. I based it on the 2 x 2 positioning maps used by Strategy Consultants. Usually the best place to be in is top left so we put the circle there. We chose orange because it was a modern branding colour. Back in 1994 the World Cup was being televised and the opening sequence showed young children with their national flags painted on their faces. I recruited my five-year-old son to have our logo painted on his face (as you can see in the photo!) and he and my daughter have been the corporate faces of TFC ever since.

✔ **I trademarked the name and identity.** We applied to register the name and our logo and even my son's painted face as registered trademarks. If my company grew we wanted to avoid being copied. It cost a few hundred pounds at the time but the extra protection was well worth it. Also research shows that the ® sign conveys value because people assume it must be valuable if it is worth protecting.

To reserve a domain name you need to go through an agent, and this can be done online. You can find out about choosing an agent on the Nominet website at (www.nominet.org.uk), the official registry of UK domain names.

If your domain name isn't available, this may affect your choice of company name. Consider the following points:

- ✔ Can you use one that matches your business name?
- ✔ Is there another word you can use associated with your service? For example, B&Q's website is DIY.com.
- ✔ Is your name available? For .co.uk domain names you can check this out on Nominet.
- ✔ Can you use hyphens or a number if your name has already been taken?

Here are a few places to check whether your proposed business name is already in use as a domain name:

- ✔ Local phone books (try www.yell.com), business directories, and the Internet.
- ✔ The Companies House website at www.companieshouse.gov.uk.
- ✔ Trademark search using the Intellectual Property Office (UK-IPO) website at www.ipo.gov.uk.

If you're in any doubt, seek advice from a trademark/patent attorney.

The Financial Stuff

If you (and your employees, if you've got any) form the brain of your consulting business, then your financial systems are the blood vessels that bring the oxygen to keep that brain healthy. Money really does 'make the world go round', and consulting businesses are no exception to the rule. Indeed, if you've got your own consulting business, you know the joy that money coming into your business can bring you, and the worry that a lack thereof can also bring.

In this section, we consider some of the financial issues of greatest importance to consultants and their firms.

Paying taxes

If there's one thing you can be certain of, it's that your consulting firm is going to owe taxes to somebody, somewhere. This is especially the case if you're making a profit. The exact amount you owe – and to whom you owe it – will depend on a variety of factors, including where you're located, the kind of business you conduct, and the form of business you select.

Here are some of the most common kinds of taxes that consultants – and consulting firms – can expect to pay:

- ✔ VAT
- ✔ National Insurance
- ✔ PAYE
- ✔ Corporation Tax
- ✔ Income Tax
- ✔ Capital Gains Tax
- ✔ Business rates
- ✔ Stamp duty
- ✔ Taxes for specific products or services, for example, insurance
- ✔ Vehicle duties

For more information about taxes, consult a competent accountant

Deciding whether to register for VAT

Value Added Tax, or VAT, is a tax that is applicable to most business transactions that involve the transfer of goods or services.

The rules (in 2009) are that registration is compulsory once your business turns over (that is, sells) more than £67,000. However you can register voluntarily if your earnings are below this level. Seek the advice of your accountant. Table 5-5 shows the advantages and disadvantages of registering for VAT.

Table 5-5	Registering for VAT
Advantages	*Disadvantages*
You can claim back some of the VAT you pay to your suppliers, for example, for stationery, fuel	If your clients are private individuals or are not VAT-registered then they'll definitely not welcome the 17.5% (standard rate) of extra cost you now put on your invoices, which they cannot reclaim.
It enhances your credibility – if your clients are other businesses they'll probably prefer dealing with suppliers that are VAT registered.	You need to complete more paperwork and records so that you can make VAT returns and payments.
If you supply other VAT-registered businesses then they can easily reclaim the VAT you're charging them.	You may be subject to periodic VAT inspections to ensure that all of your records and actions are up to scratch.

Understanding the home-office tax issues

If you've decided to run your consulting business from your home and you live in the UK then there can be big effects on your tax position, some good, and some bad.

The bad news:

- The rooms of your property that you use for work may be liable for business rates rather than council tax (contact your local authority and Valuation Office Agency VOA for advice).
- If you've set aside a room for the sole purpose of work in it then you may be liable for Capital Gains Tax when you sell your home.

On the bright side:

- Your business can claim tax relief on domestic bills for the areas of the house used for business. This can sometimes cover additional heating and lighting bills, which these days can be immense. This is because otherwise you would have left the house unheated and unlit whilst you were at work.
- If your business is VAT-registered you may be able to reclaim VAT on articles you buy for business use, for example, your desk.
- If you install a separate phone line and broadband connection it will be easier to claim back tax relief on business calls.

Obviously Her Majesty's Revenue and Customs like to look at all of these tax issues carefully, so do your research and get advice from a competent accountant to avoid nasty tax shocks.

Setting up a basic bookkeeping system

Once you're running a consulting business, or any other type of business, you're required under law to keep financial records relating to your business. The law dictates that all businesses must keep these records for six years. But you'll want to keep records anyway because:

- ✔ It saves your time (which is now quite expensive!) every time you need to provide figures, for example, to HMRC.

- ✔ You can be comfortable that you're only paying the amount in taxes that you need to.

- ✔ You can avoid going bust by keeping a firm grasp on what you owe and how much you're owed.

There are four basic sets of records you need to run a tight ship – one that stays afloat and doesn't sink:

- ✔ The cash book

- ✔ The sales ledger

- ✔ The purchase ledger

- ✔ The wages book

Sole traders with simple bookkeeping needs may simply use spreadsheets or outsource the whole task to their accountants. As your business grows you'll need an accounting package that can cover your needs well into the future. Well-known packages include:

- ✔ Sage Instant Accounts and TAS Books

- ✔ Intuit QuickBooks and QuickBooks Pro

- ✔ Pegasus Capital Gold

Above all avoid the following dreaded syndromes that many self-employed consultants have fallen into:

- ✔ **The shoe-box syndrome.** The tardy consultant does not file records regularly but periodically trawls briefcase, pockets, mantelpiece, and car for receipts and papers. He or she then dumps them in a shoe-box and asks the accountant to sort it out. He or she usually over or under pays tax and ultimately gets punished at inspection visits – so keep simple, logical, and up-to-date records and file your receipts promptly.

✓ **The home/work mish-mash.** Here the consultant mixes up personal and business finances and at the end of a period struggles to be sure which is a business expense and which is not. Here again he or she ultimately pays dearly for this error at inspection time. Remember to keep income and expenses entirely separate.

✓ **Lost in space.** Here the consultant's records are wiped off his or her computer or the files go missing. If you have no records to substantiate your tax payments, HMRC can make an assessment of what you should pay. And believe us, this assessment may well not be in your favour! Remember, keep copies, and back them up, and keeping second copies offsite in case of a fire.

Providing your own benefits

Most people who start their own consulting businesses already work for companies that provide a wide selection of benefits – everything from sick pay, to private health care, to life insurance, to pensions, and even paying for further education. However, when you start your own business, it's up to you to decide what benefits are most important to you – the ones that are essential, and the ones that are not. This means doing your homework and weighing the costs and rewards of each particular benefit.

While weighing the costs and rewards, we believe you'll find that the best solution for you is likely to involve two key factors:

✓ Be sure to price your products and services high enough to cover the cost of protecting your income if you're unable to work. Studies show that the self-employed are more frequently uninsured than other parts of the workforce.

✓ Be diligent and guard against getting taken in by what appears to be inexpensive and adequate coverage, but turns out to be inadequate.

For most independent consultants, two kinds of benefits are most important. Coincidentally, they can also be among the most difficult to deal with. Here are some options for getting past the difficulties:

✓ **Income protection:** Unlike most people who work for established companies or the public sector, if you're unable to work due to illness or an accident you won't get paid. You may need to take out an income protection policy to cover this eventuality.

✓ **Retirement Provision:** There are many different options and tax breaks in the pensions area. Be sure though that you make provision for your retirement. Get the advice of an Independent Financial Adviser, IFA, to help you select the best benefits for you.

Getting insured and managing risk

Do consultants really need insurance? Even independent consultants working out of their homes? You bet they do. Remember: The many years of hard work that you've invested in your business can be lost in mere minutes due to a catastrophic loss.

Talk with an insurance broker to determine exactly what kinds of insurance are needed for your business. Here's a list of some of the most common types of business insurance to help guide your discussions:

- **Employers' Liability Compulsory Insurance:** Mandatory if you employ people.

- **Motor vehicle insurance:** Mandatory. If you use your private car for business use you must ensure that the insurer will cover you for such use.

- **Employee or business travel insurance:** Recommended. Make sure that you and your cherished laptop or handheld devices are suitably covered.

- **Key person insurance:** Protects your business against the loss of income resulting from the disability or death of a person in a key position.

- **Premises insurance:** This may be compulsory if you buy or lease premises. If you use your home, ensure that your policy extends to business use. Contents cover, computers, and office equipment are expensive to replace.

- **Trade credit insurance:** Covers the risk of bad debt.

- **Business interruption insurance:** Payment of business earnings if the business is closed for an insurable cause, such as a fire, flood, or other natural disaster.

- **Professional indemnity insurance:** Covers you against liability, for example, for giving bad consulting advice.

- **Directors and Officers' insurance:** Covers liabilities such as non-compliance with the Companies Act.

- **Tax investigation insurance:** Covers against the cost of dealing with an HMRC investigation.

Your home insurance probably does not cover you for all the risks you may carry. As an independent consultant, you need to be sure to consult a reputable broker. For more advice and information, visit the British Insurance Brokers' Association website at www.biba.org.uk.

Do the Right Thing! Ethics and You

What would you do if your best and most profitable client asked you to divulge some new product information from another client? What would you do if a client asked you to take your payments 'under the table' and not report them to the Inland Revenue? What would you do if a potential client offered to pay you a large amount of money to do a project that you know you're not qualified to perform?

Consultants face these kinds of ethical dilemmas every day of the week. Like a double white line painted down the centre of a road, when it comes to ethical behaviour, a clear line separates good behaviour from bad behaviour. The decisions you make in response to all the dilemmas you face determine which side of the line you drive on – the right side or the wrong side. Unfortunately, just as a thick fog can roll in and obscure the lines painted on a road, so too can the line separating right from wrong become fuzzy and hard to see.

In this section, we consider some of the key elements of ethical behaviour and ways to develop and implement a personal code of ethics.

Avoiding ethical land mines

A consultant is sure to face plenty of ethical land mines in any month or year – sometimes over and over and over again. Temptations to stray from the right side of the ethical line to the wrong side are all around you. So why not take advantage of these ethical dilemmas? As long as no one gets hurt, why not make your ethical behaviour situational – that is, moving the ethical line between right and wrong depending on the particular situation, especially if a large financial reward is in it for you?

When it comes down to it, you have a simple choice: You can do business the ethical way or the unethical way.

Our advice is to do business the ethical way. Not only will you sleep better at night, but your reputation will be enhanced and your clients will be glad that they have one less thing to worry about.

Here are the kinds of ethical land mines for which you need to be on the alert. You never know when they'll make their presence known or who will plant one in your path.

✔ **Conflicts of interest:** A conflict of interest occurs when your personal interests or the interests of your business conflict with those of your client. An example is a public sector consultant who recommends that a client buy an expensive new fire-suppression system from one particular company without seeking competitive bids; unbeknownst to the client, however, the consultant is getting a commission from the fire-suppression system manufacturer for each unit that clients buy.

✔ **Personal relationships:** When professional relationships between consultants and clients cross the line into the realm of personal relationships – particularly intimate personal relationships – ethical quicksand can't be very far away.

✔ **Ability to do the job (or lack thereof):** Are you really qualified to do the work that your client is recruiting you to do? Do you already have far too many jobs lined up to be able to adequately handle new ones? Are you going to have to subcontract the work to another consultant or firm because you're too busy to do the work yourself? Your clients recruit you because they assume – either through you telling them so or through your silence – that you're able to do the work. If in reality you can't, you'll soon find yourself in a major ethical quandary. You and your clients must agree to any subcontracting of work before you commence work.

✔ **Insider information:** As a consultant, you learn a lot of interesting and confidential things about your clients' operations, business plans, and strategies. If you misuse this information – perhaps providing information gained from working with Company A to its arch rival, Company B, as a part of the work that you do for Company B – this is a serious breach of ethics with your client, Company A.

✔ **Fees and timekeeping:** Are your fees reasonable? Do you keep meticulous track of the time that you work for your clients? Do you have controls to ensure that one client isn't charged for another client's work, and that clients aren't invoiced for work that is never done (like while you were in fact out of town meeting with other clients or working on another client's project)? Ethical land mines abound in this dangerous area of your practice. To make sure that you stay on the straight and narrow path, check out our discussion on timekeeping in Chapter 17.

Developing your personal code of ethics

Ethics are important for anyone in business. They are particularly important to consultants because of the high level of trust that organisations grant them and because of the access that many consultants have to the confidential and proprietary inner workings of the companies that employ them. No uniform code of ethics has been formulated for consultants. So many different kinds of consultants exist that a set of rules that is appropriate for one group – say, training consultants – may have little in common with a set of rules that would be appropriate for a group of consulting engineers. However, some very basic ethical beliefs can and must form the basis for your personal code of ethics.

Most professional institutes, like the Institute of Business Consulting, at www. ibconsulting.org.uk, publish codes of ethics. Use the professional codes shown in the sidebar as a starting point.

An extract from the IBC Code of Ethics

This is an extract from the Code of Ethics of the Institute of Business Consulting. The IBC is the professional body for all consultants and business advisers.

As a business consultant I will:

✔ Put client interests first, doing whatever it takes to serve them to the highest possible standards at all times

✔ Consider for each potential new engagement the possibility of it creating a conflict of interest, of the perception of such a conflict, and, if such a conflict is identified, take all reasonable steps to protect the interests and confidentiality of each client

✔ Act independently and objectively, and exercise professional care to establish the facts of a situation and bring to bear an informed and experienced judgement

✔ Allow any action or recommendation made, if necessary, to be reviewed by my professional peers to confirm that I have acted in a proper way

✔ Continue to develop my business consulting competences and keep up to date with best practice.

In the interests of customers, suppliers, business partners, and other stakeholders I will:

✔ Ensure that I properly understand their interests and respond to them in a balanced manner

✔ Establish, maintain, and develop business relationships based on mutual confidence and trust

✔ Refrain from entering into any agreement or undertaking any activity which is unlawful or anti-competitive

✔ Ensure that agreements entered into or activities undertaken are consistent with the interests of my organisation and demonstrate good management practice

✔ Neither offer nor accept gifts, hospitality, or services which could create, or imply, an improper obligation

✔ Safeguard all confidential information which comes into my possession.

Here are some items that can form the basis for any consultant's code of ethics. Review them and consider using them as the basis for your own code of ethics.

- ✔ **Account for your time accurately and honestly.** If you're working on an hourly or other time-based system of invoicing, keeping track of your hours and reporting them to your clients accurately and honestly is up to you. Your client expects and trusts you to be truthful in your invoicing practices. To do any less is not only unethical but also a violation of your client's trust. And if your client can't trust you, he or she won't recruit you or refer you to friends, colleagues, or other associates.

- ✔ **Don't make promises you can't keep.** Although you may really want to impress a potential client with your amazing abilities, avoid making promises you can't keep in hopes of landing your client's account. Not only is this unethical – your client may be better off recruiting someone who has more capacity or better qualifications in a particular area – but you end up setting up yourself and your business for failure. Although a little good old-fashioned optimism is okay, don't blatantly make a promise that you know you can't keep. If you're hoping that your client forgets you made the promise or that you can change the promised action to something you can achieve after you're selected to do the work, then you're not only fooling yourself but also doing your client a great disservice.

- ✔ **Follow through on your promises.** Part of becoming a successful consultant is doing what you say you're going to do. If you say that you'll complete the project on 31 March, then you must deliver the results on (or before, if you can) 31 March – not a day later. Suppose that you promise to come up with a complete landscaping design for £1,000. Unless your client does something that causes your incurred costs to skyrocket, such as adding more work to your project but not adding more money to your project budget, you must deliver your design for £1,000 and not a penny more. If, for some reason, you can't keep your promise no matter how hard you try, then inform your client as far in advance as possible and present a plan for curing the problem.

- ✔ **Don't recommend products or services that your client doesn't need.** You may speak with clients who are absolutely, beyond a shadow of a doubt, certain that they know what is wrong with their organisation. You need only propose to do what they say they want you to do to land what could be a very lucrative contract. A piece of cake. However, if you know that this is not the proper course of action, you must tell your client so and decline the offered work. In most cases, your client will appreciate your honesty, and your reputation will be elevated a few notches in your client's mind (and in the mind of anyone else your client tells this story to).

✔ **Be candid and give your honest opinion.** Your clients pay you good money for the benefit of your skills and many years of experience. When your clients ask for your opinion, be frank and honest, and don't try to sweeten the truth to make it more palatable.

✔ **Protect your clients' confidentiality.** When you're a consultant, you may often be placed in situations in which you learn information that is proprietary to your clients, the release of which may cause them serious financial or other damage. Your clients have placed you in a position of trust. Don't violate that trust. If, for some reason, you want to publicise the fact that you're doing work for a particular firm – perhaps in a press kit or a proposal to another organisation, ask your client for permission first.

✔ **Disclose conflicts of interest.** If you're a popular consultant in your field, preventing conflicts of interest from occurring can often be difficult. As organisations vie for your expertise, you may find yourself working on the same problem for two different companies that compete with one another in the marketplace. However, as soon as you learn of a conflict – whether it is a potential conflict or an actual one – you must always disclose it to the affected client or clients and then take action to resolve it. This may mean assuring your clients that you won't transfer their confidential data from one company to the other, or it may mean signing information non-disclosure agreements. If the conflict can't be resolved through these means, then you may have to drop one of the two companies as a client.

✔ **Don't use inside information to your advantage.** While you're working for an organisation, you may learn information that is closely held within the company and unknown to others outside the organisation. For example, you may learn that the organisation is about to patent a process that will certainly lead to a huge surge in the price of the company's shares. Not only is it unethical to use insider information to your advantage – in this case, to buy a large number of the company's shares before the patent becomes public – but it is illegal as well.

✔ **Don't break the law.** At times, a client may ask you to do something that is not only against your personal sense of ethics but also obviously and blatantly illegal. Do not pass Go and collect £200. Just go. And don't come back. Ever.

These guidelines look great on paper, but in the real world, you're going to face many situations that aren't quite so black and white. Everyone has a personal set of values and ethics, and what's right for one person may be wrong for another. The challenge is to find ways to keep to your values while also finding ways to work with a client whose values may not be exactly the same as yours. If your values are too far out of sync with your client's values, then don't hesitate to pull yourself off the job and find other clients whose values more closely match your own.

If you ever find yourself in an uncomfortable ethical situation, first talk to your client about it in an effort to determine an alternative course of action that is in accordance with your own values. Most clients will respect your perspective, even if they don't share it. If you can't find a way out of your ethical dilemma by working with the client on alternative actions, walk away from the job, but in a way that doesn't offend your client. Whatever you do, don't burn bridges with your clients or poison the well for referrals to other clients.

Take some time to develop your own code of ethics. Type it up, hang it prominently in your office, and put it on your website. Above all, live the code of ethics that you've developed. A good operational rule is, if you have any doubts, don't do it!

Chapter 6

What Are You Worth?
Setting Your Fees

. . . .

In This Chapter

▶ Establishing your value

▶ Structuring your fees

▶ Changing your fees

▶ Knowing when to say no

. . . .

*T*he topic of setting fees probably makes an independent consultant more uncomfortable than any other topic. Consultants are comfortable when they are recommending the placement of columns for proper support of a massive steel beam, the implementation of a new employee performance review system, or the installation of new software to run a company's web server. After all, they are experts in those fields. But setting fees is often another matter altogether. Ask some consultants their price and watch the reaction. They suddenly get flustered and tentative. And if a client balks at a consultant's quoted price, explaining that other consultants do double the work for half the price, some of these same consultants will quickly discount their prices in a desperate effort to gain – or retain – the client's business, doing whatever it takes.

Why does discussing fees with clients make so many consultants so uncomfortable?

When you're a consultant, pricing your services is a constant balancing act. Set your fees too low, and not only might you be flooded with more business than you can handle, but also you won't make enough money from the flood of business to recover your expenses and make a profit. Set your fees too high, however, and you may get a few high-fee jobs but not enough to keep your business afloat. The end result is that many consultants are in a constant state of uncertainty when pricing their services.

Understanding your value to your clients and then pricing your services appropriately is essential to your ability to make a living as an independent consultant. So, if you're going to thrive as a consultant, you need to do three things soon after you set up shop:

✔ Develop a fee structure that allows you to achieve your goals for financial and personal independence.

✔ Become a master at understanding and selling the value that you offer your clients and at getting your clients to focus on *results* – not rates, activity, or time.

✔ Overcome any hang-ups that you have about putting a price on your time and selling your skills and services to others.

This chapter discusses putting a value on the expertise that you bring to your clients, determining how much you need to make for your business to thrive, structuring your fees, and deciding when to modify your fees and when to stand firm on them.

Deciding How Much You're Worth to Your Clients

How much do you think you're worth to your clients? £1? £10,000? £1 million? More? If we really pressed you for an answer, we probably could get you to come up with a number. However, regardless of the number you select, it's meaningless unless it is based on what your clients think you are worth.

One of the first lessons to learn about pricing your services is that you must always focus on the value that you bring to your clients and not only on your own opinion of your worth. In some cases, your clients' perception of your value may far exceed your own perception of it. In other cases, your clients' perception of your value may be disappointingly less than your own perception of it. The fact is that you really can't know how much you're worth to your clients until you talk to them and get a sense of the problems they face and the ultimate cost to them of a range of different solutions.

In this section, we consider some factors that determine your value as a consultant to your clients.

Why hire a consultant?

When exploring the philosophical question of how much you are worth to your clients, you may find it useful to explore why organisations recruit consultants in the first place.

When faced with a problem, your clients have many different options at their disposal for resolving it. The main ones include assigning a current employee to the task or hiring a new employee to take on the assignment. However, these approaches can often bring their own problems, and they may not be the most cost-effective ways to arrive at the best solution. In addition, when faced with recruiting their own employees, your clients may not be able to find any candidates with a consultant's unique credentials and high level of expertise.

So why do organisations recruit consultants? The following reasons are some of the most compelling:

- ✔ **Because consultants are experts:** Expertise and knowledge are two of the main reasons that organisations recruit consultants. Many people in an organisation may be able to take on a necessary assignment, but it's often the case that none can do the job as quickly and efficiently as an expert consultant who every day lives and breathes the issue to be addressed. The end result of hiring an expert consultant is often an overall saving in time and money – often with better results than if the assignment were performed in-house by the organisation's employees.

- ✔ **Because consultants are independent:** When an organisation recruits a consultant, it is hiring an independent contractor, not an employee. This simple fact has all sorts of implications. Consultants work closely with their clients, but they do not require the kind of direct supervision that employees performing comparable tasks do. And the client controls payment – if a consultant doesn't perform in accordance with the terms of the consulting contract, a client has the right to withhold payment, or even terminate the contract and the relationship with that particular consultant.

- ✔ **Because consultants are objective, outside third parties:** Consultants often bring a fresh point of view to an organisation that may have lost its perspective. In many organisations – especially those where employees are afraid to speak against the status quo for fear of losing their jobs – only an outsider is willing to tell it like it is. Sometimes only an outside consultant can clearly see the broken organisational systems and dysfunctional management behaviours that disable the firm. Outsiders can also make recommendations that break through to the decision-makers who most need to hear them.

✔ **Because consultants have dedicated time:** Time may be a precious element among an organisation's existing staff and in short supply. A person or group may be assigned to a project and then later taken off the project because of conflicting priorities. An outside consultant, on the other hand, can focus on the task or project full time until the work is completed.

✔ **Because consultants are a flexible resource:** Most consultants make themselves available to their clients – especially their best clients – at a moment's notice. Indeed, more than a few consultants give their very best clients their home phone numbers and 'secret' email addresses. If an organisation had to recruit someone new to take on an assignment, it could spend months to place ads, perform interviews and reference checks, make a final selection, and bring a new employee on board. On the other hand, if the organisation wants to recruit a consultant, someone just needs to pick up the phone and a consultant can often be at the organisation's immediate disposal.

✔ **Because there's no long-term commitment:** When an employee completes a special project, an organisation may find itself scrambling to place the person in another position within the organisation – or be faced with laying him or her off. When a consultant completes a special project, he or she simply goes away until the next time the organisation needs the firm's services – no two-week notice, no termination, no layoff, no severance pay, no nothing. Consultants can and do develop long-term relationships with organisations, but only when these organisations desire long-term relationships with particular consultants or consulting firms.

✔ **Because consultants are cost-effective:** When you tally up the long-term costs of recruiting an employee to take on a task versus bringing in a consultant to perform the same task for a defined period of time, going with a consultant may be more cost-advantageous. An organisation does not have to pay the consultant for private health care, holidays, pension plans, or other benefits that it typically pays its employees. Using a consultant is a cost-effective alternative for organisations that need to solve a problem quickly and efficiently. We explore why this is true in the next section.

Can you do it better, for the same price, or for less?

Although all the considerations named in the section 'Why hire a consultant?' are important for determining your value to your clients, the ultimate question is: *How much money will your client save by hiring you and your consulting firm?* The higher that number, the more value you provide to your clients.

This justifies a hiring decision in your favour – regardless of the amount of money you charge.

The point is – and we're going to keep repeating this until you believe it – that you must focus on the *value* you provide to your client, not on the hourly rate or on the number of hours that you need to complete a job. Keep this distinction uppermost in your client's mind, too. Perhaps you believe that asking for a fee of £45 an hour is very optimistic at best and insulting to your client at worst. However, suppose that a client has to invest over £50,000 a year to recruit a full-time employee to have the same effect that you can have in 24 hours each month – for £14,400 a year. In that case, you provide incredible value to your client, especially if you happen also to provide a better work product than any employee can.

Here's an example of what we mean: Say that your client wants to create a high-profile media presence for her large mail-order clothing business. She has a choice, she can recruit a part-time or a full-time employee, or she can recruit you, the public relations expert to beat all public relations experts – for a fee that, at least on the surface, appears to be pretty steep. The first thing to consider is the cost of each alternative to your client. In Case A, your client decides to recruit a full-time employee for £45 an hour. In Case B, your client recruits you for £100 an hour. On the surface, recruiting an employee seems to make the most sense. Straightaway, your client is going to save £75 an hour – yes?

Take a look.

Case A: Recruit a new employee to take on public relations chores

Hourly pay rate	£16.00
Employment costs @ 35%	£5.60
Overhead costs @ 35%	£5.60
Total effective pay rate	£27.20
Hours per year	1,958
Total annual labour cost	£53,258

In Case A, the new employee is paid a wage of £16.00 an hour. However, this wage is not the true cost to the organisation. The cost of benefits for the employee e.g. national insurance, private health care, life insurance, pension plan, sick pay, and so on weighs in at 35 per cent of the hourly wage, or £5.60. Overheads – electricity, office space, computers, and so forth – cost the organisation another 35 per cent of the employee's wage, or £5.60 for each hour worked and paid. This brings the new employee's total hourly cost to the organisation to £27.20 an hour – almost double the wage paid to the employee for each hour worked. When you multiply the hourly rate by the standard number of hours in a work year, the grand total for the new employee comes to a whopping £53,258.

So what happens if the organisation recruits a consultant to do the same job?

Case B: Recruit a consultant to take on public relations chores

Hourly pay rate	£45.00
Total effective pay rate	£45.00
Hours per year	288
Total annual cost	£12,960

Your client actually saves over £40,000 by contracting with you rather than recruiting a full-time employee to do the same work. Although your hourly rate is more than the new employee's rate in Case A, your client saves the cost of the benefits and overheads that would have to be applied to a new employee's wage. Not only that, but because you are presumably more experienced, more efficient, and better connected than the employee, you need to devote far less time to the project to get the same results – only 288 hours a year versus 1,958 for the employee.

When your client contracts with your business, you bear the employment costs and overheads. Your client has to pay only the hourly fee that you agree to. In addition, if things don't work out, your client can terminate the relationship quickly and easily; the client doesn't have to worry about messy employee dismissals.

The net result is that you as a consultant offer tremendous value to a client in this situation. Be sure you price your services accordingly.

Are you selling a commodity or a customised solution?

Part of the final determination of your value to potential clients depends on whether the service you provide has been reduced to a commodity in the marketplace. By commodity, we mean that the services offered by various providers are equivalent in clients' eyes and that price is the primary factor that determines who is going to get the job.

For example, suppose that an organisation is going to recruit a consultant to prepare a business plan. If the organisation has several business consultants to choose from – all with very good references – it will probably recruit the business consultant who offers the best price. In this case, the service that this consultant offers has been reduced to a commodity in the organisation's eyes.

Now, say that a unique organisation is looking for a consultant who shares its vision and is fully compatible with the owner's personality. The organisation interviews a variety of business consultants, but only one consultant shares the organisation's vision and gels well with its owner. This same consultant also proposes to deliver a customised solution that is unique and better suited to this particular business than the other proposals. In this case, the business consultant offers a number of items of value to the client, and price is not the determining factor in making a final selection.

These scenarios reflect the way the consulting business works. If your product is the same as everyone else's, then your clients consistently look for the least expensive solution to their problems. The eventual result of this kind of pressure is that all the consultants offering these kinds of services are forced to cut their prices until hardly anyone is making any money at all. You're stuck in the commodity trap, and you need to find a way to get out – as quickly as you can.

If you find yourself stuck in the commodity trap, there are a number of ways to make the services you offer stand out in a crowd, including:

- ✔ **Add value.** Do more for your clients than they expect you to do, and you add value to your work – the kind of value that sets you apart from your competitors. You don't need to do anything particularly dramatic; all you need to do is consistently give more – even a little more – than you promise, and your clients will know the difference. For example, if you promise to complete your project in 30 days, you can easily delight your client (and add value to your work) by delivering early – perhaps in 25 days. The little things do make a difference in the eyes of your clients.

- ✔ **Be different from your competition.** When you're caught in the commodity trap, do whatever you can to make the services that you offer different from those your competitors offer – especially in ways that your clients value. This means getting to know everything you can about your competition – the services they offer, the prices they charge, and how they deliver services to their clients. What can you do to make your clients realise that you're offering a unique solution instead of a run-of-the-mill solution? Offer free pickup and delivery? Use higher-quality materials than your competitors? Be available 24 hours a day for emergency service? Customise part or all of the products and services you deliver to each client? Decide how to make your services different from your competition and then do it!

- ✔ **Focus on customer service.** If you are in a commodity-type business in which most consultants deliver pretty much the same products or services, one of the best ways to stand out from the crowd is by providing unparalleled customer service. Unparalleled customer service starts with something that doesn't cost any money at all: a positive, can-do attitude. Your attitude says that you are making your customer your number-one priority and that you are doing whatever it takes to make your customer's consulting experience the best one possible. Follow up this attitude with action, and you're guaranteed to stand out from the crowd.

✔ **Do great work.** Despite being paid small mountains of money, some consultants simply don't do a very good job. Not only that, but some consultants deliver their products late, if at all. If you do great work and deliver on schedule at the agreed price, your clients will seek you out and will be happy to pay a premium for your work. We know from personal experience that finding consultants who are both talented and capable of following through on promises of quality and delivery can sometimes be a challenge. However, consultants who do high-quality work and deliver it on or before the deadline are well worth the extra money.

✔ **Build long-term relationships.** Nothing sets you apart from the rest of the pack more than developing long-term relationships with your clients. The more work you do for your clients and the deeper your work and social relationships with your clients, the less likely your clients are to shop around for other consultants to take your place. And the more work you do for the same clients, the better you understand their operations and their unique needs. This understanding can help you to continue to improve the work you do for them.

Setting Your Fees in Different Ways

When you go about the process of setting your fees, the first question to ask yourself is how much money you want or need to make. Unfortunately, we can't answer this question for you – you have to look at your own situation and go from there. We can, however, provide you with some general guidelines that have worked for many consultants.

Hourly rate

The hourly rate is probably the most common way that consultants price their services. Whether you are proofreading manuscripts, providing legal advice, or designing a client's website, you can charge hourly rates. Hourly rates are easy to understand and compare with one another, and clients can buy as many hours as they like. That's the good news. On the other side of the ledger, clients and consultants tend to focus on different issues. Clients generally want to reduce the number of hours that consultants work.

Consultants, however, often focus on increasing the number of hours that they work for a client.

If you decide to price your services on an hourly basis, you need to have a rationale for developing and supporting your rates. Here are some of the ways in which you can do just that:

- **Consider the market for your services.** The easiest way to set a rate for your services is to find out how much other consultants – in your area, or nationally – charge to do the same kind of work and then price your services within the same range. For example, if other consultants in your field charge between £25 and £45 an hour, then you can comfortably set your price within that range. If you step below the range, you may be swamped with low-margin business that doesn't really pay the bills. Step above the range, and you have to convince your clients that you're worth the extra fee.

- **Build your rate from the bottom up.** If you've been working in a regular job for a number of years, your goal may be simply to maintain your previous pay rate. If you were being paid £15 an hour at your job, that's where you would start. If you add the burden of paying for your own benefits that your previous employer paid – say, £7 an hour – and an additional £7 to cover your overheads, other expenses, and profit, then you end up with a rate of around £30 an hour.

- **Build your rate from the top down.** You may decide that you want to gross £40,000 a year from your consulting efforts. If that's the case, you first estimate how many hours you can work and invoice to clients in a year. For example, if you estimate that you'll work 1,500 hours, then you divide the total amount of money that you want for the year – £40,000 – by the total hours you've estimated that you'll work. In this case, you have to charge around £30 an hour to achieve your goal of £40,000 a year.

When setting your initial fee, remember that you have convinced your client that you are the best person for the task (and we're assuming you have – if you haven't, then go back to your prospective client and try again!). The client, therefore, will be relatively fee-insensitive as long as your fees are approximately 20 to 30 per cent higher than those of your competitors. Many clients consider that getting the best consultant is worth a 20 to 30 per cent premium.

Depending on the type of project, you may want to establish a minimum number of chargeable hours, such as four hours. This protects you from the client who 'just wants to get together briefly for a 30-minute meeting'. However, by the time you've driven to the client's office, met, and returned to your office, you've blown half a day – not a half hour. Remember, as a consultant, you are selling time and knowledge. For a consultant, time really is money.

And don't forget to invoice your client for any and all business expenses you incur on his or her behalf beyond those normally incurred in doing your everyday business. For example, a consulting job may require that you travel to a number of client sites nationwide and spend several weeks on the road – incurring charges for petrol, train and air fares, car hire, hotels, and dining. Remember to add these expenses to your client's invoices in addition to the hours that you are invoicing for a particular period. Be sure that you fully explain to your clients what expenses you'll charge to their accounts and any limitations placed upon them. For example, you may decide to charge a fixed per diem of £80 a day for hotel and dining expenses, or you may want to include an agreement to charge your clients only for the price of economy-class air fares, even if you fly business class.

The rule of thirds

If you are leaving a job to start your own consulting business, a common guideline says take your hourly wage rate and multiply it by three to arrive at the hourly fee to charge as a consultant. So if you are currently making £15 an hour, as a consultant you charge your clients £45 an hour.

Why so much more than your current job? Because not only are you paying yourself a wage ($1/3$ of the total rate), but you're also paying for the benefits – income protection, life insurance, pension plans, and so on – that you want to maintain as a consultant (another $1/3$ of the total rate), plus you need to set aside some extra money for profit (the final $1/3$ of the total rate).

Although you may be a full-time paid employee now, you may not be a full-time paid consultant when you make the move. Many consultants experience downtime between projects, perhaps going for days or weeks without paid work. The higher rate of £45 an hour also helps to cushion that kind of financial shortfall.

Per-item or per-project basis

Many consultants price their services on a per-item or per-project basis. For example, if you do image consulting, you may price consultations at £50 each. Or if you are recruited to audit a small electronics business, you may price the project at a flat rate of £3,000. The beauty of pricing your services this way is that you redirect the focus from the number of hours you work to the results that you achieve and – ultimately – the value that your client believes he or she has received.

For example, if you agree to conduct a full process review of the purchasing and receiving function of an organisation, you might price this project at a total of £8,000. In return for the £8,000, you promise to present a report with recommendations to improve the operation. At the end of the four-week study, you deliver your report and submit your invoice for payment. Now, your client couldn't care less how many hours you spent on the project. Your client cares only about the recommendations in your proposal – and that you performed your work within the £8,000 total agreed to. If the recommendations are good, and you haven't exceeded your agreed price, then your client will be happy and won't ask you how many hours you expended on the job. If the recommendations aren't good, you'll know soon enough.

Although you'll do much of your work – especially early in your consulting career – on an hourly or daily basis, shifting your business to a per-item or per-project basis is definitely in your interest. If you price it right, you have plenty of money left over after the job is complete, and you can focus all your efforts on creating the best product possible.

Retainer basis

Sometimes your clients want to ensure your availability to work for them, but they aren't able to define in advance exactly how much of your time they'll need or exactly when they'll need it. This kind of situation is tailor-made for setting up a retainer arrangement. A *retainer* is nothing more than a guarantee that your client will pay you a fixed sum of money each month. In return for this guarantee, you promise to be available to work for that client whenever the need arises.

Here's how it works: Say that you are recruited under an annual retainer of £30,000, giving you a monthly income of £2,500. In January, your client uses exactly £2,500 worth of services. However, in February, your client uses only £1,250 worth of services. Despite this shortfall in usage, your client pays you the fixed sum of £2,500 for February. The shortfall of usage in February is carried forward to March, giving your client a total of £3,750 to work with that month. If, on the other hand, the client exceeds the monthly amount specified in the retainer agreement, then you can invoice the client for the extra work. At the end of the year, you wipe the slate clean. If the client hasn't used all his or her money by this time, then the client forfeits the unused portion to the consultant.

Retainers are generally win-win situations for both parties. The client has a skilled expert ready to work at a moment's notice. In exchange for this privilege, the consultant gets a steady stream of income each month. And if you are an independent consultant, you know that happiness is a positive cash flow.

Keeping client value in mind

As you consider the different options listed above, don't forget that you need to base the price you charge for your services on the value that you provide to your clients, not on anyone's preconceived notion as to what a 'proper' fee is. The idea is to get the focus away from the price you charge, and onto the value you provide.

When you start out in consulting, you'll probably charge your services to your clients by the hour or day, and your clients will pay you only for the number of hours that you devote to their projects. Your clients will also probably be hesitant to pay you any more than the other consultants who offer services similar to those that you offer.

That arrangement may be all well and good, but as you gain experience in consulting, keep the big picture in clear sight and don't get bogged down trying to justify a particular number of hours or a particular rate. The goal is to move the bulk of your business into a project-based or retainer pricing arrangement. Reaching this goal may be easier said than done – especially if your clients are accustomed to dealing with you on an hourly or daily basis. But believe us – achieving your goal will be well worth the effort as you separate yourself from the very crowded pack of consultants offering the same kinds of services you do – often at lower rates.

Making Changes to Your Fees

If you are a consultant, we can absolutely guarantee that you'll eventually decide that you need to either increase or decrease the fees that you charge to your clients. Although you should never make changes to your fees without a good reason, increasing or decreasing your fees definitely makes sense at certain times.

While a client is unlikely to complain when you lower your fees – or to tell you if your fees are too low – this may not be the case when you increase your fees. Who wants to pay a higher price for something tomorrow than they're paying for it today? In either case, prepare your rationale before you make the changes and be ready to explain the changes to your clients. The following sections describe the most common reasons for making changes to your fees.

Increases

Most business people would love to pay the same amount – or perhaps even less – for the same service for ever and ever. Wouldn't that be nice? But the real world just doesn't work that way. As everyone knows, the costs of doing business continue to increase as time goes on, and as costs escalate, your fees are sure to follow. Although you may know exactly why your rates need to increase, you may not be so sure exactly when to make the change or whether to apply the change only for new customers or for both new and existing customers.

The general rule is to pass price increases on to new customers immediately. For your current customers, the answer is a bit more complex. If you are contracted to provide your services at a set rate for a defined period of time – say, six months or a year – then you need to wait until you fulfil your commitment before broaching the idea of raising your prices. If you're not bound to an agreement fixing your prices for a period of time, then give your current clients at least 30 days' notice – or more if you can anticipate far enough ahead – of the impending rate increase before you actually implement it. A notice period often softens the blow for a client, particularly if the new rate doesn't kick in until a client's new budget year. Consultants raise their fees for many reasons besides the rising costs of doing business. Here are a few reasons that may compel you to raise yours:

- ✔ **Your expenses have increased.** If your expenses increase and you want to maintain the same level of profitability as you've had in the past, then you have to pass on the price increase to your clients.

- ✔ **You've underpriced your services.** You may find that you've priced your services too low, especially if you're new to consulting, considering the high value you are providing your clients. If this is the case, you must act quickly to raise your prices for future jobs so that you don't lose money on the work that you're performing for clients – both current and future.

- ✔ **You want to test the marketplace.** Setting your fees is a balancing act. Periodically test the market with higher-priced offerings and then note how your clients respond. If your supply of prospective clients dries up as a result, it's probably not a good time to increase your rates. However, if your clients don't seem to be very concerned about the increase, and they're still clamouring for your services, then you know that you can make the change stick.

- ✔ **You need to pay for a client's 'hidden' expenses.** After you work for a client for a while, you may find hidden expenses that you didn't anticipate and that dramatically increase the amount of work that you must do to complete your assignments on time. For example, you may be expected to attend meetings that your client didn't tell you about in advance. Or you may find that obtaining access to the information that you need is more difficult and takes more time than you first anticipated. If you must take on unexpected work, you may have to increase the fee that you charge your clients to cover the extra time required to complete the project.

✔ **You don't really want to do the work.** Sometimes you just don't want to do the work. Yes, at times you would rather turn down a particular client or job than suffer through it. When a client offers you work that you don't want to do, you can price your proposal significantly higher than you normally would. If the client turns down your proposal, fine; you didn't want the work anyway. However, if the client accepts the proposal, then you're paid enough to make up for the pain and agony of doing the job or for working with that particular client.

Regardless of the reason for increasing your rates, take the time to carefully consider how you're going to implement your increase. Your goal is to keep your very best customers (the ones who pay you the most and the ones with whom you most enjoy working) while continuing to attract new business. As you attract and do business with clients who are willing to pay you higher fees, letting go of your marginal clients – the ones who aren't willing to accept fee increases – is definitely in your interest. As a rule, after you have your consultancy firmly established, you must always strive to lose the bottom 10 per cent of your business to make room for a new 10 per cent of business to move in at the top of your client list.

Decreases

Yes, believe it or not, there are times when you may actually find it advantageous to decrease the amount that clients pay for your services. However, because price decreases can potentially threaten to reduce your revenue and profit, you must carefully consider any price decrease before you implement it. You also have to be careful that you don't set a precedent for continued price decreases (unless you want to) that your clients may expect in the future.

Here are three reasons you may want to decrease your fees:

✔ **Because you've overpriced your services:** Always be suspicious that you have overpriced your services when, despite advertising, networking, and making plenty of personal contacts, your only customer is your uncle George. If you're not getting the level of business that you expected when you started your business, look closely at your rates. If they're too high, you need to bring them down to a level that is more consistent with your perceived value. Either that or improve the value that you offer to your clients so that the value matches the fees you charge.

Chapter 6: What Are You Worth? Setting Your Fees

✔ **To reward your long-term clients:** Everyone appreciates getting an occasional bargain, and this is certainly true for your clients. The most common ways of decreasing your pricing for long-term clients are either by giving them special premiums from time to time, such as reduced rates for a month, or by holding your fee constant. (You can still increase your fees for short-term and new clients.)

✔ **To get your foot in the door:** Although you run the danger of setting a precedent that will be difficult to change for future work, you may find that lowering your fees when you are trying to break into a new industry or line of business is advantageous. The simple fact is, if you can't get anyone to recruit you at the rates that you have set – no matter how fair they may be or how much value you deliver – you're not going to make any money. And if you don't make any money, then you're out of business. When you're trying to break into a new market, dropping your fees to give your prospective clients an incentive to give you a try can often pay off in the long run. Just be sure to let your client know that you are making this exception on a one-time basis only and that you'll invoice any future work at your normal rates.

One technique to address the fee issue for a new client is to quote rates as follows:

✔ Normal professional fee: £45 per hour

✔ New-client discount to demonstrate performance and build goodwill: £7 per hour

✔ Net fee for this project only: £38 per hour.

This approach establishes your normal fee in the client's mind for future projects while demonstrating that you really want the opportunity to show what you can do.

Making a Stand

Every consultant can tell you at least one or two stories about clients who wanted them to reduce their rates – on either a short-term or a long-term basis. No doubt, as a consultant, you'll have your own stories to tell. But, don't forget that this is *your* business, and *you* are ultimately responsible for deciding how you are going to run it. If you decide to reduce your rates or make other concessions to your clients in exchange for their goodwill (and business), that's fine. Just be sure that you have a good reason and definite goals in mind for doing so.

If you decide to stick to your guns, and not cave in to their requests, then by all means do so. Not only do you earn the respect of prospective clients (this reason alone often earns you their business), but marginal clients, who are more worried about fees than the results and the value you provide to them, stay away. And that's really not so bad, is it?

As you prepare to (politely) tell your clients what they can do with their demands to drop your fees, keep these tips in mind:

- ✔ **Just say no!** When you're in business, it's not fun telling your clients no, but sometimes you just have to. When you have to say no to your clients' requests to lower your fees or make other concessions, do so promptly and be firm. If you drag your feet or beat around the bush, your clients may be angered that you weren't forthright to begin with. And if you aren't firm in your response, then your clients may believe that you've given them an opening to negotiate with you – even when you really haven't.

- ✔ **Have good reasons.** When you tell your clients no, be prepared to explain exactly why. Explain to your clients, 'Those rates don't allow me to cover the expenses of doing business,' or 'I can't deliver the kind of high-quality results that I demand, and that you expect, if we compress the schedule as much as you have proposed.' Clients may not particularly enjoy being told no, but if you have a good reason for it, then at least they may understand why.

- ✔ **Be prepared with a counter proposal.** Although you may not be able to accept a client's proposed terms, you may be able to propose alternatives that you both find acceptable and that result in a win-win situation. For example, say something like, 'I absolutely can't reduce the price I proposed to complete your project, but I can get you your results faster if you like.' The more different options you can muster for your clients to consider, the better.

- ✔ **Don't forget: 'It's not personal, it's only business.'** Avoid at all costs the temptation to get caught up in arguments about your fees and prices or about why you have to decline your client's requests to decrease them. These decisions are, first and foremost, business decisions, and you must never allow them to devolve into personality clashes or conflicts. If your discussions with a client take a turn for the worse, politely cut the conversation short, tell the client again exactly where you stand, and ask the client to call you if he or she has a change of heart.

Although setting your fees can sometimes seem like a random act, there really is a rhyme and reason behind the rates that you establish and the decision to change them from time to time. Regardless of your feelings about how you set your own fees, don't forget that you're running a business: You have to make money, not lose it. Otherwise, you're pursuing a 'going out of business' plan. Set your fees so that you meet the financial goals of your business and can afford to take a few days off every now and then.

Part III
The Consulting Process

'The data collectors are here, Mr Snodley.'

In this part . . .

All consultants – whether they're experts in planting organic gardens or in managing organisational change – apply a uniform process for determining what their clients' problems are and what needs to be done to fix them.

In this part, we take a look at the consulting process: defining the problem and writing winning proposals, collecting data, problem-solving, presenting recommendations, and implementing solutions.

Become an expert at this process, and you'll be a consulting force to be reckoned with!

Chapter 7

Defining the Problem and Writing a Winning Proposal

· ·

· ·

*E*very business process has a beginning, a middle, and an end. The consulting process is no different. It begins with defining the problem, moves through collecting data, analysing that data, making your recommendations, and then ends with implementation. Because the first step – defining the problem – sets the stage for all the other steps that follow, it is particularly critical. Not only do you have to quickly determine whether your potential clients really have a problem and, if so, what exactly that problem is, but you also have to build a relationship with them and determine how to approach the problem and whether you're the best one to solve it.

For most consultants, this first step – defining the problem – takes place in a meeting with the prospective client. Although this meeting is usually in person, it can take place over the phone or even in writing, through letters or email. The process can take more than a single meeting – especially for complex problems that require complex solutions. For the very complicated problems you may be able to charge the client for working out a problem definition. For most purposes, a face-to-face meeting is best because it allows you to develop a much stronger relationship with your client and a much deeper understanding of your client's problems than you can get from other methods of communication. A face-to-face meeting may or may not make sense depending on the value of the work, how far away your client is located, and the prospects for future work. However, regardless of which method you ultimately choose, your meeting has three key purposes:

✔ To develop rapport with your client

✔ To identify your client's problem

✔ To determine whether you can be of help to your client

Note that this simple list of aims for your first meeting with your client is appropriate for any kind of consultant. Whether you teach homeowners how to recycle their refuse (and sell them the sorting systems to do it) or conduct management audits for a huge, multinational firm, the purposes underlying your initial client meeting remain the same. At your meeting, you must develop rapport with your client, determine your client's problem and decide whether you can help solve it.

In this chapter, we identify specific goals for your initial client meetings, as well as some things you can do and questions you can ask. We discuss building a partnership with your client and, finally, how to put together a winning proposal that summarises the understandings that you reach as a result of your client meeting.

Tips for Your Initial Client Conversations

At first blush, you may think that you have only one goal when you meet potential clients about a new project: to sell yourself to do the work. This may very well be your overall objective. However, you need to know much more about your clients and the problems they face before you can be sure that the work fits well within your base of experience and that you can develop the kind of partnership with your clients that is so important for ensuring a successful project.

Defining the problem – and your client

The initial conversations with your client are ones of discovery: meeting someone new and developing a basis for a strong business relationship, learning about your client's organisation, learning about the organisation's successes and challenges, and deciding whether you and your prospective client can actually work together. To help yourself through this discovery process, you need to take a series of steps in order to answer these questions. These steps represent the goals of your initial meeting:

- **Develop rapport and build a partnership.** Consulting is very much a business built on people and on relationships. If you have a talent for developing rapport with potential clients quickly, you're well on your way to building strong relationships and, ultimately, partnerships with your clients. If you find it difficult to develop rapport with your prospects, you're going to be an awfully lonely consultant. Work hard at breaking through the first-meeting jitters and establishing the kind of rapport that helps develop the foundation for long-term, fruitful relationships.

✔ **Assess your client's personality type and adjust your style accordingly.** If your client has an assertive, take-charge style, you can get to the business at hand sooner than if the client is more sociable and personable. With the latter style, the client may need to be comfortable with you personally before he or she can devote full attention to your abilities.

✔ **Help identify the challenges and opportunities and get a feel for your client's desire to change.** Clients agree to discuss consulting projects with you because they believe that you may be able to resolve significant organisational challenges or problems in their organisations, or that you can guide them to take more advantage of opportunities in the marketplace. Most likely, your clients already have some idea of what they need, and they may very well have decided what needs to be done to solve them. Already have some idea of the client's problems and opportunities, gained through your own research on the company. Your goal is to identify the real nature of your client's problems and then determine whether you can be of value in helping fix the problem.

For example, your client may be convinced that the organisation's high rate of employee turnover is related to the low wages paid to employees. You may suspect, however, that the turnover problem is actually a result of poor management skills, and through your prior research you may have discovered newspaper articles on the Internet indicating an ongoing exodus of key employees from this company who all worked for the same manager. Although your client may be willing to address the perceived problem by giving employees a pay increase, the client may not be willing to address the real problem of poor management. We have known many consultants who feel that clients initially almost never report the real problem but only a symptom of it. Clients get easily irritated by the consultant who, too early, says 'you think the problem is X but really it's Y'. Remember, nobody likes a clever dick. You'll get the opportunity to test your client's perception of the problem as well as your own after collecting data, the second part of the consulting process.

✔ **Define the project deliverables.** When you've determined that your client indeed has a problem that needs to be solved and you have a good idea what it is, you need to work with your client to define the objectives of the project and the products that you'll deliver at its conclusion. Your clients typically know the results that they want; they just don't know how best to achieve them. When you talk with your clients, ask them what results they want, and then help them translate those results into deliverables that are concrete and measurable and that can be achieved realistically. A good exercise is to ask clients to define 'what it would look like' when the problem(s) is solved. You can use this information to define the 'deliverables' you include in your proposal – perhaps a final report containing recommendations for top management, a customer perception survey, training for the client's employees, or an advertising campaign.

✔ **Agree who will do what.** To ensure that possible confusion due to overlapping (or dropped!) responsibilities doesn't come back to haunt you during the project, take time during your initial meetings to sort out exactly who is going to do what. Will you distribute surveys to your client's employees, or will your client take care of that? Will you be responsible for scheduling and setting up employee training sessions, or will your client take care of those details? Who is going to be responsible for implementing your recommendations – you or the client? Now is the time to clarify these issues – not when the ball is already in play.

✔ **Determine the information and client support that you'll need.** During the course of your initial client conversations, try to determine the information and support that you're going to need from your client and get the client's agreement to provide it. For example, suppose that you propose to redesign a client's headquarters building ventilation system to incorporate improved air circulation as well as better filtration and absorption of fungal spores and other particulates. Then you certainly need your client to provide a set of drawings that shows you the exact location and measurements for the existing system. Work with your client to mutually determine the information and support that you'll need during the course of the project and from whom specifically you can get such assistance.

✔ **Define the project schedule.** A lot of things depend on your clients' desired project schedule and your ability to meet it. When your clients decide that their problem is so serious that they need an outside consultant, they are usually in a rush to get the work done. For example, if you're an engineering consultant brought in to recommend actions to repair a leaking dam, your client isn't going to be very receptive to a completion date that is a year away. A week may not be quick enough in a situation like this, in which people's lives are at stake. Work with your clients to define a project schedule that meets their needs but that, in your best judgement, allows you sufficient time to do the project right.

✔ **Decide whether to proceed.** Despite the impression that some consultants (and clients, for that matter) may have about who decides whether a project goes forward, it is not the sole province of your clients to make that decision. In reality, the decision whether to proceed with a project is very much mutual. Just as your clients can decide that you're not the best consultant for the job or that your personality doesn't gel well with theirs, you can decide not to work for your clients for a variety of reasons. Perhaps you believe that they are not prepared to make the changes necessary for your solutions to work, or maybe you just don't like something about their personalities. It takes two to tango, and this is just as true with the consulting process as it is on the dance floor. If you decide to proceed, your next step is to develop and submit a project proposal to your clients.

As you can see, your initial client conversations are much more involved than simply trying to sell the merits of hiring your business to do some work. If you conduct these conversations in the manner we describe, you set the stage for submitting a winning proposal and for completing your project smoothly and successfully.

Meeting your client for the first time

So, you've talked with the client, broken the ice, scoped out the problem, and decided there's a fit. In some cases – where the issues are simple and your solutions are straightforward – you may next go directly to creating a proposal. However, when the problem is more complex, when your solutions are yet to be completely defined, and you have good reason to spend some time with your client, you may find it advantageous or necessary to meet your client face to face. With so much riding on the first meeting in person with a client, it's easy to become nervous or apprehensive about it. Our advice is to take a deep breath and relax. Even if you're relatively new to consulting, you undoubtedly have a lot to offer your clients, and they'll be glad to hear what you have to say.

Here are a few tips to help boost your confidence in your client meetings and leave your client with a positive impression of you and your abilities:

- **Relax!** Of course, those first meetings with your client are always critical. If they go well, you may be up to your ears in work for months, or even years. If they don't, well, you at least learn something. If you want to build rapport quickly with your clients, you must put them at ease right away. This means that you need to be confident and at ease yourself. Relax! As long as you're prepared for the meeting and you're confident in your ability, you've no need to be nervous or apprehensive. In fact, if you've done your homework, you should be positively overflowing with the excitement of having the opportunity to help your clients solve their problems. Channel your anxiety; it can inspire your best thinking.

- **Know who will be there and why.** Before you meet your client, find out who will be attending from your prospective client's organisation and what their roles are in the proceedings. After you know who will be in the meeting with you, you can prepare yourself to address any topics that may be of particular interest to individual attendees. For example, if you learn that the company's IT Director is planning to attend, you can mention that you have extensive experience working with management information systems – a topic that is sure to cause the IT Director to pay attention to what you have to say.

✔ **Make your best impression.** You only have one chance to make a first impression, and this is the time and place that you want to make a *great* first impression. The way you greet your client, the way you dress, the way you speak, and the way you carry yourself all lend weight to the fact that you're a professional. If you do financial consulting for banks, you had better look like a banker. If your expertise is in squeezing an extra knot or two of boat speed out of a 12-metre racing yacht, then shorts, a polo shirt, deck shoes, and a windcheater may be the uniform of choice. Without boasting or resorting to name-dropping, tell your client about some of the successful projects you've worked on in the past and about some of the better-known clients you've done work for. If you provide a formal reference with contact information, make sure that you get permission from your previous clients first. If you're energetic, attentive, and sincerely interested in helping your clients solve their problems, you leave them with little choice but to be impressed with you.

✔ **Be prepared.** In an effort to test your knowledge, your client may ask you highly technical questions or questions that require good judgement and expertise to answer well. The best way to handle these kinds of situations is by being fully prepared for your meeting before you turn up. If your client is new to you, you must find out everything you can about the organisation: its markets, its technology, its people, and its successes and failures. Your client will be impressed that you took the time to learn about the organisation, and that you've acquired the knowledge and understanding of how it operates. It'll be an opportunity for you to wow them.

✔ **Listen.** To understand exactly your client's problems and get some idea of how best to address them, you have to listen to your client. Some consultants mistakenly believe that they have to do all the talking in order to show their expertise. This is simply not the case. In fact, in meetings with your client – except, perhaps, ones where you're making a presentation of some sort – you need to do more listening than talking. This is the only way that you can hear what your client is really saying and understand what is really needed.

✔ **Take notes.** When you and your client decide to proceed with a project, you need to draft a proposal for the work and submit it for your client's review and approval. During the course of your first meeting and in any subsequent meetings or phone calls, you discuss a multitude of ideas, concerns, concepts, approaches, and understandings with your client. Taking notes of these critical discussions is invaluable to you both when you develop your project proposal and during the course of project performance. Not only that, but your client will be favourably impressed by the importance that you accord to what he has to say. Right after the meeting, make additional notes of your impressions while they are still fresh in your mind.

That wasn't so bad, was it? The more client meetings you participate in, the more your confidence increases, and you have less reason to be concerned about them. Before you know it, these meetings become second nature to you, and you handle them like a pro. Until then, keep working at these skills and keep meeting your clients.

Asking your clients questions that count

If you want to create great proposals, ones that have your clients reaching for their chequebooks minutes after they receive them, you need to know the answers to a lot of questions. And after your client selects you to do the work, the answers you receive in this preliminary stage of the consulting process help to guide you through the later stages.

Your job, therefore, is to ask the questions that get you the answers you need. Here are several different questions for you to try. Feel free to add to the list others if they provide you with good information:

- What is the problem that you would like me to address?
- Why do you think that the problem is occurring?
- How long has your organisation had this problem?
- Have you tried to solve the problem? How? What happened?
- What suggestions do you have about how I should approach this problem?
- What are your objectives for this project?
- Are there any organisational obstacles in the way of finding a solution?
- Are there any organisational obstacles in the way of implementing my recommendations?
- Is your management team committed to making the organisational changes needed to make this project a success?
- What measurable outcomes do you want to see at the end of the project?
- When would you like this project completed?
- How do you see your role during the course of the project? And after project completion?
- What kinds of information and other support can your organisation provide?
- Will I be responsible for helping to implement the project recommendations?

✔ Do you have a budget in mind for this project?

✔ What kind of experience would you like the consultant you select to have?

✔ What would win this business?

✔ What would lose this business?

✔ Do you have any personal concerns about this project?

✔ How soon would you like me to start?

Don't fall into the classic trap of thinking that you already know the answers to many of these questions as a result of the research you've done in advance of your meetings. The questions you ask now can and will save you lots of time and anguish down the road. Make asking questions the very core of your first client conversations and meeting.

Building Partnerships with Your Clients

You have a choice: You can either work with your clients or work against them. We're going to let you in on a little secret: The wonderful world of consulting isn't always a bowl of cherries. In fact, if you have to deal with hostile clients or with uncooperative, troublesome employees, you may wish that you had followed a different career path – taxidermy, perhaps. The problem with working against your clients is that nobody wins and everybody loses. You lose because you wasted your time on a project that no one appreciated or even wanted, and your clients lose because the original problem remains unsolved.

If something doesn't feel right or you're getting bad vibes, you may want to terminate the relationship and find clients with whom you're more compatible. If the client-consultant chemistry isn't right at the beginning, it's not likely to get better further down the road.

Clearly, building strong partnerships with one another instead of working against one another is in the best interests of both you and your clients. Your clients win and you win, too. Here are some dependable ways to build partnerships with your clients:

✔ **Collaborate, collaborate, collaborate.** Collaboration between consultant and client is an absolutely essential element in any successful consulting project. If the so-called 'expert' consultant sits up in an ivory tower – remaining aloof from the organisation and the people who work within it – the client may decide that the consultant is out of touch with the organisation and quickly discard the his or her reports and recommendations. Conversely, if the client decides to treat the consultant as just another employee – directing everything the consultant does and approving (or disapproving) every move he or she makes – then the results and recommendations will be far less credible than those that a truly independent consultant would produce. The solution is for consultant and client to work together – collaboratively – and build a partnership to ensure that the project is successful.

✔ **Make all communication two-way communication.** Good communication is not a one-way street. You can't do all the talking and expect to understand your clients' problems or what outcomes they want to achieve. The strongest partnerships are built on a firm foundation of trust and mutual respect, where each party can speak openly and the other party listens. In a real partnership, the opinion of one partner is just as important as the opinion of the other, and all communication is open, honest, and moves freely in both directions.

✔ **Discuss and negotiate the tough issues.** In any meaningful partnership – including ones between consultants and their clients – tough issues have to be addressed and dealt with head-on. Dancing around issues or avoiding them to keep a relationship 'pleasant' doesn't allow you to resolve the issues that need to be resolved, nor does it result in a better set of conclusions and recommendations. In fact, your conclusions and recommendations will be incomplete and, quite possibly, inaccurate because you failed to address crucial issues. Discuss and negotiate the tough issues with your clients directly. Be frank and straightforward. Though you can be diplomatic and respect your clients, you must confront tough issues without hesitation. The result is a real partnership – not a fantasy world version that is handicapped from the start by its artificiality.

✔ **Make mutual decisions.** Whenever possible, include your clients in making the big decisions that have the greatest effect on your project. Making them feel part of the team can help build your partnership while preventing them from feeling like they are being left out of the problem-solving process. In the same vein, encourage your clients to include you in the decision-making process for issues pertaining to your project. Doing so will also help you to build and strengthen your partnerships with your clients and achieve better project results and recommendations.

✔ **Deal with the people problems, too.** In some organisations, the consultant may be pressured to ignore people problems – weak or overbearing managers and supervisors, perhaps, or employees who consistently show up late for work. This is a mistake. If you're to reach your goal of successfully solving your clients' problems, you can't leave people out of the equation. Although faulty policies, systems, and procedures can wreak havoc in an organisation, so too can faulty employees. Be sure to discuss this potential issue with your clients at the beginning of your projects – not after you've already got them under way.

Although establishing partnerships with your clients won't necessarily deal with all of your problems and challenges, it certainly makes your relationships much easier to live with, your work more productive, and your results more meaningful.

Crafting Winning Proposals

After you wrap up your initial contacts with your client, you next need to write and present an out-of-this-world, bang-on proposal. The length, depth, and breadth of your proposal greatly depend on the nature of your business, as well as your client's expectations.

For example, suppose that you're a computer consultant and you're simply going to install a new hard drive in someone's computer. You certainly don't need to present your client with a 35-page proposal describing all the benefits of the hardware upgrade and the reasons for selecting you over the competition – indeed, your client will probably give you the go-ahead after briefly discussing your experience, your price to do the job, and how soon you can do it. However, for a complex, multi-year proposal to do some serious management consulting that will result in significant organisational changes, 35 pages may not be enough!

The Zen of proposals

A certain philosophy lies behind the crafting of winning proposals. A proposal is a document that is specifically designed to provide your client-to-be with all the information he or she needs to make a decision to move forward with you – and to do so in a very compelling way. Regardless of how long your proposals are or how much they weigh, they must always be easy to understand, attractive, and concise. Here are a few more tips for your next proposal:

- ✔ **Respond directly to your clients' needs, questions, and concerns.** Listen to your clients and determine exactly what their needs, questions, and concerns are. When you've figured them out, respond to each one with a solution.

- ✔ **Place your clients' perceptions above your own.** When it comes to proposals, your clients' perceptions count, not your own. If your clients absolutely love colour photographs in the proposals that they receive, you had better use lots of them in your proposals, even if you think they detract from your image.

- ✔ **Don't wait until the last minute to start working on your proposals.** Get to work on your client proposals as soon as you decide to do them; avoid the temptation to put them off to the last minute. Not only are you more relaxed when you write them – resulting in a better, more thoughtful product with fewer errors – but you improve your ability to get them in on time (or even early!).

✔ **Take time to review your proposals before submitting them to your clients.** Always set aside time after you write your proposals to review them before you submit them to your clients. If you submit sloppy proposals, your prospective clients will probably assume that your work will be of similar quality.

✔ **Don't ignore your competition.** Your proposals must be at least as good, or better. Keep an eye on your competitors, and don't get too complacent or settled in your ways. Plenty of competition is out there, and in most cases, your competition isn't standing still. Always strive to make each proposal better than the one that preceded it, and stay up-to-date with your competitors' innovations.

✔ **Create a database of proposals.** Our experience is that, after a while, 50 per cent of any proposal becomes boilerplate; that is, content that is used time and again. For example, CVs of key members of your consulting team will most likely only need minor updates from time to time or tweaks to highlight experience relevant to particular jobs. And this also goes for your listings of client references and project experience. Make sure though that the whole document reads well and meets your client's unique needs. Leaving other client names in the text is unforgivable.

Proposals can be of any length, but for most situations, you submit either a short, letter-type proposal or a longer, narrative-type proposal. In the following sections, we check out each approach.

The letter proposal

In many consulting situations, all you need is a brief, one- to three-page proposal that concisely and simply presents the most important information that your prospective clients need to know. This can be submitted to your clients via email, fax, or an actual printed and signed letter. Letter proposals are particularly useful for projects that are simple, short in duration, or don't cost your clients very much money.

At minimum, your letter proposals need to contain the following information:

✔ **The point of your proposal:** After a word of thanks for meeting you or requesting your work, get directly to what you have to offer, focusing on results and on the advantages of working with you and your firm.

✔ **Proposed project**: What are you planning to do for your client? Make sure that you include a brief description of your project in your letter proposal.

✔ **Anticipated outcomes:** Summarise your anticipated project outcomes. If you're going to make recommendations that will save your client money, tell him or her so. Be careful not to over-promise: In the UK your proposal letter most often becomes the basis of the contract between you and your client, so only promise what you can definitely deliver. If you're going to train your client's employees in how to use a new software program, this is the place to present that particular bit of information.

✔ **Action plan:** Briefly outline the steps you'll take to reach your anticipated outcomes, along with any assumptions that you're making and any other details that your client needs to know.

✔ **Fees:** This is a crucial part of your proposal, so be sure to explain how you arrived at the fee, any discounts you've applied, and what the fee does or doesn't include. Make the fee sound reasonable by comparing it to the outcomes mentioned earlier.

✔ **Payment terms:** It's wise to break up your payments so that you receive some of the overall total during the course of carrying out the project instead of all at the very end. Monthly payments are very common. Not only is this payment schedule better for the health of your bank account, but it also helps to ensure that you don't complete and deliver a project to a client only to have the client refuse to pay for it. Although you may have provisions in your contracts to protect you legally from this eventuality, collecting may take you months or even years if you have to take your client to court.

✔ **Next steps:** Put the ball in your prospective client's court – explain what the client needs to do to initiate the project and get you working. The simplest way is to ask your potential client to accept your proposal by signing it at the bottom and returning the original, signed proposal to you. Alternatively, the signed proposal can be faxed or scanned and emailed to you. As soon as the client signs and returns the proposal to you, you have a contract binding on both parties.

To give you an idea of what we are talking about, Figure 7-1 shows a sample proposal for a consultant who does freelance software development and troubleshooting for a living.

The narrative proposal

A proposal for a job that is complex, that you anticipate to run for a long time, or that requires a substantial investment on the part of your client, most likely needs to be a narrative proposal. In a narrative proposal – which can run from ten pages to hundreds of pages – you generally address the same kinds of information that you do in a letter proposal, but in much greater detail. For example, while the anticipated outcomes take up all of a sentence or two in the preceding letter proposal example, the section describing anticipated outcomes in a narrative proposal can take as much as five pages.

September 28
Stella Brown
Nova Games
The Old Dairy
Cowfold
East Surrey
RH77 7PA

Dear Ms. Brown:

Thank you for taking the time with me today to discuss your forthcoming software program. As mentioned at our meeting, I honestly believe that millions of computer users around the world are ready, willing, and able to pay for a Windows version of the popular children's game 'Hula-Hoops.' As I looked over what you have done to date, however, I noted many areas where I can help improve your program's functionality. Beyond the simple issues of colour and graphics, I will be able to help you bring your entire presentation into sharper focus and tighten up its response to user input. I also have questions to ask you regarding your overall vision for the program, your intended audience, and the graphic look that will best meet the needs of the audience.

As a result of my initial review of your beta program, I propose that I:

* Conduct an initial telephone interview with you to discuss your overall vision of the program. This interview will be conducted within one week of you accepting the proposal.

*Provide creative input to you in the form of a written report. This task will be completed within one week after the telephone interview with you based on the telephone interview and a further review of the beta program.

* Completely troubleshoot your beta program for functionality and aesthetics and incorporate any changes that you may approve from the previous step. I will provide the revised program to you via email within two weeks of receipt of your go-ahead.

* Provide online support and answers to your questions (limited to the scope of this project) via telephone and email.

The price for this project is £6,000. Payment will be as follows: £2,000 deposit and £4,000 upon completion of the final program. If you are interested in proceeding, please sign both originals of this letter and return one of them to me by post with a cheque for the £2,000 deposit. A copy of my terms of business is attached.

I'm looking forward to working with you on this project. I know that you will be happy with the final product. Please don't hesitate to call me if you have any questions.

Sincerely,	Accepted:
Henry Boone	Stella Brown

Figure 7-1:
A sample
proposal.

Because we don't have enough pages available in this book to provide you with a complete sample narrative proposal (sorry, but our editor says no way!), we instead summarise a typical approach to putting one together:

- ✔ **Covering letter:** The covering letter contains a brief overview of the proposed project, along with your name, phone and fax numbers, and email and website address. For some projects, you can also put the fee and the expected benefits for the client in the covering letter.

- ✔ **Title page:** As you might expect, the title page contains the title of your proposal, along with the date, the name of your business, and the name of your client's organisation.

- ✔ **Table of contents:** We told you that this proposal would be big. Your clients need a table of contents with page numbers just to find their way around this monster!

- ✔ **Executive summary:** For the client who is too busy to read the 75 pages that you laboured over for three weeks or more, this paragraph summarises the entire proposal in a quick, 30-second reading.

- ✔ **Anticipated outcomes:** As in a letter proposal, you present the anticipated outcomes here – albeit in a much more complete fashion.

- ✔ **Detailed scope of work:** A scope of work is a presentation of every task that you'll perform as a part of the project. For some narrative proposals – especially those for the government – a proposal's scope of work can easily run for 25 pages or more of highly detailed tasks and sub-tasks. We hope you have lots of toner left in your laser printer cartridge to print this one out!

- ✔ **Schedule:** In a narrative proposal, your schedule is likely to be much more complex than a simple, 'The project will be completed six months after go-ahead from the client'. In complex, long-term projects, you may assign each task presented in the statement of work a start date, a duration, and an end date. If your scope of work contains lots of tasks and sub-tasks, you must present your schedule in the form of a chart or graph that shows the information visually for greater understanding and impact.

- ✔ **Fee:** The price to your customer for the work you plan to do. You must first state your fee in the way you prefer to be paid; for example, a daily rate, an hourly fee, or a monthly flat rate. You can modify it later if your client wants you to price your work in some other fashion. In some cases, your client may want you to break down your price by task, by outcome, or by deliverable (for example, your interim or final report). If so, your pricing is going to get awfully complex very quickly.

- ✔ **Qualifications and experience:** Here's where you can go to town about all the great experience you have and all the years of training you underwent to get where you are today, as well as that great college or university you attended. If it's okay with your present and former clients, you can even mention their names if you want to augment your credibility.

- ✔ **Curriculum Vitae (CV):** If you feel that it will help support your proposal, include a copy of your CV along with the CVs of other key project personnel. One word of caution: Make sure to tailor your CV to the kind of work you're proposing!

- ✔ **References:** If any of your clients were so overwhelmed by the work you did for them that they were moved to write you letters of thanks or reference, include those letters or quotes from them here.

After you submit your proposal, follow up with your clients to be sure that they received the proposal and that they have what they need to make a decision. Don't forget to ask when you can expect a reply – but don't put too much pressure on your clients, or you may not like the answer you receive: 'No!'

Seven proposal success secrets

A proposal can be anything from a one-page email message, to a more formal letter proposal, to a multivolume tabbed, perforated, and indexed extravaganza. Because proposals are so important to the financial wellbeing of your consulting business, they deserve your utmost attention and care. This section gives you seven of our favourite (and most effective) proposal success secrets.

Know your competition – inside and out

If you're competing with other firms for the same business (and what firm isn't competing with other firms for the same business?), you have to become very familiar with your competition. However, not only do you need to know how many competitors you have and who they are, you must also become knowledgeable about your competitors' pluses and minuses relative to your own business if you expect to survive and prosper. Ask your clients what they like and dislike about the consultants they've worked with (your competitors). Scour the Internet for information about your competitors' pros and cons. Get to know your competition inside and out. In the UK and Europe it's considered bad form to directly criticise other consultants. However, you can do so indirectly without naming them. For example, if you're a training firm and you want to mention that your main competitors load the fee by charging through the nose for training materials, you can write: 'Unlike many other firms we do not charge extra for the training materials.'

Set up a file folder for each competitor. When you get some information or an article about a competitor, file it. If you review the file every few months, you see a picture begin to emerge.

Help your client to develop the specs for the job

Salespeople have known for aeons that if they can help you develop the specification for the product you want to buy, then you're more likely to buy the product from them. Why? Because they define your problem in ways they can address. Few of your clients have your technical expertise – that's why they hired you. The wealth of knowledge and experience that you possess can save your clients time and money in trying to figure out how to describe their problem and what needs to be done to fix it. Volunteer your services freely – and for free – when asked; that small investment of time will undoubtedly pay off in a big way down the road.

Talk through the proposal with your client first

Before you submit your proposal, talk through your concepts with your client. Drop in for a visit, make a phone call, or send an email to seek feedback on your ideas. Although you may be certain that your proposed approach is the right one for the particular situation, you may be surprised to find out that your client doesn't agree. Discovering this before you submit your proposal is better than finding out after you've submitted it. Not only that, but whether or not you get the work, you begin to develop a relationship and rapport that make you a welcome bidder in the future.

Include great references

If you were going to hire someone to advise you in some aspect of your business – say, an accountant to help you do your taxes, wouldn't you prefer to hire someone who had years of experience and a list of satisfied clients about half the size of your phone book? Your ability to show prospective clients in a proposal that you have an established and successful track record in your field goes a long way to prove that you can do the proposed work. A successful track record can directly result in your being hired for a job; this is especially the case when clients you've worked for in the past are in the same line of business as your prospective client. Make a point of including the names of your best clients in your proposal – after getting their permission to do so. Asking satisfied clients to call new clients on your behalf is often a good idea.

Offer to submit your proposal in person

Posting or couriering over a proposal to a client is okay. Your client will most likely get it on time, and everyone will be happy. Delivering your proposal in person, however, is much better. Why? Because you not only ensure that the proposal is delivered promptly and accurately, but you also demonstrate to your client that his or her business is important to you. Delivering a proposal in person also allows you to answer your client's questions on the spot and to leave a good parting impression. Unless the cost is prohibitive, or the job is to small to merit it, always offer to deliver proposals in person.

Be prepared to answer every question

When you develop and submit a proposal to a prospective client, you must be prepared to answer any question that the client may ask you. This requires you to know what you wrote in your proposal (don't laugh – all three of us have met consultants who hadn't read their own proposals). By knowing what's in your proposal, you're prepared to address your clients' needs and concerns with thoughtful responses tailored to their specific situations. Don't forget: You're the expert, so don't be unprepared when your clients expect you to act like one!

Be sure to follow up!

After you deliver your proposal to your prospective client, setting up a definite time and process for follow-up is important. First, call your client within two days after you deliver the proposal to ask whether you can answer any questions and when the client expects to make a decision. When the decision date arrives, call your client again to ask whether he or she has made a decision. Continue with this approach until your client makes a decision. If the decision is favourable, congratulations! If it's not, ask what you can do to win the business. A new approach? A tighter schedule? An extended payment plan? Whether you win or lose a job, be sure to ask your prospective clients what led to their decision and what you can do to improve your proposals in the future. Then fine-tune your approach accordingly.

After your proposal is accepted, you can proceed with the next part of the consulting process – data collection – which just happens to be the subject of the next chapter of this book.

Chapter 8

Data Here, Data There, Data, Data, Everywhere

In This Chapter

▶ Selecting sources of data

▶ Enlisting your clients in the data-gathering effort

▶ Watching out for data disasters

*W*hen you meet your clients to help determine whether they have a prob-lem and, if so, what that problem is (see Chapter 7 for more informa-tion about this step), your opinion of what your clients' problems are and why they're happening are preliminary. It's sort of like being a doctor examining a patient complaining of chest pain: The patient (the client) may be convinced that a heart problem is causing the pain, and you, the doctor (the consultant), may suspect that something else is actually at work – perhaps heartburn or acid reflux – but until you run some tests and gather further data, you don't really know for sure what your patient's problem is. The heart problem may turn out to be a simple case of indigestion! You use the data you gather to test your assessment of what is wrong or determine the best approach to achiev-ing your clients' goals. The data could prove you right or prove you wrong, but whatever the results, you need complete, accurate, and timely data to diagnose your client's problem and know one way or the other.

In any data-collection exercise, you face a dilemma. Every organisation gener-ates an incredible amount of information – internally in the form of memos, reports, plans, graphs, and so on, and externally in the form of investor rela-tions materials, newspaper and magazine articles, and other documents. When deciding what information you need, you can easily get bogged down in a flood of information, much of it irrelevant to the problem. On the other hand, if you're too selective in your approach, you may miss an important source of information. The challenge is to obtain just the information you need – no more, no less. This is often much easier said than done, but you must always make it your goal.

Another problem with collecting data is that you often have to dig deep into the organisation – and into its hierarchy – to get to the real answers. As you speak to people in an organisation, their awareness of a problem moves from an external focus to an internal one. When you first question your client, for example, she may perceive that the 'payroll system is all messed up.' If you press her a little bit, she may move down one level and provide you with example symptoms of the perceived problem: 'I am fed up with complaints about payslip errors.' If you continue to press your client, you may get to some potential causes of the issue: 'Well, we don't always get our time sheets in on time but why are we filling in bits of paper in this day and age?' Questioning a variety of people throughout the organisation – employees at all levels and with all types of jobs – invariably leads you to the truth.

Collecting the kind of data from your clients that is useful in your efforts on their behalf is an art. In this chapter, we describe the most common and reliable sources of client data, and we tell you how you can involve your clients in helping you collect that data. Finally, we consider some of the most dangerous data disasters and explain how you can take steps to avoid them.

Identifying Key Data Sources

Selecting the sources of data you need and then obtaining that data in an accurate and timely manner is a critical step in the consulting process. The secret to knowing what data to gather is simple: You must have an analytical model – a hypothesis – to explain the problem or demonstrate your preferred approach. Start by gathering data that can prove your idea or model true or false. The initial identification of the problem or approach gives you a starting point for which specific data to gather.

For example, let's say that you've got a client whose salespeople can't meet their monthly sales goals to save their lives. Your client wants you to figure out why. After some initial discussions with your client – and preliminary observations of the sales organisation – you may have a hypothesis in mind for what the problem is. In this case, it may be because the organisation's customer relationship management (CRM) software is out of date and the salespeople are therefore not using it. By gathering data of the right kind from the right places, you can test your hypothesis and prove it right or wrong.

Keep an open mind so that you can research a range of hypotheses in case your first pet theory doesn't hold true. Also ask open questions of key stakeholders to get their hypotheses. For example, the sales people themselves or their customers or the sales managers may have worthwhile views.

When you look at the universe of places from which you can gather data, your task can seem incredibly daunting. (Indeed, when you're pulling together a large quantity of complex data from a variety of sources, the job can be very difficult.) However, if you work with your clients to determine the exact information that you need – and where to find it, you have a much easier time completing your task successfully.

Fortunately, the number of sources for gathering data is not unlimited. The following six categories pretty much sum them up:

- **Interviews and focus groups:** Any data-gathering exercise worth its salt includes interviews with people in the organisation as a basic foundation. Interviews can take the form of one-to-one question-and-answer sessions ('What do you do after you weigh the package on the postal scale?') or small focus group meetings ('Do you have any idea why so many accidents are occurring on the night shift?'). Interviews must always include the people who are directly involved with the problem, as well as others who aren't directly involved but who may have a good perspective on it. One-on-one interviews are often better than group meetings because the participant can tell you what's on his or her mind without fear of retribution from management or co-workers. However, group meetings often offer their own insights – especially when they reveal rivalries between individuals or departments or expose raw nerves in the organisation. One method of dealing with extensive data is to use these sessions as opportunities to get the participants' interpretation of the data. For more information about these and other potential land mines in the data-collection process, check out the 'Watch Out! Data Disaster Ahead!' section at the end of this chapter.

- **Direct observation:** One of the best ways to gather data – especially when you want to know how people really carry out a job, task, or procedure (not how they say they carry it out) – is to actually watch people do their jobs. It's amazing how people's perceptions of how they do their jobs can differ from the reality of how they do it. The only way to get past the discrepancy is to directly observe them in the business environment.

- **Internal documents and records:** Every organisation – no matter how large or how small – has internal documents and records that document the way it does business: accounting records, purchase orders, internal company memos, policies, procedures, product marketing plans, vision statements, and many others. As a part of your data-collection efforts, you need to determine exactly which internal documents and records are most useful for your project and then work with your clients to obtain those items. For example, if one hypothesis is that your client's security problem is a result of security guards who aren't performing their duties in accordance with prescribed policies, then you can seek security logs and similar data that indicate the daily activities of the security guards.

✔ **External documents and records:** Every organisation distributes numerous external documents and records outside the company, including such things as press releases, magazine and newspaper articles, radio and television interviews, licences and permits, health inspections, and tax records. In your search for external data, libraries, government offices, and research services are invaluable assets. And as you most likely know if you've ever logged onto the Internet, a heck of a lot of information is out there in cyberspace just waiting to be grabbed. You may be surprised at what comes back when you do a global Yahoo! or Google search on the name of your clients' organisations or the names of the people in charge.

✔ **Surveys and questionnaires:** Surveys and questionnaires, especially anonymous ones, offer a structured and confidential way for an organisation's employees and for your client's customers, vendors, bankers, and other business associates to provide you with data. As with interviews, you get to decide exactly what information you need and what questions you need to ask to get that information. And because you control the way the questions are asked, you can direct the response – from a simple yes or no to a more expansive response. For example, if you're trying to find out how your client's customers rate your client's efforts at customer service, you can design a survey with questions that help you gauge the opinions of your client's customers. To conduct the survey, obtain a list of your client's customers, call them – using either the entire list or a sampling of the list – and ask them to answer your questions. Their responses can provide valuable data for your investigation.

✔ **Personal experience:** The longer you've worked in your field of expertise – whether as a consultant or as an employee, the more personal experience you have to draw on. For example, you may have 15 years of experience in designing composting facilities for organic farmers and gardeners and may have written scores of articles on the topic. Your own opinions and experiences can be important sources of data, supplementing the other data you gather directly from your clients. In some cases, you may have seen identical problems in other organisations. If you have extensive experience in a particular field, take advantage of it!

Of course, gathering data from all these different sources, depending on which ones you finally settle on, can involve an incredible amount of time and effort. Make sure your proposed fee takes account of and will cover all of the effort. You can also save time by getting your client to help gather the data for you! Not only do you save time and money, but you have the opportunity to cement further the relationship with your client. Why? Because you and your client will naturally work together more closely as you strive towards a common goal: obtaining the information that you seek. Thus, you strengthen your relationship with your client while you reduce your own effort. That combination is hard to beat.

Getting Help from Your Clients in Collecting Data

Collecting client data is an important part of the consulting process, but it's often an incredibly time-consuming part of the process as well – for both consultant and client. If you allow it, you can quickly get bogged down in your data-collection efforts – slowing or even halting your progress on a project. Not only is this outcome potentially expensive and frustrating for you, but it can also make your client question whether you're the right consultant for the job.

One way to avoid getting bogged down in the data-collection process, while improving the quality and timeliness of the data you collect, is to enlist your client's help. The old adage that many hands make light work applies in consulting, too. If you're concerned that your client may tamper with the data, then you may not want to ask your client to help you collect data. But if you decide that getting your client involved is in your best interests – and in the best interests of your client (and it generally is because you get better access to the data you seek), then ask your client to do the following to help you through the process:

✔ **Assist you in deciding what data is best.** After you have a general idea of the data that you need to get, decide with your client the kinds of data and the sources that are the best for what you're trying to accomplish. For example, you and your client may determine that the organisation's weekly sales reports are a better source of near-real-time data than the quarterly financial reports released to shareholders. After you determine what data is best, then you can turn your attention to finding it.

✔ **Identify where the data you need is located.** Who better to know where the data you seek is located than your client? You can play detective all you want and try to track it down yourself, but you can save yourself (and your client) a great deal of time and money if you ask your client to help direct you to the data you need. If, for some reason, the data is not what you expected or is incomplete, then you can dig more deeply in your own search for it. However, getting your client to direct you to the right source to begin with is certainly worth a try.

✔ **Prioritise your effort with employees.** If you're an experienced consultant, you probably already know that many employees (that is, anyone in the organisation besides the person or persons who brought you in) look forward to dealing with consultants about as much as they look forward to trips to the dentist. As an outsider, you can be stonewalled, misled, obstructed, and otherwise thrown off track by employees who not only don't want to cooperate with you but also may be actively fighting your efforts. Your client can help to smooth out these little bumps in the data-collection road by explaining to employees that their cooperation is not only encouraged but also expected.

✔ **Help you physically obtain the data you need.** The data you need may be archived in an organisation's warehouse, or it may be squirreled away at a variety of sites scattered around the country. When you know exactly what information you need, your client can pull it together for you. All it takes is a simple memo or a phone call to your client, and before you know it, you have everything you need, when you need it. Not only do you save the time and money that it would have taken you to physically gather the data yourself, but you avoid organisational red tape and employee resistance that may otherwise have caused you problems.

✔ **Ensure the ongoing support of those responsible for the data.** Sometimes you need one or more of the people responsible for an organisation's data to, in essence, act as your guide and translator as you review the many different pieces and sources of data that you uncover during your project. This person can be an invaluable resource as you try to understand the context of the data that you're reviewing. When was this policy last updated? Why was it updated? Was it intended to address some sort of organisational problem? Find the individuals and departments responsible for generating the data and have them tell you two things: what it means and how it was used. If necessary, your client can grant you the help of one or more employees on a part-time or full-time basis.

In some cases, your clients may be very willing to help you collect the data you need – perhaps even undertaking the entire effort. Alternatively, your clients may expect you to take responsibility for data collection yourself. Which is the better approach? It depends.

If it is important for the data to be collected by an independent, outside party, then you must collect it. This would be the case when administering employee opinion surveys where employees may not provide candid answers to their own managers or human resources department for fear of retribution, or when collecting financial or other data for auditing purposes. If it doesn't matter who collects the data – or if the process would be particularly cumbersome for an outside party to collect – then consider asking your client to collect it.

The best way to solicit the assistance of your clients in the data-collection process is to include this discussion in your initial client meetings and impress on them the benefits of involving them in the search. You can encourage your clients' involvement by pointing out two benefits to them. Firstly, the quality of the data-collection efforts is enhanced (thus enhancing the quality of the results of your efforts). Secondly, you can pass on the savings that result from the reduced number of hours that you devote to collecting data. You're much more likely to get your clients signed up if you make data collection a part of the original contract instead of springing the request for help on them during the course of the project. Be sure to include in the contract a section listing the exact support that the client is to provide.

Watch Out! Data Disaster Ahead!

If you aren't careful, you may conduct an involved data-collection effort only to find that key data is missing, incomplete, or suspect because the source was biased. These data disasters not only can cause you additional work and heartache, but when they become a part of your project assumptions, they can also destroy the validity of your work as well as your credibility as a consultant. For these reasons, it's especially important to validate your sources and to examine them closely for problems that could lead to data disaster.

Here are some of the most common data issues together with suggestions for ensuring that they don't cause you problems:

- **Overlooking key data sources:** It's easy to overlook a source of data – perhaps a disgruntled employee who has been moved to an offsite location or a dishevelled box full of audiotapes recorded at executive team meetings. Such an oversight may occur because your clients direct you to information sources that are less embarrassing to them or simply because you inadvertently omitted some information. Unfortunately, the data you overlook may be a crucial link in the success of your project. Be exhaustive and relentless in your search for the data that you need to complete your project successfully.

- **Overlooking client biases:** Regardless of what they may say or think, every employee – from the postroom worker to the chairman of the board – comes with a unique set of biases. For example, a design engineer may tell you that the problem with product development is absolutely, positively the result of late input from the marketing department. But you may not be aware (and you won't be aware until you start digging into the problem more deeply) that he harbours a personal grudge against the head of marketing because she got a bigger bonus than he did last year. The secret to gathering accurate data from interviews with employees, group meetings, and questionnaires is to recognise that most data gathered directly from employees is susceptible to bias, to understand the source and nature of this bias, and to filter it out of the data that you've gathered.

- **Overlooking personal biases:** Believe it or not, you may harbour a bias or two yourself. Perhaps your client is from Tierra del Fuego, and you've never trusted anyone from Tierra del Fuego. Or maybe you don't think that your client knows what he's talking about, and you think that you have all the right answers. Take a close look at yourself and any biases that may colour your data-gathering efforts, and work to overcome them and make your approach as balanced as you possibly can.

✔ **Accepting incomplete data:** Sometimes you know exactly what information you need from someone and you ask for it – but what you get in return is incomplete or not what you asked for. You may be greatly tempted – especially when you're under a lot of pressure to complete your project or you have tons of data to analyse – to simply let it pass and accept what you're given. This can be disastrous to the successful outcome of your project. When you get incomplete data – or no data at all, follow up with your source and insist on getting what you need. If you meet with continued resistance in obtaining necessary information, ask your client to help prioritise the effort with the difficult employee.

✔ **Failing to fully document data:** When you're in the middle of fast and furious data gathering, the sheer amount of data that comes your way can be overwhelming. Before you know it, you can find yourself focusing your efforts on data that is already documented for you – reports, policies, staffing plans, product schedules, and the like – at the expense of data that isn't documented, such as employee interviews and surveys. Often, the data that you gather from your sources turns out to be the most useful in getting to the heart of an organisation's problems. Don't let these important sources of information slip through your fingers; document your conversations, interviews, and other interactions with client personnel as soon as you can after they occur.

Before we bid adieu to this chapter, we need to consider one more kind of data disaster to consider: when a client gives you intentionally false, misleading, or even fraudulent data. Not only can this cause you to draw the wrong conclusions in your analysis, but your consulting firm may become entangled in the fraud as well. You may recall that not too many years ago, a company by the name of Enron made a fine art of regularly providing misleading financial information to its outside auditor, Arthur Andersen – at the time one of the top five accounting firms in the world. When this approach to doing business was eventually revealed, it led to a number of events, including a drop in the company's stock price from more than ÷90 to below ÷1 a share, and Enron's eventual bankruptcy. Not long after Enron filed for bankruptcy, Arthur Andersen – which was being prosecuted by the US Department of Justice for its role in the Enron disaster – surrendered its licence to practice as a Certified Public Accountant (CPA) firm, and was forced to lay off 85,000 employees. The long-standing brand built on a proud heritage no longer exists.

So, the lesson is this: There are times when a client may give you false, misleading, or fraudulent data. If you can determine that such data was given to you unintentionally and with no intent to mislead you, then you may decide to continue your project with this particular client. If, however, it seems clear that your client is intentionally trying to mislead or lie to you, then run – don't walk – to the nearest exit. If your contract agreement has a termination provision, then seriously consider invoking it.

The data that you collect in this phase of the consulting process forms the basis for the ensuing steps of the process. Be sure that the data you collect is accurate, complete, and timely, and check it thoroughly before you send it on to the next step of the consulting process: problem-solving and developing recommendations. In Chapter 9, we consider how to take the data you gather in this phase of your project and start making sense of it.

Chapter 9

Problem-Solving and Developing Recommendations

· ·

In This Chapter

▶ Organising client data

▶ Problem-solving and weighing alternatives

▶ Developing, prioritising, and selecting your recommendations

· ·

*T*he first step in the consulting process is defining the problem. The point of collecting data, which is the next step of the process, is to test assumptions about the nature of the problem. For example, if you and your client make a preliminary decision that the organisation's problem is a lack of training for line supervisors, the data you collect either supports that conclusion or points you in a different direction altogether.

Now, what are you going to do with all that information you gathered?

Before you can tell whether the data supports or refutes your conclusions, you need to organise it and make sense of it. This means sorting it into recognisable categories and then looking for commonalities and trends. Through this process of sorting data – discarding irrelevant data along the way – and then focusing on the data that is most compelling, a range of possibilities for problem-solving naturally opens up.

The point of this exercise is to arrive at the very best recommendations for your client. By considering your client's needs, the cost of your recommended courses of action versus the benefits to be derived from them, and the organisation's culture, you can arrive at recommendations that not only solve your client's problem but also are right for your client's organisation. In our experience, if your recommendations don't mesh with the organisation, its culture, and politics, then your report gets filed away and is soon forgotten.

In this chapter, we consider how to take a flood of data and organise it so that it makes sense to both you and your clients. We explain how to apply an effective model for problem-solving and discuss the best way to go about deciding which recommendations you present to your clients.

Making Sense of All That Information

After a week or two (or three) of collecting data, most consultants find themselves up to their ears in data of all kinds, sizes, and formats. Surveys, interviews, focus groups, archives, management reports, and much more are available to you. This is good because the more data you have to draw from, the higher the probability that you're going to get to the bottom of your client's problem. However, all this information can be overwhelming. If you don't have a good system for organising it and separating what's important from what's not, you're going to find yourself drowning in a flood of data. And if you can't pull yourself out of the flood, your project progress is going to slow to a crawl, and your client is going to begin to wonder whether engaging you was the wrong choice. This is not the best outcome for you or your client.

It's up to you to make sense of all that data and identify the trends and patterns that point you to solutions. Here's a hint: Just follow the steps listed here, and before you know it, you have the right information at your fingertips.

Sort and consolidate the data

After you pull together all the data, you're likely to be faced with a stack (or perhaps a small mountain) of information from many places: project status reports, computer files, printouts, sales forecasts, promotion plans, internal memos, discs full of email messages, and the like. Your first task is to synthesise all this data by sorting it into collections of similar kinds of information. For example, you can organise a year's worth of data detailing an organisation's financial performance into monthly categories. Within each month, you can further organise the data into the categories of 'sales', 'expenses', and so on. How you decide to organise your information is up to you; you must base your decision on the nature of the project and your personal preferences.

When you've sorted your data into collections of related items, you can consolidate it. You may have multiple copies of the same data or the same data from several sources; if so, discard the duplicates.

 If you use surveys to collect data, first read the ones on which the respondents made numerous comments. Because those respondents cared enough to take the time to give you additional information, you may get the most productive and thoughtful feedback from them.

Put steps and processes in time sequence

When people take on a task, they normally do so in a logical and stepwise fashion. Part of organising and synthesising your data is to figure out the sequence of the steps your clients take to carry out tasks and processes. What do employees say they do first, second, third, fourth, and so on? Now, what do they *really* do first, second, third, fourth, and so on? What then are the differences between what employees say and do, and why are there differences?

For example, a postroom worker may claim that he delivers all courier deliveries to employees first, then processes incoming regular post, and finally prepares all outgoing post. However, upon personal observation, you may discover that courier post is actually handled second, causing delays in the receipt of urgent correspondence.

 A great way to work out time sequences is to draw the steps and processes on flowcharts or write the steps on stick-on notes and then stick them on a wall in sequence. This technique is commonly known as *process mapping*. Using computerised flowcharts or stick-on notes makes it easy to rearrange the steps as you enter the problem-solving and recommendation phases of the consulting process.

Look for patterns, trends, and themes

As you pore over all the data you pull together, you may soon begin to notice certain patterns and themes emerging. For example, if you're reviewing a company's employee attitudes, you may notice that employees are happier towards the end of the calendar year – towards Christmas time, when bonuses are traditionally given out – but then consistently dip at the beginning of the next calendar year. Or you may notice that more accidents occur on an assembly line during the night shift than during the day. These emerging trends tell you where to delve deeper when it's time to problem-solve.

Ignore and set aside irrelevant data

As you begin to refine your data further, noting which information is starting to point to recurring themes and possible solutions, you notice that some of the data you collected is irrelevant to your efforts. Set that data aside and remove it from further consideration. Doing so allows you to focus your efforts and attention on the most promising data while ignoring the information that has little or no bearing on your recommendations.

Focus

Concentrate your full focus on the most relevant data, and consolidate it to the lowest common denominator – that is, the information that keeps coming back to you as a possible solution. For example, suppose that you're investigating the reasons for the poor morale of an organisation, and a large amount of the data that you're collecting through employee interviews and one-on-one meetings points to uncaring managers as the source of the problem. In that case, you focus your efforts on the information that tells you exactly which managers are at the root of the morale problem and what they are doing to cause it. Focused information forms the basis of your problem-solving efforts, which are at the heart of this process.

Phew! Organising your data is a tough job, but somebody has to do it. Fortunately, now that the heavy lifting of collecting your data and sorting it into recognisable collections of information is out of the way, you can begin having fun with this phase of the consulting process.

How to Problem-Solve

So far you've defined the problem and collected data to analyse so that you can get pointers for the solution; next you must actually solve the problem.

In consulting, problem-solving is really what it's all about. While problem-solving, you review the data that you sliced, diced, and otherwise processed in order to develop a set of solutions, one of which will ultimately become the recommendation that you present to your clients. Because of this, you want to open the net as wide as possible at the beginning of the problem-solving process – sucking in as many possibilities as you can. Then you need to throw some of your catch back into the sea (and keep the good ones for yourself) by weighing the alternatives until you're left with the best possible courses of action. At this point in the process, you aren't narrowing the field down to one possible course of action, but only down to the few best ones.

There's a right way and a wrong way to develop solutions. Fortunately for you, we present the right way here:

1. **Brainstorm possible solutions.** The first step in the process is to take the data that you collected and consolidated and to brainstorm possible solutions to the problems that the data identifies. Although you can brainstorm by yourself or with other members of your firm – if there *are* other members of your firm, you get a much wider variety of options when you include your clients in your brainstorming sessions.

The secret of conducting productive brainstorming sessions is to encourage every possible idea – no matter how weird it may seem. This means suspending judgement for the duration of the session and welcoming everyone's input. Record every idea on computer, paper, flip charts, or a whiteboard so that you don't lose track of any of them.

2. **Consider the implications of each possible solution.** Isolate each option that was generated during your brainstorming sessions and follow it to its logical conclusion. For example, if a client has a problem with the quality of the circuit boards leaving the factory floor, one possible cause is that workers are not using the correct soldering techniques. If you follow this possibility to its logical conclusion, the solution may be to provide more training to employees on soldering correctly or to provide better supervision and to monitor employees' work more closely.

3. **Weigh options and narrow your focus.** When you're working through all possible options, weigh them one against another to determine which are most likely to be relevant to the outcome and which ones are least likely to be relevant. As a part of getting to your final recommendations, you have to focus your efforts more sharply at this point and move ahead on a few fronts instead of many. Discard the options that are least likely to become viable recommendations, and continue to narrow your focus to those that are the most likely.

4. **Pick the best courses of action.** By this time, you need to have your list of possibilities narrowed down to a manageable number. Continue to work through this list with your client until you whittle it down to no more than about five of the best courses of action. If you look up for a moment, you should be able to see the light at the end of the tunnel. After you complete this step, you're ready to start developing your recommendations.

So you managed to wade through all your data, problem-solve, and arrive at a reasonable number of options from which to draw your recommendations. This is the reason your clients called you in: so they could take advantage of your expertise, obtaining your advice and recommendations on ways to solve their problems. Don't worry – you're almost there!

Developing Your Recommendations

Your clients hire you to get your recommendations on how they can solve their problems. However, you have to test every set of recommendations to ensure that they are in the best interests of your clients and that your clients will readily accept and implement them. All the most wonderful recommendations in the world – bound in attractive report binders and accompanied by lush PowerPoint presentations – are worthless unless they are heeded and implemented.

The best client recommendations are effective and honest but take into account clients' budgets, needs, resources, and culture. Here are some guidelines to help you develop recommendations for your clients:

✔ **Evaluate the best courses of action.** At this point, you have approximately five possible best courses of action resulting from the problem-solving phase of your effort. Take another look at them in light of the following criteria:

- **Cost versus benefit:** Before settling on your final recommendations, consider each in terms of its cost versus ultimate benefit. If a recommendation is potentially very expensive for your client and the benefits are marginal at best, it may not deserve a high position in your list. However, a recommendation that costs your client relatively little and has a high payoff is worthy of priority status.

- **Client needs and resources:** Your best recommendations not only address the very real and concrete needs that your research and brainstorming uncover, but they also address the unique situation that your client's organisation and employees are in right now. Each client has particular needs and can muster differing amounts and kinds of resources. Whereas some companies may be short on cash and long on employees, other companies may have plenty of cash to throw at their problems but have no excess personnel to assign to the necessary repairs and solutions. Be sure to account for these kinds of differences as you finalise your recommendations.

- **Client's organisational culture:** Every organisation has a unique culture, and your client's culture is an important consideration in moulding your final recommendations. You may have the greatest recommendations in the world, but if they run counter to the organisation's culture, at best they'll be adopted only grudgingly. Much more likely, they'll be discarded altogether. For example, if you recommend making part of a company's workforce redundant to pay for your recommended new system but the founder is rightfully proud that throughout the company's history no employee has ever been made redundant, your recommendation is likely to be quickly discarded.

- **Client's people and politics:** Politics plays a major role in how things are done in every organisation. Your recommendations have to take into account your client's political landscape and the way that people relate to one another to get things done. If they don't, your recommendations may look great but be unworkable in the organisation. For example, you may determine that an organisation needs to get its employees much more involved in the decision-making process. However, if the middle managers in charge of implementing this change are dead set against it and they have the political power to block it, the recommendation will die a quick death.

✔ **Draw up draft recommendations.** After taking the preceding criteria into consideration, the next step is to draft the recommendations to present to your clients. Although you still have a little bit of time to rework them before you make your client presentation, they need to be fairly definite, settled, and stable at this point in the process.

✔ **Rank your recommendations.** After reviewing all the potential recommendations and running them through the gauntlet of criteria such as cost versus benefit, client needs and resources, and organisational politics and culture, you're ready to take the last step: ranking your recommendations in order of practicability. After you do that, you're in business. Provide options for your client. Let the client choose among lower price, faster completion, and higher quality. It's best to use a 'min-max' approach: Build a first-class, top-of-the-range strategy, and then build a bare-minimum strategy. Doing so helps your client to select a solution between the two viable options.

Well, you've made it through one of the most difficult, yet most rewarding, parts of the consulting process. After you compile your draft recommendations, you're ready for the next step: presenting them to your client. Coincidentally, we address that very topic in Chapter 10.

Chapter 10

Tell It Like It Is: Presenting Your Recommendations

In This Chapter

▶ Giving feedback to your clients

▶ Designing your feedback meeting

▶ Building client ownership of your recommendations

▶ Making great presentations

*A*t some point in your consulting project, you're going to develop a set of recommendations for your client. This, after all, is what your clients pay your fees for. So how do you go about presenting your recommendations to your clients? Should you write them a letter, or drop them an email message? Although those are certainly options you can pursue, you're more likely to communicate your recommendations in the form of both a written report and a presentation. As a rule, always give your clients a tangible product of some sort at the end of the project – in most cases, at minimum a written report. And to ensure that your clients understand and ultimately act on the recommendations in your report, presenting your recommendations personally – whether directly to your client or to a group of managers or other members of your client's organisation – is definitely the way to go.

Your primary goal in this phase of the consulting process is to get your clients to accept your recommendations. Bringing your clients around to the point where they are ready to embrace your recommendations is very much a selling process; running through a few charts is usually not enough. You have to be passionate about your recommendations and feel strongly about your clients' need to adopt them.

In this chapter, we consider the importance of presenting your recommendations to your clients, plus we give you some tips for making the feedback meaningful and lasting. We also review the steps involved in presenting your recommendations in an effective and successful client feedback meeting and discuss ways to help your clients take ownership of your recommendations to build the momentum necessary to carry them out.

Giving Client Feedback: Setting the Stage

 You can have a great impact on whether your client ultimately accepts and implements your ideas. Keep these tips in mind as you prepare for your presentation; they'll pay you back many times over in the form of happier clients and a greater probability that your recommendations will be implemented. And don't forget, a happy client is a client who will most likely contract with you again – and refer you to new clients.

- **Remember your selling hat.** The point of communicating your recommendations to your client is, or course, to explain exactly what the organisation needs to do to solve its problems, whatever they are. However, making your recommendations involves more than that. In most cases, presenting your recommendations to an organisation is as much (or perhaps even more) a selling job as it is a telling job. No matter how much an organisation wants to solve its problems, you always come across at least some resistance from some of the people within it. As you present your recommendations, keep this in mind and be consistent in highlighting the benefits to be gained by the organisation and the people who are part of it. Your case must be compelling!

- **Keep your clients involved.** If you've been playing your cards right throughout the consulting process, your clients are very much a part of your presentation and the recommendations you make. They are involved because you keep them abreast of your findings as you encounter them and you ask for their feedback and input. Not only do you gain great insight from their feedback, but you give your clients the opportunity to begin buying into your recommendations before you formally make them. By keeping your clients involved – and, actually, an integral part of the process, your recommendations are likely to be better suited to the organisation, and so accepted and implemented, than those that are created in a vacuum and announced to a resistant audience. You can anticipate objections and have that information incorporated into your solutions.

- **Don't spring surprises.** You may like surprises, but chances are your clients don't – especially when it comes to your recommendations. If your recommendations will shatter your clients or embarrass any of the principals of the firm, you haven't involved your clients enough in the consulting process. If your clients have been adequately involved, not only will they not be surprised by the recommendations, but they will already be sold on them before you make your presentation. Make that happen by involving your clients closely in the problem-definition, data-collection, and problem-solving phases of your work.

That said, if, for some reason, you do have a surprise or two up your sleeve, first present it privately to your client or to a key member of the client's organisation.

✔ **Be honest and frank.** Sometimes the truth hurts. Despite the fact that you probably would much rather give your clients good news than bad, you're getting paid to lay it all on the line. Be sure that your client gets the complete benefit of your expertise – not just the parts that will make your client feel good, are politically correct, or easy for you to communicate.

✔ **Don't be judgemental.** Avoid being judgemental or overly critical about the decisions your client made that got the organisation into its current mess. Opening your presentation by saying something along the lines of 'In all my years of consulting, I have never seen such a mess as this!' is definitely not the way to build more business with your client. Not only are you unlikely ever to work for that particular firm again, but also your recommendations will find their way into the bin sooner than you can say, 'Oops!' Maybe the management team has some problems, but you have a much better chance of helping if you present your findings in a way that doesn't insult your client.

✔ **Support your client.** Change is tough for any organisation, and the recommendations that you present may set the stage for tremendous change in your client's organisation. Restructuring, downsizing, stream-lining, and more are often inevitable results of consultant recommenda-tions. Support your client – both emotionally and organisationally – in preparing to confront the need for change.

Now that you know some things that you must definitely do when you pres-ent your recommendations to your clients, the next step is to plan and con-duct your client feedback meeting. In the section 'Conducting a Feedback Meeting,' we review each step of this very important meeting.

Conducting a Feedback Meeting

Hours and hours of work – defining your client's problem, collecting data, and problem-solving – bring you to this point: your client feedback meeting. In this meeting, you present your recommendations to your client, and you plant the seeds for the eventual acceptance or rejection of your results. If the meeting goes well, your client will most likely move to implement your recommenda-tions. If not, they're destined for the proverbial rubbish heap of history.

Client feedback meetings are first and foremost *your* meetings – you set the agenda and control the pace and flow of your presentation. Sure, you can and must be responsive to your client's needs and allow for some flexibility in the agenda, but be sure to get back to the topics that you planned to discuss.

Here are the five steps for conducting a successful client feedback meeting:

1. **Present the project background, goals, and methodology.**

   The first part of your presentation consists of a brief description of the project, including the problems you were hired to tackle, your project goals, and the methodology you applied to arrive at your recommendations. Be sure to highlight your client's role in the problem-solving process and in helping you arrive at the recommendations you're presenting. Everything here must have been agreed to beforehand.

2. **Present your recommendations.**

   Getting to this point has taken a while, but, finally, here you are. At this point in the presentation, you give your key recommendations along with the reasons why they are the most likely solutions to the problems your client faces. Be sure to have some different recommendations for your client to consider (including options such as lower price, faster completion, and higher quality), and explain why you didn't select them as your primary recommendations.

3. **Encourage client discussion.**

   Getting your client to talk about your recommendations is a critical part of this phase of the consulting process. You want those at the meeting to ask questions, challenge your assumptions, consider the alternatives, request further information, or do whatever it takes to help decide on an appropriate course of action. If your audience is silent after your presentation, encourage a healthy exchange of ideas by asking the participants whether they understand your recommendations and whether they have questions about anything you presented.

4. **Help your client decide on a course of action.**

   Your recommendations are exactly that – recommendations. Your job is not to make your clients' decisions for them – they have to absorb the data you present and make up their own minds. However, you must press your client to make a decision of some sort – preferably while you're around to help facilitate the process. After conducting your project, you're likely to be the person who is most knowledgeable about the problem and the fixes that have the best chance of working. You can offer your clients a great deal of help as they decide which course of action to take.

5. **Determine your role in future activities.**

   In some cases, presenting your recommendations to your client may be the last step of the project. In other cases, your client may want you to stick around to help implement your recommendations. In any case, use the client feedback meeting to determine what, if any, role you'll play in further activities related to your project.

After your client has your recommendations, all that's left to do is to implement them. Of course, countless filing cabinets around the world are stuffed with recommendations that were never implemented. Part of the process of getting yours implemented is helping your client gain a sense of ownership of them. Like passing the baton in a relay race, you need to make your recommendations your client's recommendations.

Would it surprise you to hear that we address that very topic in the next section?

Building Client Ownership of Your Recommendations

You can directly influence the chances of your recommendations being implemented by working with your clients to build ownership of them. Although you've been setting the stage for this transition since the beginning of the project by creating partnerships with your clients and involving them in the consulting process, now is the time to press your point home.

Your recommendations are only as good as their implementation by your clients. Even the best recommendations miss the mark if they remain unimplemented. Here are some ways that you can help your clients take ownership of them:

✔ **Push for consensus.** Don't allow issues to remain unaddressed or unresolved. For example, suppose that you recommend instituting a mandatory quality programme for all the businesses that sell parts to your client's manufacturing operation. However, if one or more of the participants in your feedback meeting is opposed to your recommendation because such a programme may lead to increases in vendor-supplied part prices, don't just drop the issue. Work with your client to find a compromise between the two positions and come up with a consensus that can then be implemented. If you let the issue drop in your meeting, your recommendation may be ignored.

✔ **Push for decisions and commitments.** The client feedback meeting is the perfect time and place for you and your client to work out the details of an action plan for implementation. It's also the perfect time for you to push your client to make the commitments that ensure that the action plan is followed. After all, unless you've completely missed the point, implementing your recommendations is the only step that helps your client.

✔ **Offer to continue your partnership through the implementation phase of the project.** Do you still have that selling hat we asked you to put on at the beginning of the chapter? That's okay; we'll give you a minute or two to dig it out of your closet. Your client may or may not want your help in implementing your recommendations. If implementation wasn't a part of your original client contract (and you almost always must try to make it a part), you can suggest it now.

You have two good reasons for offering. Firstly, you can help ensure that your recommendations are actually implemented and that the implementation is indeed what you recommended. Secondly, you can continue to reinforce and build the relationship that you've already developed with your client by continuing your work through the implementation phase. If the implementation goes well, your client will surely ask for your help when other problems arise in the future.

Congratulations! For some of you, this is the end of the consulting process. Your clients are now going to take your recommendations and implement them on their own. If this is the case, be sure to call in on your clients periodically to see how it's going and offer to help them in any way you can. You never know when your clients may want to take you up on your offer.

The rest of you – the consultants whose clients have engaged them to participate in the implementation phase of the consulting process – still have work to do. In Chapter 11, we discuss working with your clients to implement your recommendations.

You Can Make Great Presentations

Making successful presentations is a key skill for every consultant. But, although some people seem to be natural-born presenters, others struggle with making presentations before groups of any size or shape. If, like most of us, you think you fall in the second category, the good news is that you can dramatically improve your presentation skills with a little preparation and practice. And the better your skills, the more confident and credible you are when you make your presentations.

Getting prepared to present

Preparation is the key to giving a great presentation. In fact, for 'knock 'em dead' presentations, you can figure on spending anything from 30 minutes to an hour of preparation time for each minute you're actually presenting. In addition to the hints presented in the section that follows, be sure to check out *Presentations For Dummies* (by Malcolm Kushner), published by John Wiley & Sons, for a wealth of information on making great presentations.

The following tips can help you in preparing your presentation:

- ✔ **Describe what are you trying to accomplish.** What are the goals of your presentation and what are you going to have to do to achieve them? For example, the goals that you have in mind when you pitch a project to a prospective client (sell, sell, sell!) are substantially different from the goals you have in mind when you present an interim progress report on an ongoing project (to inform and to seek the commitment of the client). And because your goals are different, your presentations will be different, too. Be sure to tailor your presentation to achieve the goals you set and the outcomes you require.

- ✔ **Assess your audience.** You want your presentation to be as effective as it can be, so you need to think carefully about your audience and write the presentation exactly for those people. Although an audience of scientific researchers is likely to expect and appreciate a jargon-laden, highly technical presentation, the same presentation would quickly put a group of general managers to sleep. Before you make your presentation, be sure to assess your audience.

- ✔ **Develop the heart of your presentation.** Start writing your presentation by outlining the major points that you wish to communicate to your clients. After you've developed your major points, note any sub-points and visual aids that you'll use to support your presentation. Don't get over-ambitious; limit your major points to between three and five. If you have more information to communicate than you can 'fit' into the actual presentation, convert the extra information into handouts that you give to your audience at the beginning of your presentation.

- ✔ **Write the introduction and conclusion.** The introduction of your presentation needs to do three things:

    - Grab your audience's attention

    - Provide a brief overview of the presentation

    - Sell the members of your audience the idea that the presentation is important and of benefit to them

The conclusion of your presentation is just as important as the introduction. Your conclusion needs to do three things:

- Briefly revisit your key points

- Remind the members of your audience why your presentation is important to them

- Leave your audience feeling energised and inspired

✔ **Prepare your notes.** If you've given the same presentation many times before, you can probably get away without using notes. However, having notes in your hand is a real help if you momentarily lose your place and they also ensure that you don't forget to cover any of your planned topics. Notes must be brief and specific; they aren't a word-for-word script of your performance, but merely a reminder of your key points. Many people use computer PowerPoint slides for the same purpose. We address this in the next section.

✔ **Bring in reinforcements if necessary.** Depending on the nature of your project, its complexity, and the number of people you have working on it, you can consider bringing other project participants from your business into the presentation. This idea is particularly good when your project is highly technical. If you have experts on your staff who can add credibility to your recommendations and solutions, ask them to address specific aspects of the project as part of your presentation.

✔ **Remember that 'practice makes perfect'.** Depending on your personal comfort level or on the complexity of the information that you plan to present, you may find it advantageous to run through your presentation a few times before you present it. At one end of the spectrum, you may be comfortable simply running through your notes a few times the night before the big event. At the other end of the spectrum, you may prefer to rehearse your presentation in front of another person or even a video camera.

You can't be too prepared for a presentation. Make the most of the time that you have before your presentation because it pays off in a big way when the time comes to get up in front of your audience and start your performance. And believe us, every presentation you make is a performance, and, each time, you're the performer.

Using visual aids

Did you know that scientists have proven that approximately 85 per cent of all information received by the human brain is received visually? Think about that the next time you make a presentation. Though your spoken remarks may convey a lot of valuable information, the people in your audience are likely to understand and retain far more of the information when you present it to them visually.

Here's an example of what we mean. Peter actually saw someone make an hour-long presentation to the executive team of a high-tech computer software development company using screen after screen full of tiny little words and numbers. If you were sitting anywhere farther away than the centre of the front row, the text and numbers became a blur of hieroglyphic-like gobbledygook. What really iced the cake was that the presenter read each and every figure directly from the screen. Ouch!

A much better alternative: Convert the mass of text and numbers into some simple graphs that convey the very same information. Your audience then has an instantaneous, visual understanding of the numbers. As the presenter, you can concentrate on explaining the meaning behind the numbers instead of wasting time just reading them to your audience.

It took us many years of concentrated effort, but we eventually captured the essence of the visual element in presentations. Here for your consideration is the Albon/Nelson/Economy axiom of visual learning:

> Information seen is remembered; information not seen is easily forgotten.

So how does this handy little axiom impact your presentations? It means that you must always give the same consideration to your visual presentation as to your spoken presentation. Whenever possible, think of ways to present your information visually. Maps, displays, product samples, prototypes, photographs, charts, and graphs are just a few of the many options available to you. Here are some of the most common kinds of visual aids used in presentations:

- **Handouts:** Providing your audience – no matter what size it is – with handouts of the information that you plan to cover – both text and graphics – can sometimes help them better follow your presentation. Sometimes, for a smaller group, using slide copies rather than a projector creates a more intimate and friendly atmosphere. But heed this warning: Don't fall victim to the practice of providing handouts and then reading from them word for word; nothing is more boring to an audience than getting stuck in such a presentation.

- **PowerPoint:** Using Microsoft PowerPoint or similar presentation software, you can put together a complete multimedia presentation on your laptop computer and then take the resulting file anywhere you like (on your computer, a CD-ROM, or a flash drive) and project the presentation onto a full-size projection screen. Remember to inject variety to your PowerPoints. Death by bullet point is tedious, so include a mix of pictures, graphs, quotes, and numbers as well as bullet points.

Before you go mad with your visual aids, keep a couple of things in mind. Firstly, don't try to squeeze too much information into any one aid. Use a large typeface (font), keep the number of words and numbers to a minimum (16 words or less, please!), and use colour to improve the professionalism and readability. Secondly, have your presentation ready before you show up to make it! You definitely won't impress your clients if you start your presentation by spending five minutes fumbling with your computer or paging through a disorganised stack of handouts. Finally, don't forget that *you* are the heart and soul of your presentation – not your visual aids. Visual aids help to support your presentation, but they won't make up for a lack of preparation or for not being an informed presenter.

Making your presentation

Okay, the time to prepare has come and gone, and you're ready to make your presentation. All your hours of hard work and preparation are about to pay off. Heed this advice as you start your presentation and you're sure to do a great job:

- ✔ **Relax!** Breathe deeply and visualise making a successful presentation before your audience. There's no need to be nervous. Don't forget: Your client is paying you because you're an expert in your chosen field. And you are – yes?

- ✔ **Use flipcharts if necessary:** Flipcharts are hardly ever used now for formal presentations. However, you may need to record client ideas or expand on points by drawing diagrams on the spot, so make sure one's available.

- ✔ **Greet the members of your audience.** Besides making sure that everything is in order for your presentation, the opportunity to meet your audience is one of the main reasons for arriving early. Before you start your presentation, try to greet, introduce yourself to, and shake hands with as many members of the audience as you can. Not only does this practice help you break the ice with your audience – reducing any nervousness you may feel – but as a result, it helps generate more interest in you and what you have to say.

- ✔ **Wait for your audience's attention.** When you make a presentation, try to capture the full attention of your audience right at the start. You can ask for your audience's attention, or you can seek it by standing up in front of them and saying nothing until everyone's attention is focused on you.

✔ **Make your presentation.** Jump in with both feet and don't look back. One thing: When presenting, move about the stage a little and try to make eye contact with the critical decision-makers. Moving around helps make your presentation much more interesting to your audience. Making eye contact enables you to pick up on critical cues from your key clients. (For example, if your client rapidly draws a finger across his or her neck, you have a big problem!)

As we have seen, getting your ideas across to your clients in an organised and effective fashion is a real art. Don't expect to be able to just wing it – it takes a great deal of work and preparation to prepare and execute killer reports and presentations. Fortunately, computers can do much to make preparation easier than ever before. But, don't forget: You're the one who determines whether a presentation will be just okay, or one that dazzles your client. So, what's it going to be?

Chapter 11

Implementation: Making Your Prescriptions Work

....

....

*Y*our recommendations to your client represent the fruits of your labour. Much hard work – both on your part and on your client's part – goes into producing them. However, if your recommendations are filed away in a drawer or set aside on some manager's desk, then the fruits of your labour soon rot away to nothing. And although you're being paid to do the work anyway, no consultant alive can honestly say that it doesn't hurt just a little when after all that hard work the client fails to act on a recommendation.

As a consultant, you're in a difficult position. You may know exactly what needs to be done to solve your client's problem but, ultimately, you're not the one who decides whether or not to implement your recommendations – your client is. Indeed, your client may decide to pick apart your recommendations and use only the ones that he or she wants to use at any given moment. That's the client's prerogative. All you can do is push hard for your point of view – that is, after all, what your client is paying for – and back off only after you're certain that your client has given your point of view due consideration.

You can participate in the process of getting your clients to adopt and implement your recommendations. This is, after all, the most satisfying reward for all your hard work – to see your recommendations implemented and to watch your clients' problems disappear as a result. And, indeed, as an outsider, you may be the only one who can make the necessary changes without getting tangled up in nostalgia for the status quo or with office politics.

In this chapter, we show you how to work with your clients to put together implementation plans, and we give you some tips on making the implementation go more easily for everyone involved. Finally, we consider why and how to assess the results of the implementation of your recommendations.

What Gets Planned, Gets Done

To ensure the ultimate success of the implementation of your recommendations, you and your client need a plan that details the exact steps that have to be undertaken, who is responsible for carrying them out, and when they have to be done. Depending on the size of your project and the extent and complexity of your recommendations, your plan may be only a few paragraphs long, or it might go on for many pages. The best plan you can have is one you've worked out with the close participation of your client. Participation builds commitment, and commitment greatly increases the chances that your recommendations will be implemented successfully and completely.

As you work with your clients to put together project implementation plans, make sure you do the following things:

- ✔ **Define the implementation tasks.** Every good plan includes tasks that spell out each step in its completion. A plan for implementing your recommendations must also contain the tasks that ensure that the implementation phase of the consulting process is completed successfully and with a minimum of confusion and client resistance. Because your client plays such a critical role in bringing your recommendations to fruition, be sure that he or she plays a big part in defining the specifics of implementation.

- ✔ **Define implementation task schedules.** For a plan to be effective, it must have schedules for completion. Otherwise, the people who are assigned implementation tasks don't have a sense of their priority, and they tend to let other priorities – ones with specific deadlines – take the front seat. For every task in your implementation plan, make sure to establish a start date and an end date.

- ✔ **Assign roles and responsibilities.** Every task in your plan needs someone who takes responsibility for its successful and timely completion. The best way to avoid confusion in the implementation process is to assign the responsibility for each task to one and only one person. When you assign responsibility for a task to more than one person (or, heaven forbid, to a committee), no one is truly responsible for the task. Given the way that human nature often works, this can lead to confusion, dropped tasks, missed deadlines, and project failure. And that's one result you won't want to be blamed for as a consultant – you're supposed to be solving existing problems, not creating new ones.

Note: For employees to carry out their assignments effectively, they must also have the authority to do so. Ensure that your client gives his or her employees the authority to do the tasks they are assigned.

✔ **Consider pilot projects.** If you're working on a fairly minor set of recommendations for a fairly small organisation, you can probably implement your recommendations in a straightforward manner with little or no need to do extensive testing along the way. However, as the size of the implementation phase grows, along with the possible impact on your client's employees and customers, it often makes sense to create a pilot project to test the implementation of your recommendations before they are actually put into service. For example, if you're a web design consultant, you may want to set up a test web page for a client before actually posting the real website on the Internet. The test page lets you check all text and graphics so that they look the way you (and your client!) want them to look and gives you a chance to ensure that the site looks good and functions well, and that the links and other features function appropriately. Pilot projects are a virtual necessity if the changes you recommend impact particularly important client business systems, such as computer-based accounting systems and stock control systems.

✔ **Define how you'll assess the success of the implementation.** The final part of your implementation plan is a description of the baselines, measures, and outcomes that you'll use to decide whether your implementation was successful. These link back to the original baselines, measures, expectations, and goals that you worked out and agreed to with your client at the beginning of the project. What are your client's expectations for success? What are *your* expectations? If there are differences in your client's perspective and your own, make sure that both points of view are incorporated in the overall plan. If your implementation isn't successful, you need the information from this assessment to determine why.

Although you can follow any variety of formats to present your implementation plan, the plan must at least address each one of the points discussed in this section. Figure 11-1, shown on the next page, is a sample implementation plan, based on the recommendations of an audiovisual consultant, for the installation of a new public address system in an auditorium. Note how the plan specifically incorporates the activities that need to be part of an implementation plan, as described in this section.

Regardless of how extensive the implementation is or how long it may take, a plan helps to ensure that no confusion arises over who is supposed to do what, and when. Of course, every implementation programme can have its ups and downs. In the section 'Just Do It! Implementation Tips', we give you some advice on avoiding the downs and maximising the ups of your implementation.

Cowfold Conference Centre Public Address System Upgrade Implementation Plan

After a thorough study of the acoustics of the Cowfold Conference Centre and a review of the adequacy of the current public address system, the project consultant – Sussex Audio Associates – recommended that the current system be upgraded with the Freitag Model 1000 public address system. Implementation of this recommendation involves accomplishing the following tasks:

Task 1: Purchase new Freitag Model 1000 public address system. Sussex Audio Associates will seek competition to obtain the lowest price on the Freitag equipment, purchase it, and take possession of it no later than 25 May.

Task 2: Remove the current public address system from the Cowfold Conference Centre. Employees of the Cowfold Conference Centre Trust will remove the current equipment and repair any resulting damage to the facility no later than 1 June.

Task 3: Install new Freitag Model 1000. Sussex Audio Associates will install, mount, and wire all components of the new public address system no later than 5 June.

Task 4: Perform system testing. Sussex Audio Associates will completely test the installed new public address system, ensuring that it meets all published specifications for power output, signal-to-noise ratio, and distortion, no later than 7 June. Sussex Audio Associates will be responsible for making any required adjustments to bring the equipment within specified performance limits.

Task 5: Train Cowfold Conference Centre employees in the operation of the new public address system. Sussex Audio Associates will have trained all Cowfold Conference Centre employees in how to operate the Freitag Model 1000 public address system by no later than 10 June. Consultants will also be available for retraining of employees as required.

Success Measures:

Sussex Audio Associates will be considered to have successfully completed the project when all of the following events occur:

New Freitag Model 1000 public address system is installed, mounted, and wired no later than 5 June.

New Freitag Model 1000 is tested to meet all published specifications for power output, signal-to-noise ratio, and maximum distortion no later than 7 June.

All Cowfold Conference Centre employees have been trained in the operation of the new Freitag Model 1000 public address system by no later than 10 June.

Figure 11-1:
A sample implementation plan.

Just Do It! Implementation Tips

Wouldn't it be nice if you could snap your fingers and get all your recommendations implemented, just like that? Unfortunately, the implementation phase of the consulting process can be difficult – for both you and your client. If you aren't careful to attend to the details, the whole thing can unravel very quickly, and your client's organisation quickly moves back to where it is most comfortable: the status quo.

You can actively do several things to help ensure that your implementation comes off without a hitch (well, at least with only a few hitches here and there). To facilitate the implementation of your recommendations, you need to do the following as you work through the implementation process:

- **Deal with resistance.** If you thought that your client's employees were resistant during the data-collection phase of your project, you haven't seen anything yet. Now that your recommendations are soon to become reality within your client's organisation, the people who have the most to lose through the coming changes will be sure to rally their forces against you and your supporters or sponsors in a last-ditch effort to preserve the status quo. If you hope to make your recommendations last, you have to identify all the possible sources of organisational resistance and then neutralise them one by one.

- **Be realistic in your expectations.** Organisations don't change overnight. Even after a massive reorganisation, employees still do their jobs in pretty much the same way as they always have. Lasting change takes time to bring about, and you must have patience as the organisation slowly moves in the right direction. Be realistic in your expectations for the implementation of your recommendations. As you develop your implementation schedule, allow plenty of time for employees to soak up the changes and incorporate them into their day-to-day work routines.

- **Watch out for dropped responsibilities.** The successful implementation of your recommendations requires close attention to the performance of tasks – ensuring that they are completed when they are supposed to be – and to the continued participation of all personnel assigned to carry them out. Employees resisting change commonly do so by conveniently 'forgetting' to carry out their assigned duties or by simply ignoring them or by allowing other tasks to take priority. The best way to prevent this type of behaviour is to establish clear tasks, assign definite responsibilities to specific individuals, track task completion closely against the established schedule, and hold individuals accountable.

- **Nurture your client partnership.** You need the complete and committed participation of your client to make the implementation of your recommendations work and ensure that it lasts. The ongoing care and feeding of your client relationship is an important factor in getting your recommendations implemented. You can demonstrate this care by keeping in touch with your clients, inviting their input and suggestions, and maintaining a good working relationship. If you find yourself in your clients' bad books, your recommendations probably will soon find themselves there, too.

✔ **Beware of the perpetual implementation syndrome.** Some implementations drag on. And on. And on. Before you know it, the whole project – recommendations and all – falls off the radar screen and everyone forgets that it ever happened. By allowing implementations to drag on without end, you risk letting all your work go to waste. Be sure to work closely with your clients to establish a firm implementation schedule that has a clear beginning and a clear end – one that is written in terms of weeks or at most months, not years. Exact timetables depend on the nature of the project – its complexity and the desired speed of implementation, along with the availability of required client resources and support.

By following this advice, you're doing just about everything you can to play your part in the implementation process. Don't forget that your clients must do their part, too. As the old saying goes, you can lead a horse to water, but you can't make him drink. You can't force your clients to implement your recommendations. All you can do is to point out the many benefits to their organisations by following your prescription for change. If they decide to ignore your advice, the decision is theirs to make, and you have to accept it and move on. As we mentioned earlier, however, don't give up until you're convinced that your point of view has been given serious consideration by your client.

The final step in the implementation phase of the consulting process is to assess the results of the project. We just happen to cover this topic in the next section.

Assessing the Results of the Implementation of Your Recommendations

So you've reached the end of your consulting project. It's been a long haul, but you managed to develop a great set of recommendations with your client. In addition, those recommendations were implemented just as you planned. How do you determine whether they had the effect you intended? You do so by assessing the results of your project implementation and then comparing the results to your original plan.

Fortunately, assessing the results of your recommendations is fairly simple because you took the time at the beginning to develop a detailed implementation plan that you can now use to measure the results. (You did do an implementation plan, didn't you?) Here's how to assess the results of your project implementation:

1. **Gather data.**

   Just as you gathered information in the data-collection phase of the consulting process, you need to gather data that tells you whether your recommendations are working. Some results of your recommendations may be readily apparent; others may take months or even years to come about. If, for example, you're implementing changes that impact employee morale, surveys may tell you within a few weeks whether morale is improved. However, changes to large and complex manufacturing systems to improve product quality may require many months of gathering product quality data to show whether the recommendations are working. Whatever the case, you don't know how your project turned out until you collect the data that tells you whether it was a success.

2. **Assess progress against plan.**

   Keep close tabs on the progress of all implementation tasks, comparing it with the plan you created. Depending on the nature of the project – its complexity and speed of implementation – daily or weekly checks wouldn't be too often. Assess whether some tasks need to be accelerated and whether the schedules for other tasks need to be lengthened.

3. **Assess your client's satisfaction and view of your effectiveness.**

   One of the most important measures of success (some may say the only measure worth worrying about) is how satisfied your client is with the implementation of your recommendations and his or her view of your effectiveness as a consultant. Ask questions; send surveys; call your client. How you choose to solicit and measure your client's satisfaction is up to you. The important thing is that you ask.

4. **Assess your own satisfaction and view of your effectiveness.**

   Project satisfaction is a two-way street. Consider whether you were satisfied with the project. Did you handle your client in the right way? Did you approach the project in the most effective way possible? Would you change anything about what you did and how you did it? Do you want to do future work with this client? Did you make any money on the project, or did your work turn out to be 'pro bono'? Ask yourself these questions and others like them to gauge your own level of satisfaction.

5. **Use feedback to adjust future projects.**

   As you obtain feedback on the way you conducted the project and implementation, note the information that you need to keep in mind for future projects. Use this feedback to adjust the way you approach the different steps of the consulting process – defining the problem, collecting data, diagnosing, presenting your recommendations, and implementing them. No one knows everything there is to know about consulting, and you can always find out something new that helps you do an even better job the next time.

6. **Write an impact study.**

   This is a definite discipline of top-quality consulting firms. Writing an impact study forces you to document lessons, both positive and negative, that ensure that your process improves consistently, and that provide valuable marketing data for future clients.

As you can see, assessing your project – whether it is the most successful project you ever pulled off or the least – is the way that you and your client's organisation gain valuable information. By obtaining feedback and using it to figure out what you did right and what you did wrong, you improve your services to clients and become a better consultant. You can always find out something new from a project you participate in and from clients you work with, and doing so is always in your best interests.

Part IV
Selling and Marketing Your Consulting Services

'And a free sample to all our clients, we're giving away tee-shirts!'

In this part . . .

It's one thing to have a great idea, but it's another thing altogether to attract the attention (and money!) of the clients you need to make your consulting business take off and grow over a sustained period of time.

In this part, we explore the sales process and present strategies for publicising your business and building business through referrals and with new clients.

Chapter 12

The ABCs of Selling Consultancy

So you're up and running as a consultant. Either you're working for a consulting firm, or you own and operate one yourself. Either way, you'll quickly notice that if you want to stay afloat, you've got to keep a steady flow of new business coming into your firm. To accomplish this often means becoming a pretty competent salesperson. This is especially the case for those of you who have your own consulting businesses – you may be the one and only person who sells projects to clients, signs the agreements, and delivers your company's services. If you sell new work, whether to current or new clients, then the cash you need to run your business and pay your bills will keep making its way into your bank account. If you fail to sell new work, however, that bank account will soon be a very dusty and lonely place.

But even consultants who work for someone else are often called upon to participate in the selling process – sometimes calling on prospective clients to pitch the merits of your firm or your approach to doing business, and often selling to current clients through your great project performance and excellent service. Indeed many consulting firms expect their consultants to take a leading role in the selling process.

Whatever your own situation may be, your future success – and the future success of your consulting firm – may very well depend on your own ability to sell. Which is why we devote an entire chapter to this important topic.

The Selling Process

So, what exactly is this selling process we keep talking about? The classic process for selling consultancy comprises eight stages:

1. **Prospecting for leads.** Before you can sell your services, you've got to find prospective clients. Prospecting for leads is all about finding those prospective clients.

2. **Qualifying your leads.** All leads are not created equal. Some may want to buy your products and services but can't afford them, while others may be able to afford them, but not see a compelling reason to buy them. Qualifying your leads will help you figure out whether or not they are ready, willing, and able to buy from you.

3. **Preparing for sales meetings.** Once you've got a qualified lead, you need to find out more about your prospective client – and his or her organisation's needs – and you need to get his or her commitment to meet you.

4. **Running a successful sales meeting.** You need to find out what's hurting this client and how you can help to take away the pain. You begin to scope out the solution with the client and get commitment to go on to the next stage.

5. **Making your pitch.** Whether in person, or via letter, telephone, or email message, you'll eventually submit your proposal to your prospective client – explaining what you'll do, how long it will take, and how much it will cost – and try to convince him or her to contract with your consulting firm to do the work.

6. **Overcoming client objections.** Your prospective client may have questions and concerns after you make your pitch – this is where you address them in hopes of making the sale.

7. **Closing the sale.** After your client's concerns have been sufficiently addressed, you should be able to convince him or her to sign an agreement, thereby closing the sale.

8. **Following up.** The best clients are happy clients. Make sure that your clients are happy clients by following up with them after the sale to address any issues that may arise while setting the stage for additional future work.

In this section, we consider the selling process in detail. We also give tips and advice for each step and finally talk about how to sell on (and on) once you've successfully landed a client.

Prospecting for leads

For many salespeople, prospecting for leads – that is, locating prospective customers and clients – takes up a significant portion of their day-to-day schedules. Generally, the more leads you can gather – especially *qualified* leads – the greater your chances are of making a sale. This first step in the sales process is so important that some companies have dedicated staff whose sole job it is to generate leads.

Leads can come from a number of different places – some expected, and some not, including:

- ✔ **Networking.** Selling is a very social process, built on relationships. Who do you know that might be interested in buying what you've got to sell? Who do *they* know who might be interested in what you've got to sell? Are there professional groups, clubs, or associations you can join that will increase your exposure to prospective clients? Many people join chambers of commerce, industry associations, and the boards of local nonprofit organisations for this very reason.

- ✔ **Referrals.** Are you taking care of your current clients? If so, it's highly likely that they'll become an excellent source of referrals – prospective clients who to some extent come to you already sold to. Because you come recommended by your clients, much of your selling work has been done for you.

- ✔ **Cold calls.** Making cold calls to prospective clients – that is, contacting prospects who you don't already know to see if they are interested in your services – is a time-honoured and sometimes effective tradition in selling. Truth be told, your chances of landing a client as a result of cold calling increase dramatically when you've done your homework and limit such calls to prospects who you've determined will be most likely to need your services. A shotgun approach of contacting hundreds or even thousands of prospects who are unlikely to buy from you is a waste of your time and money.

- ✔ **Promotions.** Promotions cover a wide variety of different ways of enticing prospects into giving you the information you need to contact them, including contests, coupons, and freebies. For example, you can offer prospects free admission to your investment seminar as a way of attracting prospects and then gathering their contact information, or you can offer visitors to your website a free subscription to your online newsletter in exchange for their email address. Not only will you get the contact information for people who are interested in your offers (which you can then use to make follow-up sales calls), but anyone who follows through can be considered a solid sales lead.

✔ **Mailing lists.** There are a number of companies that sell mailing lists of individuals and companies that may find your consulting services of interest. You can buy or rent these lists, and use them for client prospecting. Be sure you narrowly define your selection criteria to improve your chances of prospecting success.

✔ **'Walk-ins'.** Believe it or not, every once in a while a prospect will contact you out of the blue – perhaps as a result of seeing your name in the newspaper, or running across your website, or reading the comment left on a blog by a happy client. Again, there's a good reason why he or she decided to contact you first. Be ready for walk-ins, and treat them well.

Before you go running off to look for prospects, however, first take a few moments to focus your efforts by considering who your ideal client really is. You can do this by asking questions like these:

✔ What kinds of problems can my consulting firm solve?

✔ Who needs these problems solved?

✔ Are they individuals or businesses?

✔ What are their exact needs?

✔ What is most important to your prospects?

✔ What is least important to your prospects?

✔ What advantages does your firm offer over your competitors?

✔ Can you communicate these advantages effectively to your prospects?

Use the answers to these questions and others like them to build a model of your most likely prospects – who they are, where they are, what their needs are, and how you'll address them. While you don't want to be too narrow in your focus, which might cause you to overlook many likely future clients, you also don't want to cast your net too widely. Doing so may overwhelm you with prospects who aren't really right for you or your business – wasting your time and theirs.

Qualifying your leads

Truth be told, some leads – and some clients – are better than others, and it's important to understand which are which. Why? Because not only is chasing every single lead possible a waste of your limited time and money, but bad leads often make even worse clients. The idea is to focus your efforts on the ones that will pay off for you.

Philip's marketing team prioritise sales leads in the following way:

- ✔ **First priority:** Sell existing products/services to current customers

- ✔ **Second priority:** Sell related products/services to current customers

- ✔ **Third priority:** Sell existing products/services to new customers

- ✔ **Fourth priority:** Sell new products/services to new customers

The point here is that your strongest – and most highly qualified – sales leads are almost always going to be your current clients. This makes sense because they already know and trust you. And – chances are – you'll have much better luck selling them something they're familiar with than trying to introduce them to something new. So, keep your primary focus on your current clients – make sure they're happy with your services, and give them good reasons to want to purchase even more of what you're selling (and to refer their own colleagues and associates to you).

Of course, you always need to keep a constant inflow of new clients – not just to grow your business, but just to keep up, as some current clients inevitably fade away. For that reason, you need to qualify your leads. Here are some questions to ask for doing just that:

- ✔ **Do they need what you've got to sell?** Be honest now – does your lead really need what you're selling? Let's say you're a management consultant for fast-growing technology businesses. It wouldn't make much sense for you to try to sell your services to a slow-growing government agency – would it? (Hint: No.) Be sure your prospects really need you and your consulting company.

- ✔ **Do they have the necessary funds?** You may find a lot of prospects who need your excellent consulting services, but who really can't afford the price. When you run into a prospect like that, you've got essentially two choices: move on to a different prospect, or lower your prices. Unless your prices are entirely out of step, then it's probably better in most cases to move on.

- ✔ **Can you get to the decision-maker?** Generally, if you hope to gain success in your consulting sales efforts, you need to get your proposal in front of the right person within your client's organisation – someone who is empowered to make a decision in favour of contracting with your company. Countless salespeople have wasted billions – perhaps trillions – of their precious hours barking up the wrong tree, and trying to sell something to someone who does not have the authority, budget, or responsibility to buy it. If you simply can't get to a decision-maker, then you probably need to write off that particular lead.

✔ **Will you be able to convince them of the value you bring?** While you may never truly know unless you ask, some prospects will be easier to convince than others – and some will never be convinced, no matter how much value you bring to the table. Unfortunately, some prospective clients will focus on your hourly rate – even when you can potentially be saving them millions of pounds. If they can't see the value, then these leads may ultimately be a waste of your time.

✔ **Are they in a position to buy from you?** In some cases, a client will need to have already purchased and used certain products or services for whatever it is you sell to be appropriate. For example, it would be hard for you to optimise a organisation's computerised customer relationship management (CRM) program if it was still using index cards to track sales contacts.

There is an old sales maxim – the **8-4-2-1 rule**. According to this rule, out of every eight qualified leads you bring into your business, you get four sales meetings, that result in two sales proposals, that ultimately lead to just one sale. While we don't know if this particular rule is precisely accurate, we do know that it is true in a general sense. Out of any group of qualified leads, only a fraction will actually turn into clients, and the higher the quality of your leads, the higher that fraction will be.

When it comes to qualifying your leads, be smart, and be sure to take off your rose-tinted glasses. Not everyone is qualified to be your client. Some don't need your consulting services, some can't afford them, and some will never understand just how much they really need them. In any case, your job is to focus on your very best prospects, and to ignore the rest. Ultimately, you're the one who has to decide which are which.

Preparing for sales meetings

Before you present a proposal or quote to a prospective client, there are a number of things you need to first consider and take care of. As the old Boy Scout saying goes, *be prepared*! Here are some things to do as part of your preparation to meet a prospective client:

✔ **Figure out who the decision-maker is, and how best to get to him or her.** You may be wasting your time if you meet someone who can't give the go-ahead for work with your company. Take time to research who the decision-makers are in your targeted organisation, and then chart out a strategy for getting in touch. Many managers and executives have assistants (also known as *gatekeepers*) who specialise in keeping salespeople away from their bosses. There are many ways to deal with this obstacle – from schmoozing the gatekeepers to making a direct approach to the decision-maker via phone call or email to simply making an appointment. The best approach is the one that works best for you and your prospective clients.

✔ **Research, research, research.** Using Internet search engines such as Google and Yahoo!, you can find a lot of information about prospective clients – information that can provide you with insights into their challenges and opportunities, and help guide the development of your proposal. This research can turn up information about the products and services they buy, organisational structure and leadership hierarchy, key contacts and phone numbers and email addresses, news, and much more. Not only can this information help you understand better your prospect's potential problems, but it can also provide you with ideas for structuring solutions.

✔ **Make initial contact.** When it's appropriate, you can make initial contact before your sales call to discuss your client's issues and then scope out a solution. This may enable you to shape a solution at your first client meeting rather than using the meeting to scope a problem and then delivering a proposal later. If your solution and pricing are straightforward enough, then you can do this relatively easily. However, if your solution is complex, and the pricing is not standardised, then you most likely need to actually meet your client – in person, or on the phone – before you can draft an effective proposal.

Running a successful sales meeting

You're now at the point where many consultants go wrong. Other consultants go in with a definition (their own definition) of the client's problem fixed firmly in their mind together with one solution (their own solution). They then tell the client precisely what his or her problem is and precisely what would solve it. Every now and then they get it right but 99 times out of a hundred they succeed only in alienating the client. Philip had this tendency beaten out of him as a young consultant at Coopers & Lybrand (a predecessor firm of PricewaterhouseCoopers) and he can still hear experienced partners' words ringing in his ears: 'You sell consultancy by questioning not by telling – seek don't tell.' Your goal at a first meeting is to get the prospective client to ask you for a proposal or presentation. The time for telling clients things is when you write your proposal or make a sales presentation. By then you're able to tell your client things you know he or she wants to hear about.

Here are the main things you need to cover at a first sales meeting:

✔ **The history:** What's the background to the issue? For example, if you want to sell your client advice on Quality Assurance, ask what the organisation's approach has been so far and how that approach has worked out. Probe to find out what he or she likes or doesn't like about how it is currently managed. Listen for what sales people call *pain points*; these are things that are hurting clients and are where they need help (your help).

✔ **Concrete examples:** Once you find a pain point, get real examples. Why is it a problem for the organisation? How much does it cost them? How often does this happen?

- **Diagnostic questions:** Okay, so you've established where the organisation needs help but do they have any ideas about what may solve their problem? These types of questions can lead you in one of two main directions. Either they know exactly what they want, and brief you on all the help they require (bingo!) or they don't know so they ask for your advice (if you can offer credible advice and make a solution sound real and desirable, bingo again!).

- **Scoping questions:** Now you and your client are both heading in same direction, you need his or her help in scoping the work. How many people do you need to interview, and who? How often would you need to visit the client's office? How many people need to be surveyed? If this goes well you can map out a plan together.

- **Buying process:** At this stage you need to find out how the client will make the decision to buy your consultancy service and who will be involved. In an ideal scenario he or she can buy it without asking anyone else; in other scenarios many departments or managers may need to be involved. Making assumptions about the buying process is a mistake, so ask thorough questions.

- **Buying concerns:** These questions have two main purposes: firstly, to identify any concerns the client has so that you can address them in your proposal; and secondly, to find out what would make the solution you offer even more desirable. For example, what sort of consultants does he or she prefer to work with? (If the answer is 'pragmatic', guess what you say in the proposal. Hint: that you're very pragmatic.)

- **Commitment questions:** To save yourself wasted effort you need to see what your client really wants you to do next. When would he or she want you to start? What would be the best next step? Get some commitment from the client to do something that will get you closer to the sale. Some salespeople call this tactic *ABC, Always Be Closing*. Don't misunderstand – this closing doesn't always mean the final close, but a series of stage closes along the way. If the client commits to get his or her boss (the real decision-maker) to meet you, that's a stage close. If he or she commits to reading your proposal and meeting again to refine it, that's a stage close. Philip calls these *commitment questions* because if you cannot close on them the final sale is unlikely.

The better prepared you are for your sales meeting, the better the chance you have of finding success with your prospective clients. Take time to work your way through the above list before your next client sales call. However, don't over-prepare and fall into the trap of assuming you know all about a client's problem and exactly how to solve it without listening to him or her carefully first.

Making your pitch

Once you've outlined your client's issues and problems – and you've developed solutions and prices to implement them – then it's time to make your pitch. Again, the better prepared you are for this moment, the better your chances of success (see the previous section for more details on getting prepared). Every step in the selling process has led you to this point – now go and get 'em, tiger!

We have the following advice for making effective sales pitches:

- ✔ **Know what to say, even if you don't say it.** Understand your approach and solutions fully – from the most basic parts, all the way up to those detailed specifics that clients love to ask about when you least expect it. Rather than fumbling for an answer that you just can't seem to pull out of the depths of your mental archives, be ready for whatever questions come your way.

- ✔ **Organise around your key selling points.** You don't have much time to grasp your prospect's attention – according to research, the first 30 seconds is pretty much the limit. Lose his or her attention, and you'll have one heck of a time ever getting it back. Be sure that your sales pitch is organised, with a natural flow that takes your client from problems to solutions in a logical manner.

- ✔ **Be flexible.** The one thing you can expect during the course of almost any sales pitch is the unexpected. Be ready at any time to take your carefully prepared proposal and throw it out the window when a prospective client wants to move in a different direction. This is a common occurrence, and it's something you must be prepared to deal with. Be light, be nimble, and be always ready to change your approach to adapt to your client's needs.

- ✔ **Be honest.** To make a sale, some salespeople end up over-promising to their prospective clients. Don't fall victim to this temptation – it's always better to be honest about what your consulting firm can and can't do, and what your client can reasonably expect as a result of hiring you. Most clients will respect your honesty and trust you more. It's better to lose a sale or two than to be set up to meet unrealistic expectations, which will ultimately have worse consequences for you in the long term.

Making your pitch is perhaps the most important step in the sales process, and your ability to do it well will go a long way in determining your success as a consultant. Believe us, practice makes perfect – the more sales pitches you make to prospective clients, the better you'll get at it. Always be on the lookout for ways to make your pitches better and become alert to the approaches that work – and the ones that don't. Then do more of the former, and less of the latter.

Overcoming client objections

While some sales pitches will go smoothly, with your prospective client perhaps only asking a couple of minor questions here or there, other sales pitches can have you feeling like you've just gone through the Inquisition. Some clients are bound to feel that your proposal doesn't address their needs, or that you've missed the mark on describing the problem, that your solution is the wrong one, that your price is too high – or your schedule is inadequate. Now what?

 Be aware that when a client expresses doubts or concerns, that shows that he or she is listening to what you've got to say and is not just tuning you out. This is a good thing, so don't dismiss the concern too quickly. You want to empathise so that the client knows you understand the concern – this will make him or her more receptive to your responses and explanations. Therefore reframe the objection as a constructive question. For example:

> **Client:** Two days for the training course is way too long; we've got a call centre to run.

> **You:** I see your point. I can understand that you would want to minimise time out from the front line. If we were to split the training into shorter sessions, when would be good times to run these in order to avoid problems?

Next, here are some tips for addressing client concerns:

- ✔ **Deal with misunderstandings.** Some client concerns are simply the result of misunderstandings – of your approach, of your pricing, or of some other aspect of your proposal. Dig deep to identify any misunderstandings that may have crept into your client's mind, and defuse them immediately – before they can become permanent obstacles to your proposal being accepted.

- ✔ **Deal with lack of urgency.** Some clients may not fully appreciate the importance of dealing with a problem before it grows larger – or capitalising on an opportunity while it is still available. Or they may simply be too busy dealing with other matters to focus on the problems that you bring up in your proposal. Clearly explain the issues or opportunities that you've unearthed, and explain how ignoring them will cause the problems to grow, and the opportunities to disappear. Build a sense of urgency in your prospective clients.

- ✔ **Deal with lack of perceived need.** Prospects may not make the connection between the problems or opportunities that they have, and your proposed approach. If this is the case, then you've not done an adequate job of presenting the issues – nor the value that you bring to the table. Pay close attention to your client's resistance in this area and use objective data and responses to help tip the balance in your favour.

✔ **Deal with funding issues.** Sometimes a client has a real lack of funding – and nothing you do will solve that – but sometimes a client has a *perceived* lack of funding. In this latter situation, you can do a lot to help your prospective client realise that he or she does have the resources available to pay for your consulting services. Show your client how much money the organisation will save when he or she brings you in – far more than the fee that you'll charge. Offer to allow monthly progress payments or other payment arrangements that make it easier for your client to say 'yes'.

✔ **Deal with lack of trust.** What if your prospective client doesn't think he or she is dealing with the right person (you!), or the right consulting company (yours!)? Perhaps you haven't spent enough time with your prospect to establish the strong foundation of trust that you need in order to sell effectively, or maybe there are other concerns that need to be addressed before you can build trust. Ferret these out and deal with them so that trust is built – and this source of objections is no longer an obstacle to your sales efforts.

Once you've successfully addressed your client's concerns, you can move on to the next step in the selling process: closing the sale. Many sales are lost in this transition – much as a fish will often jump off the hook and escape as it is being reeled in. It's your job to reel those prospects in and close the deal.

Closing the sale

Reaching agreement with a client – that is, closing the sale – is a powerful, and sometimes mysterious, part of the selling process. This is where all your powers of persuasion and understanding of human nature will be put to the test. As the moment approaches, you've got to be ready for it by saying the right thing at the right time – making a very specific offer to your prospect while observing his or her response closely.

The best closings are ones where your client is the one who initiates the closing process of his or her own volition – for example, 'You're right – we can't wait any longer to get you on the job. I'll send out a purchase order to you tomorrow with the terms you set out in your proposal.' Music to any consultant's ears.

The worst closings are the ones that require you to push your clients into an agreement that they seem not to actually want to enter into. In this situation, you've got to decide if simply dealing with the client's sales resistance (as outlined in the previous section) will get you to your goal, or if you need to back off, fold up your tent, and move on – before your prospective client throws you out.

If you decide to move to closing – the normal situation in most cases – then here is some advice:

- **Look for signals that the client is ready to buy.** If your prospect is interested in your pitch, asks good questions, and indicates that he or she wants to move forward, then you know that it's time to close the deal.

- **Overcome any final client concerns.** If there are any lingering client concerns, now is the time to deal with them.

- **Don't be too pushy.** Again – if you've moved your client through the preceding steps in the selling process, and the client is still interested, then you won't need to push him or her to get the deal you seek. Pushing clients too hard will either anger them, or convince them that what they need to do is find a less obnoxious consultant.

- **Shake on it.** When you reach agreement, seal the deal by shaking hands with your client and expressing your thanks. These simple actions will help encourage your client to follow through with your agreement and set the stage for building a strong, long-term relationship.

- **Reassure your client.** Let your client know that he or she is making the right choice in hiring your consulting firm to do the work you've proposed, and support them throughout the process. This final step is to help the client overcome what psychologists call buyer's remorse.

If you don't close your deal and reach agreement on a contract for your consulting services, then you've potentially spent a lot of time with nothing to show for it. If this happens with a number of prospects, then it can be devastating for your business. However, if you've followed the selling process to this point – and have willingly brought your prospective client along with you – then chances are that the closing will happen quickly and with little prodding from you. And that's really a dream come true.

Following up

Although there might be much celebrating and back-patting when at long last a sale is made and a new client is signed on, or an old client signs up for more work, the sales process has not ended yet. In fact, in many ways, it has just begun.

Following up with clients after you've sold them your consulting services is a key ingredient in the recipe of developing long-term client relationships – the kind that every consultant worth his or her salt dreams of – and it's the never-ending part of the sales process. You see, if all you care about is landing a client – at the expense of following through to make sure the client is satisfied with the results you provide – then your client will eventually figure that out, and act accordingly. In most cases, acting accordingly means either cancelling your contract or rejecting any future contracts with your firm.

However, when you treat clients like partners, and keep up with their projects and the state of their satisfaction – or lack thereof, you build clients for life.

Of course, as with anything else, there's a right way and a wrong way to follow up with your clients. Here's a list of the right ways:

- ✔ **Work on that relationship.** Now that you've got that client you've been chasing, you can work on building a solid, long-term relationship. You can achieve this first of all by doing good work – and doing it on time and within budget – and then following up by building an ongoing dialogue with your client. Ideally, you'll establish a mutually beneficial partnership, where you look out for your client's interests, and your client looks out for yours.

- ✔ **Drop in for a visit (or two or three).** Of course – you can give your client a call on the telephone, or you can send out an email, letter, or fax, but nothing tells a client that you really care more than taking time out of your schedule to visit his or her offices. You can do this on a regular basis, whether or not you've got a presentation to make or business to do. While you're there, it wouldn't hurt to get your client out for lunch or dinner either.

- ✔ **Use the telephone!** When you're miles away from your clients, driving for miles every time you want to say hello isn't always going to be your best option. A good substitute is a simple phone call. With the proliferation of email, social networking sites, and other online forms of communication, telephones have taken a bit of a back seat. Don't neglect your phone – call your clients on a regular basis to check in on projects, gauge satisfaction, suggest additional solutions, or simply say hello. Your clients will appreciate the personal touch – and you'll appreciate their business.

- ✔ **Write letters instead of email messages.** While letters and handwritten notes are increasingly finding themselves on the endangered species list, email messages have become the standard form of communication in most organisations. While it's fine to use email to communicate with clients and follow up after the sale, the best option is to mix it up with letters and handwritten notes and cards. A handwritten note signifies something special – and he or she will notice, which is a good thing.

The sales process doesn't end when you sign a contract with a client – it continues as you deliver your consulting services, and often beyond. Make following up with clients a regular part of the way you do business – the relationships you build will make the time you spend doing this very well worth your while.

Selling In and Selling On

The classic selling process described in the previous section will take you a long way towards achieving your goals of winning new clients or, in consultancy-speak, *selling-in*. Next you need to focus on one more thing: building long-term relationships with clients. Focusing on selling-in (which brings in new clients) as well as selling-on (which focuses on building ongoing, long-term relationships with clients) helps consulting firms to increase sales overall and decrease selling costs.

Consider the example of a pushy, used-car dealer who will seemingly stop at nothing to get you to buy a car – *any* car – right now! Your credit's bad? No problem – we do our own auto financing. Don't like the colour? No sweat – we've got every colour of the rainbow on our forecourt. You want a 2-door and not a 4-door? Nothing to it – we'll have our body shop weld two of the doors shut for you. And, of course, the ultimate weapon of the hard sell technique: This offer is available today only.

When you're engaged in relationship-based selling, you're focused on:

- Building long-term relationships with clients
- Being totally committed to clients
- Talking to your clients continually
- Selling the benefits of your services to clients
- Consistently providing the highest levels of customer service.

If you're ready to make the move to relationship selling, then your quickest way there will be through building trust and creating bonds with your clients while being empathetic to their needs and challenges. The idea is to focus on your client – and your client's needs – first and foremost. Once you build a strong, long-term relationship, selling-in will come naturally.

Chapter 13

Getting the Word Out: Promoting Your Business

In This Chapter

▶ Promoting your business with personal selling

▶ Using public relations and publicity

▶ Boosting business with advertising

▶ Using sales promotions to promote your business

*P*romotion is informing your potential clients that you have a product or service that they need. Unfortunately, very few products (with the possible exception of whatever product Apple happens to have on its drawing board for next year) sell themselves. Most products – including consulting services – need to be promoted in order to sell in quantities sufficient to maintain a business. Although some consultants exist strictly through word-of-mouth advertising and referrals, an element of promotion is still involved when the prospective client contacts you, because then you, as the consultant, must convince the client of the wisdom of paying you to do the proposed work. You promote yourself by using various channels of communication to inform and to persuade prospective clients.

You can promote your firm and its products and services in four main ways:

▶ **Personal selling:** Personal selling is promotion by person-to-person communication directly between you – or representatives of your firm – and your prospective clients. Methods include telemarketing, personal meetings, and proposal presentations.

▶ **Public relations and publicity:** Public relations involves promotion by communication methods that create favourable public images of your firm and your products or services. Publicity entails promotion by placing non-paid organisational messages in the media through press releases, media packs, media events, television interviews, and other communication materials and techniques.

✔ **Advertising:** Advertising is promotion through paid, non-personal channels of mass communication, such as newspapers, direct mail, radio, websites, and television.

✔ **Sales promotion:** Sales promotions are short-term promotional techniques used to stimulate an immediate purchase of your product or service. Such techniques include discount coupons, product samples, and competitions.

Some consultants use a mix of all four categories of promotional techniques, and others pick and choose from the list. We suggest that you develop a mix of techniques from each key promotional category. Experiment with different combinations of techniques and measure the results. What works best for you and your business depends on the nature of the consulting you do and the buying habits of your target market.

For example, if you're an interior design consultant and advise clients how best to decorate their homes, you probably want to advertise your business – perhaps in the Yellow Pages and in interior design magazines and via a website – and also employ sales promotions, such as discount coupons or free offers. However, if you're a political consultant who advises political candidates on how best to raise money for their campaigns, you probably want to rely on personal selling, public relations, and publicity to promote your business. For some reason, most political consultants don't use buy-one-get-one-free coupons or give away free samples to promote their services, but they definitely get a lot of their work from referrals.

One thing to keep in mind: You have to weigh the cost of promoting your products or services against the benefits. Buying a big display ad in the Yellow Pages or building a professional-looking website may be an expensive proposition, but if it works, it's worth it. The key is to discover what works for your particular consulting business and then to use it to your greatest advantage. The best way is to experiment and then measure your results. How? One of the most effective methods is to ask your clients how they found out about you. For example, if you've placed an expensive Yellow Pages advertisement but a survey of your clients tells you that none of them came to you as a result of this, that might indicate that your valuable promotional budget could be better spent elsewhere.

In this chapter, we review each of the four ways of promoting your business and its products and services, and we look closely at the many different promotional methods that consultants use. Although the listings are quite comprehensive, you can promote your business in other ways. Be creative and try something new!

Personal Selling

Consulting is built on relationships, and personal selling is the cornerstone of many consultants' promotional efforts. Networking – or building contacts with new clients through personal selling and referrals from current clients or associates – is a very effective way for you to promote your consulting business. Some kinds of consultants – legal, financial, and medical consultants, for example – primarily use personal selling to find qualified prospects.

Here are some of the ways that consultants promote their services through personal selling:

- **Face-to-face meetings:** There's nothing like a good old-fashioned, one-to-one meeting with a client to promote your business and its products or services. The advantages are endless: You can tailor your message to the individual client you're meeting, gauge his or her reaction in real time, and then adapt your message to address any concerns that your client may express. In these days of 'technology this' and 'technology that', people seem to find the human touch very comforting.

- **Telephone calls:** If you can't meet someone in person, you can use the telephone to promote your business. If you have new information of interest to your clients or just want to keep in touch, most clients will welcome your call. Although you miss the nonverbal cues that you pick up in a personal meeting, you can call far more clients in a day than you can meet in person.

- **Letters and email messages:** Keep in touch with your clients and your highest-potential prospective clients by occasionally writing them a personal letter or email message. Your clients will appreciate that you took the time to keep in touch, and they're much more likely to remember you when they need to hire a consultant. If you can include a newspaper or magazine cutting, brochure, or link to your website highlighting your business or products, or something they may be interested in professionally or personally, then by all means do so – it's a small investment to make for a potentially high reward.

- **Blogs and Internet forums:** Today, you can find blogs and Internet forums on just about any topic you can imagine. There are blogs and forums for small-business owners, scriptwriters, engineers, doctors, and just about every other profession you can imagine. Shrewd clients search these boards for talented consultants to do work for them. More than a few consultants receive unsolicited requests to perform consulting work because of their posts on blogs and Internet forums dedicated to their particular line of work.

- **Association memberships:** Most industries have trade groups and other associations that you can join for a nominal annual fee. These associations offer opportunities to promote your business by networking with other members and potential clients at events including regular meetings, conferences, and trade shows. Locally based groups, such as the chamber of commerce or Business Link offer the same kinds of opportunities.

- **Talks:** Giving talks – before community groups, clients, or groups of your peers – is a great way to network with potential clients or with firms that may offer you subcontracting possibilities. You may even attract the attention of the print or broadcast media, and in may be useful to employ a public relations specialist to ensure that your appearances get the attention they deserve. Not only do you enhance your personal credibility and image by giving talks, but you also may generate numerous qualified leads.

- **Seminars and workshops:** Many consultants find great success in promoting their businesses by offering seminars and workshops – often for free – to prospective clients. For example, stockbrokers and financial planners love to drum up business by offering personal finance seminars to people who are interested in learning how to handle their finances better. A certain number of attendees then naturally turn to the broker for help in executing and managing their personal stock transactions.

- **Social events:** Loads of business is done informally at cocktail parties, golf tournaments, and other social events. Picture this conversation: 'What do you do for a living?' 'I'm a chiropractor.' 'Oh, are you ? I've had this kink in my neck for weeks. Is there anything you can do for it?' It's usually advisable to avoid making a sales pitch at the event or asking your prospective client to lie down on the dining room table for an impromptu adjustment, so simply hand over your business card instead and approach your prospect during normal business hours. But you can certainly be ready to respond if you're asked for your opinion.

- **Telemarketing:** Although many people cringe when the phone rings at dinner time, telemarketing must work or the telemarketers would stop doing it. (Big hint: Telemarketing *does* work!) Telemarketing can be an effective way to drum up business if you can reach your intended market. Just be sure to use a targeted list of people who are most likely to want your product – random phone calls do little to bring you qualified prospects – and consider hiring a qualified and properly licensed firm to do the calling for you.

- **Community events:** Community events – everything from village fetes to museum openings – are great ways to network with members of the community who may need your services. Be sure to bring plenty of business cards to hand out to your new friends and acquaintances!

Personal selling adds a human touch to your promotional efforts. Because consulting is so dependent on the care and maintenance of personal relationships, most consultants discover that personal selling techniques are the most effective way to promote their products and services. They can also be a lot of fun! Ensure that you make personal selling a big part of your marketing mix.

Public Relations and Publicity

Public relations and publicity are the fine art of building and enhancing your public image through a variety of carefully crafted techniques, all aimed at getting a positive message about your business and its products and services into a variety of media outlets. Whether you just won the Nobel Prize or you're simply volunteering your time to help a good cause in your community, public relations and publicity make sure that you're not the only one who knows what you've done.

Here are some proven ways to ensure that you get your 15 minutes of fame:

- **Press releases and media packs:** If you're serious about getting a publicity campaign off the ground, you need to send out press releases and media packs to a list of media outlets that have the greatest probability of reaching your prospects. Media packs – folders that include a photo, biography, and information of interest to readers, listeners, or viewers – are a definite must if you want to line up print, radio, and television interviews.

- **Articles and books:** Writing articles or books on your field of expertise is a great way to both build your credibility and get your name in front of a wide range of potential clients. Many trade journals and association magazines are particularly hungry for articles written from an insider's perspective. They probably won't pay you for your efforts, but you reap some free publicity. Just make sure that the publications that you write for have a large readership among your target prospects. A public relations professional can help you place articles in the best print media to obtain maximum exposure.

  Writing a book can make you an instant expert in the eyes of the media and gain you entry for interviews and other opportunities to get your word out.

- **Web pages and blogs:** The Internet has exploded as an opportunity for promoting your services and products. A web page can be a showcase of your business and the unique skills and expertise that you offer your clients. (See *Building a Website For Dummies* by David Crowder for more information about creating your own website.) In addition, putting together a blog – and posting to it regularly – can create a much more dynamic and interactive experience for your clients and your clients-to-be. (See *Buzz Marketing with Blogs For Dummies* by Susannah Gardner for more details.)

✔ **Newsletters:** Newsletters are a particularly effective way to generate favourable publicity for your business and keep your clients informed about the latest happenings and innovations in your field and in your consulting practice. Not only can you keep in touch with your current clients, but you can also reach out to new ones. The good news is that instead of spending a lot of money to print and send hard-copy newsletters, nowadays you can simply email an electronic version to your clients for little or no money.

Bob reaches out to a very focused group of clients, potential clients, and media outlets with his Tip of the Week newsletter. Once, as a special thanks to his loyal subscribers, he sent each one a personally autographed copy of one of his books.

✔ **Media interviews, talk shows, and podcasts:** The various media – newspapers, magazines, radio, television, and now the Internet – have an insatiable appetite for interviewing interesting, informative, and entertaining people. You can either approach the media directly with story ideas or hire a publicist to take care of the heavy lifting for you. Every media outlet that you may want to target is looking for one thing: a personality who is entertaining to an established audience. If you're entertaining, informative, and engaging, you should have no problem getting the attention you desire. What do you have to offer? And even if the media doesn't come knocking on your door, you can easily create your own podcasts and place them on your website or blog for visitors to download and listen to. Be sure to pick up a copy of *Podcasting For Dummies* by Tee Morris, Evo Terra, Dawn Miceli, and Drew Domkus for lots more information on this topic.

✔ **Community service:** By offering your services to non-profit-making community organisations for free, you're helping them obtain the kinds of services that they may not otherwise be able to afford. You also have the opportunity to network with other businesspeople who often inhabit the boards and leadership of these types of organisations.

✔ **Independent surveys:** Some consultants are very successful in garnering tons of publicity by conducting surveys and then publishing the results in a press release. If the results are newsworthy, the media may pick up your study (and the name of your business) and distribute it nationwide.

✔ **Sponsorships:** By sponsoring an event in your community – perhaps a charity fundraiser or a job fair – you help create a positive public image for your business in the community and have the opportunity to draw media focus to your efforts. Imagine the value of explaining on camera to your local television news programmes why your event is so important to the community and why you feel so strongly that you should sponsor it.

✔ **Awards and honours:** Many consultants seek professional awards and honours, not only for the prestige that they bestow upon the recipients but also for the value of the publicity that they generate.

Successful consultants (and other businesspeople, for that matter) pay close attention to their public image and are always on the alert for new ways to get their message out to the public through the media. Don't forget: If you don't create your public image, you may not end up with the one you want.

Controlling Your Message: Advertising

For many businesses, advertising is necessary for survival. For other businesses – including many different types of consultants – advertising is an effective adjunct to their primary sources of qualified prospects. For example, although stockbrokers and estate agents depend on referrals from satisfied clients as their primary source of new client leads, advertising is an important supplement to this source, and it helps build their image in the community at the same time.

The best thing about advertising is that you can exercise a large degree of control over the message that your prospective clients receive and when and where they receive it. You can send your message to the public in shotgun fashion – gaining exposure to a huge number of people, only some of whom may be interested in what you have to sell – or you can direct it with rifle-sharp accuracy at only those potential clients who are your best prospects. And you can repeat the message often for maximum impact.

Advertising may or may not be for you – not every consultant will benefit from it. However, it can be a powerful part of your overall marketing mix, and you mustn't write it off too quickly. Here are some of the most common forms of advertising available to you:

- **Newspaper and magazine advertisements:** Newspaper and magazine advertising can be an effective way for certain kinds of consultants to promote their services. One thing is for sure: You get your message out to a lot of potential readers, although your message may be of little interest to most of them. While a newspaper may not be the best place for an aerospace consultant to advertise, for example, it may be a great place for a home audio and video consultant to advertise – especially in the weekly television guide. The wide variety of narrowly focused special interest magazines on the market today – as well as trade journals and association magazines – can make magazine advertising a particularly effective way to reach your targeted audience.

  Note: Newspapers have a very short shelf life of just one day, whereas magazines tend to hang around for weeks and even months. So your message may have a greater chance of being noticed in a magazine, unless you run newspaper ads on a daily basis.

✔ **Direct mail:** Direct mail is the sending of advertisements in the form of letters, flyers, brochures, coupon books, or other offers to your prospective clients. This is one of the best ways for consultants of all sorts to reach a large audience of qualified prospects. The real beauty of direct mail is that you can target your recipients with extraordinary precision. If, for example, you make your living as an advertising consultant, you can buy mailing lists from magazines and associations whose subscribers and members contain a high percentage of individuals likely to be interested in receiving your message. The mailing lists – complete with names and addresses – are available for direct download over the Internet, on CD-ROM or DVD, or even as ready printed envelope labels.

If you can profile your clients, a mailing list specialist can, for a modest fee, produce a list of other clients whose characteristics match those of your clients. For consultants, customised mailing lists are both effective and efficient. And apart from attracting new clients, direct mail can also help you keep in touch with existing clients.

✔ **Yellow Pages and other directories:** For certain types of consultant the Yellow Pages and industry-specific directories may be a useful way to reach qualified prospects. Most professional and industry associations list member firms in their directories for free. If you have a business phone line, you are provided with a simple telephone listing in your local business telephone directory. However, if you want to buy a display advertisement, be prepared to pay a lot of money for this form of advertising. Not only do readers of these publications have a need when they pick up a directory, but they are also usually ready to buy in the very near future. One possible downside with Yellow Page advertisements is that an increasing number of people are turning to the Internet for their information instead of the old paper-based directories.

✔ **Search engine advertising:** No company can survive these days without ensuring it comes up on Internet searches. Most search engines produce two listings: the natural listing found by the 'spiders' searching for key words and freshest content and the paid listing where advertisers pay to get onto the first page. Check out the Google Words tutorial for a beginners guide. In this high tech age, if your firm is not being found in Internet searches it will soon wither.

✔ **The Internet:** Those of you who are already online have probably noticed advertising on the Internet – on websites and blogs, and via email messages, both solicited and unsolicited.

As you may already know from reading your own Internet email inbox, unsolicited advertisements can be very annoying to recipients. How many get-rich-quick schemes and cheap replica watch advertisements can you tolerate before you're ready to unplug your computer once and for all? Use such methods at your own risk! If you do decide to use the Internet to advertise your consulting business, choose your recipients very carefully, be sure they want to receive your message, and provide them with an easy and reliable way to permanently opt out if they so desire.

✔ **Radio and television advertisements:** As with newspaper and magazine advertisements, radio and television advertisements can reach a large audience; everybody has at least one radio or television at home or at work. However, your message may be of interest to only a very narrow market. Cable and satellite television – with special interest channels such as National Geographic, MTV, Bloomberg, Nickelodeon, Bravo, and more – and radio stations that specialise in news, talk shows, and different music formats offer you the opportunity to aim your message at specific demographic groups. However, the relatively high cost of placing advertisements in these media outlets and the complexity and expense of putting together a quality advertisement make such advertising too daunting a task for most consultants.

✔ **Outdoor advertising:** Unless your last name is Goodyear and you're in the tyre consulting business, sticking an advertisement on the side of a balloon or on a billboard is probably not the best way to drum up business. However if you're a consultant who helps people get jobs then advertising in buses and trains may work. For the rest of you, at least you know that outdoor advertising is always an option should you choose to pursue it.

Make sure that you consider advertising when you develop your marketing plan. It's one of the best ways to get the exact message you want to send to your most likely prospective clients.

Sales Promotion

What do you do if you want a potential client to buy your product or service right now or at least to make sure he or she keeps your name and phone number handy for the time he or she needs you? Independent consultants use sales promotions – coupons, logo coffee mugs, free samples, and the like – to fulfil this task. Many sales promotions are fun and exciting for your clients, and they help to generate excitement about your business and its products.

Sales promotions come in all kinds and all flavours, so you surely can find something that fits your business and its clients. Consider some of these options:

✔ **Business cards:** Business cards are probably the ultimate low-cost way to promote your business. For less than £15 (even less if you print your own), you can have a box of 250 cards printed to your exact specifications. Once you have them, use them. Hand them out at parties, give them to your clients, staple them to proposals and reports, and always carry extras when you're out in the field. Some consultants print messages on the backs of their business cards, such as The Rules of Negotiating or other tips that may be valuable to prospective clients. If you have employees, give them business cards, too.

✔ **Brochures and sales materials:** If you're actively selling your product or service to others, then you've probably already developed your own promotional brochures and sales materials. They're easy to design and inexpensive to have professionally printed. If you're not on board yet, you're missing out on a great opportunity to promote your business. Few clients are ready to hire you immediately; most would prefer to look over your promotional literature first. Of course, your brochures and sales materials need to be as attractive and inviting as possible, and they must be easily available via your website as well as on request via the post.

✔ **Discount coupons:** Discount coupons are a time-honoured tradition for promoting consumer goods and certain kinds of services, such as car maintenance and carpet cleaning. There are a number of ways to distribute them to your targeted clients: through newspaper or magazine advertisements, through direct mail, or via the Internet. Depending on what kind of consulting you do, discount coupons may be worth a try.

✔ **Advertising freebies:** How could we live without coffee mugs, pens, pencils, refrigerator magnets, calendars, and the like – all bearing the name of your business and your phone number or Internet address? Handing out inexpensive and useful promotional freebies can help you keep your name in front of your clients all year round.

✔ **Free samples:** Everyone loves to get something for free. Offer free samples – a free home inspection, a free newsletter, a free web page – in exchange for trying your product or listening to your sales pitch.

Now that you've had the opportunity to review many of the different ways to promote your business, you need to develop a marketing plan that incorporates your selected mix of the approaches and techniques. All these approaches must be integrated to present and reinforce the professional image you're trying to project. Don't forget to closely monitor the results of your promotional efforts and to fine-tune your approach based on your market feedback.

Chapter 14

Building Business and Referrals through Current Clients

. . . .

. . . .

*E*very consulting business needs new clients to thrive and to grow. Firstly, as you lose clients – and every business is bound to lose some each month and each year for a variety of different reasons – you need new clients to replace the revenue that is lost. Secondly, new clients can play a crucial role in helping you grow your business in the future. While you may be able to grow your business to some degree by expanding the projects you do for current clients, you can't rely on them for 100 per cent of your future growth prospects. Your future success depends on maintaining a balance between keeping your current clients happy and devoting time and resources to finding new ones.

Building your business is an activity that must never stop. Sure, you have to attend to your current clients and your current projects (after all, the very first place you need to look for new business is with your current clients), but always be looking down the road – a month, six months, a year into the future – for new clients.

Just as there are many different ways to drive a car from Land's End to John O' Groats, there are many different ways to bring new clients into your business. You can place advertisements in magazines, in newspapers, or via the Internet and hope that your prospective clients see them and decide to contact you; you can go door to door and sell your services personally; you can conduct public presentations and workshops that attract interest to your services; you can stage a competition or give away free samples and gather leads that way; or you can choose any one of an almost unlimited number of different approaches for attracting new clients.

However, there is another way to get new clients – a way by which some consultants derive almost all their new business but that others overlook entirely. This way of building your business is through referrals. *Referrals* are prospects sent to you by someone outside your own business. For example, say you're a successful nutrition consultant. If your clients are happy with the work you do for them (they *are* happy, aren't they?), then your clients are bound to want to tell their friends about their positive experiences. In fact, they may think they're doing their friends a favour by telling them about that great consultant they found (you!). When your clients' friends call you as a result, they are considered referrals. Referrals are a fantastic way to obtain new clients, and you must not overlook this method.

The benefits of referrals to your business are many. Here are some specific reasons why referrals are worth pursuing:

- ✓ **Referrals are a major source of new business for many consultants.** Although some consultants depend on referrals to identify almost all their new business leads, others may not have tapped very deep into this vast resource. If you've not taken advantage of this important source of new business to the full extent that you're able, you can increase the number and quality of your referrals easily by following the advice in this chapter.

- ✓ **Referrals are easier to close than other kinds of prospects.** Because the people who send you referrals have most likely already told the referrals who you are, what you do, and – hopefully – what a great job you do, a large chunk of your work in selling to them has already been done. The fact that they are talking to you means that they have a need. The hard part of attracting their attention and getting them to listen to what you have to say has already been accomplished, so you can focus on identifying the solutions they need.

- ✓ **Referrals cost less to market than other kinds of prospects.** Because referrals are sent to you by other people, you don't have to spend much of your promotional budget to get their attention. This is marketing of the very best kind – targeted, and in many cases costing you little or no money. And because these prospects are to a large degree already favourably inclined towards you and your business, convincing them to buy your product or services doesn't take you as much time as convincing a prospect who was not referred to you.

In this chapter, we help you determine who are the best sources of referrals for your business, and we consider the importance of keeping your current clients happy with the work that you're doing for them and the way that you do it. We look into the very best ways to get referrals and then tell you what to do with them once you have them.

Deciding Who to Approach for Referrals

Referrals can come from anyone at any time. Your best and most obvious source of referrals is likely to be your many current, happy clients. Assuming you've been doing good work for your clients – and you've delivered your services or products on time and within budget – then they'll generally be the ones most loudly singing your praises. However, referrals can pop into your life from the least expected places at the least expected times. Every consultant has received a call from a friend of a friend of a friend. A positive mention by the press or on a blog or website can also generate referrals. Of course, like anything else in business (and in life, for that matter), you can greatly improve your chances of getting referrals by making a conscious effort to seek them.

You have two choices: You can either choose to wait for people to make referrals to you or your business, or you can actively work for them. Which of these choices do you think will improve your chances of getting the referrals your consulting business needs? (Hint: If you're sitting around waiting for people to make referrals, then you had better be ready to do a lot of sitting around.)

Assuming that you've made the decision to seek referrals (good decision!), whom must you approach for them? Although you can approach almost anyone, the following sources of referrals are likely to be your best bets and therefore the best use of your time:

- ✔ **Current clients:** Your current clients are without a doubt your best source of referrals. Not only do they know the quality of your work on a firsthand basis, but they are often your biggest fans and champions. And when your clients are out looking for new clients for you, your own marketing and promotion efforts are multiplied many times. The best approach with your clients is a direct one. Simply tell them that you would be happy to work with any associates of theirs who may also need your services. The best time to make the approach is after you complete a project successfully for your client – when the glow of the great work you did is still fresh in his or her mind. Be sure to take care of your current clients first, and they'll be sure to take care of you.

- ✔ **Other consultants:** Consulting can be a very cyclical business. One week you have hardly anything to do, the next week you're so busy you don't know how you're going to get all your work done. The fact is, other consultants are in much the same situation, and juggling projects is a skill that almost every consultant finds essential. Many consultants, when temporarily overwhelmed with business, contract out some of their work to individuals and firms that they know and trust. Doing so enables them to get the work done on time without having to hire permanent employees. Some consultants actually refer their clients to other consultants when they are already booked up. By getting to know other consultants – and helping them get to know you – you can pick up referrals that help you get through your slow times. Just be absolutely sure that you can trust the other consultant to do the same high quality of work that you do yourself. If you have to go back and fix the work that the other consultant did, then you're wasting your time – and money. And if the other consultant makes a bad impression on your client, then your client may not be that anxious to work with you again in the future.

✔ **Business associates:** During the course of a typical business day, you probably interact with a number of business associates – perhaps your accountant, an assistant at your favourite office supply store, or even your postie. Do they know about the products and services that you offer? If not, you have another opportunity to bring an entirely new group of referral opportunities to your business. Your solicitor and accountant can be terrific sources of referrals because they're likely to be plugged in to your local business community. You just need to give them the information about your business and explain what you can do for them (and for *their* clients) so that they know. Here's where having a good website for your business can be a real asset. Simply send them a link to the site and your work is done.

✔ **Family and friends:** Unless you just recently arrived from another planet or galaxy, you have lots of family and friends who also can be a great source of referrals. Be sure to remind them periodically of what you do for a living and invite them to tell their families and friends. Keep them up to date by sending them copies of newspaper or magazine articles about your business and by sending them copies of your brochures or other sales materials. And be sure that they know how to find your website.

How you find referrals is really up to you. If you're more comfortable waiting for your contacts to make referrals to you and would really rather not push them in that direction yourself, then that's what you must do. However, if you want to enjoy the benefits of a greatly enhanced quantity and quality of business referrals, take a close look at the people with whom you're acquainted and do business, and ask yourself whether they would be good sources of referrals. You may be surprised by how many of your clients, friends, and other associates are more than happy to refer new clients to you, if only you ask them to do so.

Setting the Stage with Current Clients

Because your current clients are your most likely source for referral business, you want to focus your efforts on them before you explore the other possibilities – such as the bloke who runs your local kebab shop or the lady who walks by your home office every morning at 8 a.m. with her dog. You can do a number of things to keep your clients happy and set the stage for the referrals your business needs so that it can grow. Here are some ways that you can help to motivate your clients to send those referrals your way – and keep them coming:

- ✔ **Do great work.** We've said it before, and we'll say it again. One of the best ways to keep your clients happy is to do great work for them. If you do, they'll probably be so happy that they'll want to tell all their associates about the great job you did. Similarly, if you *don't* do great work, why would anyone bother to tell friends and associates about you? Believe us, they won't.

  Years ago, a house painter did a job for Peter's next-door neighbour. The painter did such a great job for such a great price that Peter immediately asked him to paint some rooms in his house. When Peter recommended him to another neighbour, she asked the painter to do some work for her. This went on and on until the painter – who had been completely unknown to anyone in the neighbourhood – had done work for almost everyone on the street.

- ✔ **Do your work on budget and on time.** What are two things that your clients hope they'll never hear from you? That you're going to be late and that the project is going to cost more than you originally estimated. One of the best ways to keep your clients happy and ensure that you're at the top of their list of referrals is to do your work at the price you originally agreed to and on time. But what if you underestimated the price to do a consulting job – shouldn't you try to recover the additional cost? Our advice is – depending on your contract – probably not. When you quote a firm price – and sign an agreement to provide a defined amount of work for that price – then you must honour it, regardless of what the project ultimately costs you to complete. Honouring your commitments builds strong bridges of trust with your clients and, for most consultants, trust is one of the most important things they've got. Of course, few clients will fault you if *they* do something to make you go over cost or deliver your results late and in that case you can pursue remedies according to your contract terms and conditions. But even if they do something that creates a problem for you, do everything you can to keep things on track. You'll be a hero!

✔ **Keep your clients well informed.** When you're working on projects for your clients, you can earn their everlasting and undying affection (and their continued business) by taking the time to keep them informed about your progress and notifying them if you encounter problems or difficulties that require their attention. Indeed, consultants who make a habit of surprising their clients with bad news are consultants who soon find that they have a lot fewer clients than they had the year – or even the month – before.

✔ **Be reliable and dependable.** If anything impresses a client, it's being reliable and dependable. On the flip side of the coin, one of the biggest turn-offs for clients is a consultant who is unreliable and who can't be counted on to do what he or she promised to do. If you promise your clients that you're going to do something, then they expect you to do it – nothing less and nothing more. Believe us: There is a very real shortage in this world of consultants who do what they say they'll do – who meet their deadlines at the high level of quality and price that they promised they would. If you're reliable and dependable, you'll have more business – and more referrals – than you can imagine. However, if you aren't, you'll have plenty of spare time on your hands to do other things (maybe look for a new way to make money, for a start!).

✔ **Be flexible.** In any business, change is usually the rule and not the exception – especially in these days of fast-changing global markets, and even faster-changing telecommunications and computing technology. It seems that if you're not changing, you're not going anywhere – and you probably aren't. The best consultants are able to quickly adapt their approaches, schedules, and project staffing when required to meet their clients' needs. As a result, not only do they earn their clients' gratitude, but also their ongoing business – and their referrals.

✔ **Be liked.** People like to do business with people they like. If two consultants perform equally but one has built more rapport with and is liked by the client, guess which one wins? Devote enough time (but not so much as to interfere with your work and theirs) to building rapport with all of your clients at all levels.

✔ **Thank your clients for their referrals.** Be sure to thank your clients whenever they refer you to a prospective client – whether or not you end up doing business with the prospect. This gesture of gratitude demonstrates to your clients that you've taken note of their assistance on your behalf, and that you appreciate it. This reinforcement makes them more likely to refer again.

Your good work sets the stage for more work with the same clients and for your clients to refer others to you. When you do good work, your clients will want to tell others about you. When you do bad work, your clients will be sure that others know about that, too. Do everything you can to keep your current clients happy with the work you do for them, and you'll be a very busy consultant indeed.

How to Get Referrals

You can either wait for your associates and acquaintances to refer new clients to you, or you can actively seek them. In our humble opinion, it's always best to actively seek them. Referrals are a great thing for any business to have because they are much easier to sell to and cost less to obtain. You can increase the number and quality of your referrals by pursuing them through a variety of different techniques.

The following sections describe a few different approaches for you to try in your quest for new clients.

Use the direct approach

In life and in business, the direct approach is often the best approach. Why beat around the bush when you can ask your clients and acquaintances directly to send you referrals? How? Simply tell your clients that you would like them to refer any of their acquaintances and business associates to you if they need services of the sort that you offer, and that you would be grateful for their assistance. You can do this in person or by telephone, letter, email, or fax. Figure 14-1 presents an example of a letter soliciting referrals from a client directly. Remember: If you're doing good work for them, most of your clients will be very happy (and perhaps even honoured) to refer others to you.

Keep in touch with your clients

How does the old saying go? Out of sight, out of mind? Everyone today is incredibly busy, doing more with less and doing it more quickly and with less time to think about it than ever. If you don't keep in touch with your clients, your clients will soon forget you as they turn their attention to the crisis of the day. Every salesperson worth his or her salt knows that keeping in touch with clients – both old and new – is a key approach for generating future sales. When you're between jobs with your clients, drop by their offices to say hello every once in a while, or send them a note, a newspaper or magazine cutting, or a link to a story or website on the Internet that they may find interesting. By keeping in touch with your clients, you are the first consultant they think of to refer to a colleague who needs help with a problem or opportunity.

October 25, 2009

Ms. Sara Blanc
Blanc & Associates
5 Howard Road
London, SW1

Dear Sara:

I'm pleased to let you know that we successfully completed the redesign of the aqueduct, and we finished the project a week early. I have you to thank for helping us cut through wads of red tape, and I am personally very proud of the partnership that we developed during the course of the project.

I look forward to our next project. Until then, if you know people who need the services of a good civil engineering consultant, I hope you'll send them my way. I'll be sure to make sure that they get the best service possible for the best price possible.

Thanks again for your help.

Best wishes,

Jane Bennett

Figure 14-1:
A sample letter soliciting referrals.

Reward your clients for referrals

Think for a moment how you feel when someone takes the time out of their busy day to thank you for doing something to help them – makes you feel good, doesn't it? Now, imagine how your clients feel when you take time out of your busy day to thank them for something they've done. Guess what? It makes them feel good, too. Always reward your clients when they refer business to you. The reward you select depends on the kind of consulting you do; it can range from a simple thank-you note – handwritten or delivered via email, to a gift basket or bottle of their favourite beverage, all the way to commission based on a percentage of the fee that the referral pays you. At a minimum, call your client and thank him or her personally. As an extra show of thanks, you can send a gift of nominal value – say, a coffee mug with your name and telephone number printed on it, or a nice flower arrangement – or you can allow your client a discount on your next job.

In some cases – especially for a particularly valuable referral – you may want to pay your client a fee for finding you the work (a flat amount) or commission (an amount that varies depending on the size of the fee that you charge the client) for his or her consideration. If you decide to pay a referral fee, be sure that you're not violating your client's company policies or the law by doing so. In some cases – for example, if your client is a government body – the fee may be considered a bribe or an inducement, and that's the last thing you want to get wrapped up in. In such cases, a simple thank-you note may be the best – and safest – approach for all concerned.

Build a contact database

How many different clients and potential clients do you meet every year? 15? 150? 1,500? The problem is, after you've met more than a few people, forgetting the personal details about each one is easy. This is where a contact database earns its weight in gold over and over again. After you set it up, you can target your referral efforts at specific clients with great precision. At a minimum, your contact database must include your contact's name and title, company name and address, telephone and fax numbers, business needs, personal interests, and any other information that you believe will help you in your efforts. While you can build such a database yourself relatively easily using programs such as Microsoft Excel, there are many terrific customer relationship management (CRM) software programs available today. Do an online search for the latest-and-greatest CRM packages, and be sure to check out our discussion of CRM software in Chapter 15.

Make referrals yourself

Here's an important lesson that can help you both in business and in your everyday life: What goes around comes around. This is the idea of *karma* – that a person's deeds actively create their past, present and future experiences. What does this digression into Hindu and Buddhist philosophy have to do with getting referrals? A lot. Just as you hope that your clients will refer you to *their* associates, you can refer your clients to *your* associates. Say you're a travel consultant and are doing work for an accounting firm. If an acquaintance tells you that he is looking for a good accountant, then it only makes sense to refer your acquaintance to the accounting firm for which you're doing work – assuming, of course, that it is a quality firm. Of course, the accounting firm will be grateful for the referrals that you make to them, and they'll most likely make even more referrals of their clients to your own firm. It's really quite simple: The more referrals you make, the more referrals you receive.

Following Up on the Referral

After you receive a referral, you need to follow up on it to determine whether you have a qualified prospect or just a dead end. Leads are a bit like a loaf of bread sitting on your kitchen shelf. The longer your leads sit on a shelf – while you take no action to follow up on them – the more stale they become. Eventually, when they start to grow green hair and smell bad, you have to throw them in the dustbin.

Referrals are an important part of your new business and your future. Do the following to ensure that you have plenty of referrals for months and years to come:

- ✔ **Follow up your referrals immediately.** Whenever you get a referral from a client, friend, or acquaintance, be sure to follow up immediately. Get on the telephone and return the call – do it now! Nothing is more embarrassing to a client who has made a referral than to hear that you never returned the call or responded to the message. You can bet that that client won't bother making any more referrals to you!

 When you contact the referral, provide a brief summary of what you offer and then press for a face-to-face meeting to define the problem. Respect your referrals and your clients by responding to referrals quickly. Even if you can't help, you at least leave the door open for future referrals from your clients and also for future business with the referral you couldn't help out at this time.

✔ **Follow up with your clients.** Keep your clients in the loop about how the work with their referrals is going. They'll appreciate the update, and the communication helps to remind them that you're ready, willing, and available for additional assignments.

Try an approach like this:

> You: I just wanted to thank you for sending me the referral for Text 3000 Ltd – I landed an interesting deal with them as a result.

> Client: We're pleased with the work you do for us so I was delighted to recommend you. I know quite a few people who are crying out for your type of expertise – watch this space.

> You: That would be great. I always have room to accommodate a few more valued clients like you. I'll make sure that we do a good job for them.

Chapter 15

Building Business with New Clients

. . . .

. . . .

*A*ttracting potential clients to your business is a definite must if you expect to sell them your product or service. (Chapter 13 details the kinds of things that you need to do to bring potential clients to your door.) Now that they're at your door – or on the phone, or in your email inbox – what do you do next?

The next step is to convince your clients that they need to do business with your consulting firm. Or rather, that they've got a problem that needs to be solved, and you – and perhaps only you – can best help them with their needs. So much so that your business has the clear edge over all your competitors.

In this chapter, we explore exactly what you need to do after you get the attention of prospective clients. We tell you about the importance of the personal introduction and the significance of quickly establishing good rapport and a strong basis of trust and goodwill. We walk you through the process of making a pitch to your clients and then following up – and we talk about the importance of keeping your commitments.

The Personal Introduction

In many ways, the personal introduction of a prospective client to your business is one of the most critical points in the process of selling your services. Blow it here, and you probably won't have to worry about seeing that client again. However, if you make the right impression, you have a client for life.

We know that you're not necessarily in business to make friends. You're in business to make money. But you have to remember that business involves much more than just pounds and pence (or dollars, euros, or whatever your monetary persuasion). Consulting is first and foremost a social activity, and it is built on a foundation of one-to-one relationships.

In the sections that follow, we consider the things that go into this most important beginning phase of your consulting relationships: the personal introduction.

Make a good first impression!

The first experience that a potential client has with your consulting business may be anything from leaving a message on your voicemail, to visiting your website, to meeting you personally through a mutual acquaintance. We can't emphasise enough the importance of a potential client's first experience with your business – in many cases, it may be your only opportunity to impress on that client the benefits of working with your organisation. Consider these two scenarios:

- ✔ **Scenario A:** The client of your dreams calls the freephone number listed on your website. The creaky, old answering machine in your home-based office picks up, 'Hi, this is the Acme Consulting Group. Sorry, we can't take your call right now, but leave a message and we'll get back to you as soon as we can.' The client of your dreams leaves a brief message expressing his urgent need and asks you to return the call as soon as possible. Unfortunately, you're halfway across the country at the time, working with another client, and you don't get the call until you return home several days later. When you finally return the call, the client of your dreams has already found someone who can meet his urgent schedule.

- ✔ **Scenario B:** One of your best current clients refers the client of your dreams to you. When the prospective client drops by your office unannounced, she is warmly greeted by your receptionist – who offers a cup of coffee or a soft drink – and is steered to the waiting area while you're paged. Because you always have time to meet a new client, you drop everything and come out to the waiting area to greet her. After you take her on a brief tour of the architectural models of some of your most involved and successful projects and then review her needs and make a rough pricing estimate, your new client asks how soon you can start.

What kind of initial impression does *your* organisation make with your clients?

There's never been a valid excuse for sloppy service – and there still isn't one today. What's more, in these days of email-enabled mobile phones, and Blackberrys, you have less of an excuse than ever before to be hard to reach – even if you're a one-person organisation. If you can't get your introduction right, why should a client trust you to get anything right?

If you want a quick reality check on the first impressions that your organisation is making with your clients, pretend that you're a new client and do the following:

- ✔ **Call your business phone number and see what happens.** Does someone answer the phone on the first few rings, or does it take longer? Is the initial greeting upbeat and cheery, or is it the kind of greeting that makes you feel like the receptionist would rather be doing something – anything – other than taking the call? If the receptionist is out, does another employee pick up the phone quickly and courteously? Do you end up in voicemail hell with no chance of escape?

- ✔ **Take a close look at your facilities.** If you're a freelance advertising copywriter, your clients may not be surprised (or disappointed) to visit an office that is located in a spare bedroom of your home. However, if you're a tax accountant, your clients may prefer to see that you have a real office in a real office building with a real employee or two – indicating that your practice is financially stable and viable.

- ✔ **Take a close look at your marketing materials and work output.** Does your website look professional and modern, or does it look like something your 9-year-old child put together for you? Are your company brochures and other marketing materials of high quality? Are your letters and work samples laser-printed on high-quality paper? Would *you* pay your hard-earned money for your products?

- ✔ **Take a close look at yourself.** It probably goes without saying that you need to be well groomed and dressed appropriately for the kind of consulting you do. Although your clients may expect their investment advisers to wear pin-striped suits, the same clients might accept their design consultants being dressed more casually or even flamboyantly.

Seriously consider the answers to these questions and then make any changes necessary to ensure that all your clients and prospective clients have a positive first impression of you and your organisation. Don't forget: You have only one chance to make a first impression!

Ask and listen

The best professional salespeople know that their primary responsibility is to help potential clients find the best solutions to their needs. This means asking questions and then listening – really listening – to the answers.

In their book *Selling For Dummies* (published by Wiley), master salespeople Tom Hopkins and Ben Kench present a very useful rule:

> *Listen twice as much as you talk and you'll succeed in persuading others nearly every time.*

Think about why this is true:

- ✔ *Everyone* **likes to be listened to.** Not only does listening show respect, but it also makes the speaker feel important. However, good listening skills go way beyond simply stroking a client's ego.

- ✔ **Good listening helps you do your job better.** Why? Because when you listen, you hear exactly what your clients want, and you can respond with the exact answers that your clients need.

The simple fact is that you can't possibly understand what your potential clients need unless you give them the opportunity to tell you. And you can't possibly hear what your client is telling you unless you take the time to listen! To make sure that you both ask clients the right questions and listen to their answers, we have developed the following four steps to effective asking and listening:

1. **Ask open-ended questions that define the boundaries of the opportunity.**
   When you first meet potential clients, you really have no idea what their needs are, how extensive those needs are, and what addressing them will require. Therefore, your first task is to ask the kinds of open-ended questions that help you define the big picture, the rough boundaries of their opportunities, and thereby the rough boundaries of your solutions. For example, you might ask, 'What results do you want to see from this management training?' or 'Exactly what would you like our firm to do for you?'

   Avoid asking questions that can introduce an element of trepidation into your relationship. Questions along the lines of, 'Do you realise how incredibly expensive it's going to be to straighten out this mess?' or 'Who's responsible for designing this mess?' are to be avoided at all costs.

2. **Use active silence.** When it comes to listening, silence is golden – not the disinterested silence that comes from having more pressing matters on your mind, but the active silence that tells your clients that you're involved in what they have to say and are interested in, thinking about, and putting your all into understanding their issues and perspectives.

When your clients appear to have ended a thought and seem ready for you to respond, first prod them to give you deeper understanding with a nod of the head or by saying 'Go on' or asking 'Is there more?' before you launch into your side of the discussion.

3. **Ask clarifying questions.** Clarifying questions take you from the big picture to the little picture and help you to refine your understanding of your clients' opportunities. For example, asking, 'Do you want a full review of your entire quality assurance system, or do you think that a random sampling of products might accomplish the same goal?' is a good way to help define the extent of the effort required to accomplish a task.

4. **Confirm your understanding.** An important part of the process of asking questions and listening to their answers is periodically confirming your understanding with your clients. For example, you can say, 'Now here's what I'm hearing that you would like me to do . . .' or 'Correct me if I'm wrong, but I believe that what you would like me to do is to create a website for your firm that illustrates and explains all your products and then to keep it updated on a regular basis – am I right?'

Never forget to listen before you leap! You'll have plenty of time for talking after you land your client. For now, content yourself with asking a few questions to help draw your client out, and listen, listen, and listen some more.

Tell them about yourself

Your clients want the best service that their money can buy. Your job is to give it to them. However, before you get the opportunity to do so, you have to prove that you've got the right stuff. And just how can you do that? Here are a few ideas to get things rolling. You don't want to overwhelm your potential clients at this point in the process – you just want to set the stage for your relationship.

- ✔ **Related experience:** Of the firms you've worked with, whose needs were most like those of your prospective client? How large or small were the firms, and what was your part in the project's success? Why will this experience help you deal with your prospective client's needs?

- ✔ **Personal credentials:** What are your personal credentials for doing the job that your client needs to get done? What firms have you worked for and with? What college and professional degrees do you have? What major projects have you been personally responsible for, and what are the quantifiable measures of their success?

✔ **Company credentials:** Who are the key clients of your business? What do you do for them, and how long have they been associated with your company? What are some of your business's most prominent successes, and what was your role in making things happen? Keep your descriptions brief and relevant to your clients and avoid droning on about your career – keep an eye on their reactions as you describe yourself and your experience.

Building Relationships with Prospective Clients

Because of the nature of person-to-person interactions, every consulting relationship involves a certain amount of chemistry. If the chemistry is good, a consulting relationship can be long lasting and beneficial to all. If the chemistry is bad – like a lab experiment at school careering out of control – you can count the length of the relationship in nanoseconds instead of years.

Consulting relationships are built on trust and on an honest desire to help clients to succeed. Sure, every consultant has something to sell, whether it's dragging a company kicking and screaming through a long-range planning process, conveying a lifetime of expertise in finding underground oil deposits, or setting up a company's website. But the best consulting relationships are based on wanting to share your unique skills and expertise to help someone who needs them.

In this section, we consider some techniques to help you establish good relationships with your potential clients. We discuss how to build rapport with your prospective clients, get your clients what they need, and build a firm foundation of trust to carry your relationship forward into the future.

Establishing rapport

Before you enter into a business relationship with prospective clients, you have to establish some degree of rapport with them. *Rapport* is the connectedness that individuals in a relationship feel for one another. Rapport comes from shared experiences. A shared experience can be as simple as a shared joke or as complex as a common lifelong interest. In some cases, a relationship is established between people instantly; in other cases, a relationship never really blooms. If rapport doesn't develop between the parties of a relationship, you can bet that the relationship won't last.

Here are the basics of building rapport with prospective clients:

✔ **Be friendly.** Everyone likes people who are friendly and who seem genuinely interested in them. When you take the first step to reach out to someone, they're likely to reach back.

✔ **Assess your client's personality.** Does your client want to chat and socialise for a bit before getting down to business, or does he or she want to skip all that and keep business at the very top of the agenda? If your client is oriented towards socialising first, allow plenty of time for getting to know one another before getting down to business. However, if your client is the kind of person who wants to forego social pleasantries and get right to business, do that.

✔ **Find something in common with your client.** Do you share a common interest or hobby with your client – perhaps fishing, playing Bach fugues on the harpsichord, or collecting beer mats? Common interests can break the ice between you and a client faster than a Russian icebreaker at 30 knots. You never know until you ask, so ask!

✔ **Be sincere and down to earth.** Don't try to pretend to be someone you're not. Just relax, be sincere, and, above all, be yourself.

Helping them get what they want

Helping your clients get what they want is really your number one job, and you have to be particularly vigilant to avoid letting *your* needs take priority over *theirs*. It's not uncommon for a consulting business to develop certain assessment or training tools or products and to then feel a lot of pressure to make clients fit these tools or products – even if it means pushing the clients into a box that really isn't their shape or size.

For example, a firm that conducts long-range planning sessions with the top management teams of private sector corporations may have developed an assessment model that works great for them, but if a local not-for-profit agency asks for help in its long-range planning, the same assessment model may make no sense at all because the fundamental nature of the organisation is quite different. It may make perfect sense from the consulting practice's cost perspective to use the same model (why spend the money to adapt the assessment tools for a one-off project, after all?) but not from the perspective of getting the best results. In a case like this, if the consultant is unwilling to take the time or spend the money to tailor its approach to the needs of the client, it would really be better for all concerned to refer the work to someone else.

Some consultants allow their egos to get in the way of building relationships with clients. If you see that ego is starting to get in the way – either with you or with an associate – step back for a moment and take a close look at what your clients really need. Then push that big bad ego out of the way, if only for a few moments, to determine whether what you're offering is really what your clients need. If it is, great – you're on the right track. If it's not, go back to the drawing board and come up with an approach that does meet your clients' needs.

On the flip side of this coin, you may need to tell your clients things that they just don't want to hear but that reflect the truth of a situation. For example, while speaking with your client about a problem he's having with the response rate for direct-mail advertising, you may quickly realise that the problem is the poor quality of the advertising piece that the client's firm is sending out. Ask him if he would like your feedback on what the cause may be. If he says yes, then give your honest opinion. Even if your client disagrees vigorously (after all, he created the ad personally and knows what works and what doesn't) he asked you for your opinion and you told him what you thought. To do any less would be to do a disservice both to you and to your client. A good consulting relationship is built on trust, and part of building trust is being honest with your clients – even if occasionally the truth hurts.

Building a foundation of trust

Although many things go into making a good consulting relationship, trust is probably the most important factor of all. Trust is the glue that holds a relationship together. Without it, a relationship quickly falls apart – crumbling into little bits and pieces before your very eyes.

So how do you build trust in a consulting relationship? At this early phase of the consulting relationship, doing the kinds of things that set the stage for the development of a strong, long-term relationship is most important. Here are some quick and easy ways to build trust with your clients:

- **Make commitments – and keep them.** One of the easiest ways to build trust in a relationship is to make commitments and then keep them. If, for example, you tell a client that you will be available at 3:00 p.m. on Wednesday for a conference call, then, when you're ready and waiting for the call at 3:00 on Wednesday, you're sending a message to your client that you can be relied on. Whether the commitments that you keep are big or small, they add up to increased trust. Make commitments and then keep them.

- **Give your honest opinion.** If your clients have a problem, tell them that they have a problem. Sometimes you may be tempted to sugar-coat problems in the hopes that your clients will find them easier to swallow. However, this tactic can backfire when your clients finally realise (and most eventually *will* realise) the full extent of their problems and wonder why you kept them in the dark. Trust is built on honesty. Be honest with your clients at all times.

✔ **Keep secrets.** When you're hired as a consultant, you may have access to some of the organisation's most important information and secrets. Never disclose this confidential information outside your business or outside the circle of individuals with whom the client decides you need to work. Not only can leaking confidential information destroy the trust you've worked so hard to build, but it can also expose you to an expensive lawsuit. If you keep secrets secret, you prove your trustworthiness every day.

✔ **Do great work.** When you do a great job for your clients, you demonstrate that you value their work and their organisations and that you can be trusted with taking on even more important responsibilities in the future. Do great work, and the trust that you've established with your clients continues to build.

Using software to manage your customer relationships

A *customer relationship management* system (CRM) is a computerised database that tracks information about customers. Years ago, important customer information – names, addresses, phone numbers, and so on – was filed away on index cards, or on sheets of paper stapled into file folders. No longer. Today there are loads of computer-based systems available that allow you to quickly and easily capture, store, and analyse customer information.

What can a good CRM software package do for your company? Plenty. Here's a list of the functions you find in a typical CRM system:

✔ Company and contact management

✔ Lead management

✔ Activity management

✔ Opportunity management

✔ Charting

✔ Reporting

✔ Email marketing and mailing lists management

✔ Sales forecasting

✔ Microsoft Outlook email integration

✔ Notes

✔ Business Intelligence management

✔ Diary reminders

As your consulting business grows, a good CRM system can be a real asset. Standard packages are really not that expensive. Choosing the right CRM software is a critical decision for your business and it's important to take your time when researching the right product for you. Ask your colleagues or industry contacts what system they use, or read the reviews on the Internet. Finally, when you select a system and implement it, monitor the results closely to make sure it's doing exactly what it's supposed to do. Philip's company installed CRM right from day one and he swears by it as a tool not just to support sales and marketing but also to provide professional client service on an ongoing basis.

Meeting Clients

It's very likely that your first contact with a potential client will not be in person but will be by phone, email, letter, or other mode of communication. However, after you get past the initial introductions and find a clearly mutual interest in proceeding, you have to take the relationship to the next step, which usually means a face-to-face meeting. Don't get us wrong – we're not saying that you have to drive 300 miles across the country for a meeting whenever a prospect calls. In fact, we have all established relationships and done business with clients without first meeting them in person.

Your decision to meet face to face with a client depends on many factors. But, as we have said before, consulting is a people thing. Although you can establish and carry on a long-distance business relationship with your phone company or with a mail-order bookseller for years without a face-to-face meeting, consulting is a different animal.

Whether to meet in person, or not

The world is a big place. We understand that the potential rewards of a business relationship don't always justify the expense of setting up a one-to-one meeting. And we also understand that the Internet, email, voicemail, mobile phones, and all those other nifty technologies make it easier than ever to communicate with anyone you want, anytime you want. But despite all these great innovations, nothing can replace the power of a face-to-face meeting.

The question is not _whether_ to meet with a prospective client. The question is: Do the benefits of meeting outweigh the costs? For example, it may make sense to drive 300 miles across the country to meet a client who could pay you £25,000 to do a job – with the promise of more work to come if the project is a success. However, it may not make sense to drive 300 miles across the country to meet a client whose job is a one-off deal for just £400. When you consider your options, take the time to weigh the potential benefits of a face-to-face meeting against the costs.

Tips for successful face-to-face meetings

Personal face-to-face meetings can be a particularly effective way to sell yourself – and your consulting business. However, to take full advantage of the benefits of face-to-face meetings, you've got to be sure you're meeting the right person, you're meeting at the right place, and you've picked the best time to meet. Here are some tips to help you make your face-to-face meetings all they can be.

Who to meet?

It's quite simple – the best person to meet is the one who can decide whether or not to hire you or your firm. Why? Because if you're dealing with anyone else, you may be wasting your time. However, the next best thing to meeting the person who can make the decision is to meet the people who can favourably influence the person who makes the decision.

Who are some of the people you need to meet? Before you schedule your next meeting with your prospective clients, make sure you see how they stack up according to the following list:

- **The boss:** Whether this person owns the company or is a top executive or manager, this man or woman usually has responsibility for a budget and the authority to hire you. Not only that but, after you're hired, this person can clear a path through the organisation's obstacles for you, making it much easier to get your job done.

- **The personal assistant:** Because they've earned the trust of their bosses, personal assistants wield tremendous power in their organisations. If you can't get to the boss, his or her personal assistant is definitely a close second in priority.

- **The specialist manager:** Often bosses delegate the task of getting specialist help to the manager of the relevant function, so if the payroll is causing a problem, guess who gets the task of briefing consultants? That's right, the payroll manager. As the key user of your service he or she can be a good place to start. Two points though: Firstly, be sure not to compete with his or her expertise (telling the payroll manager that the payroll department is in a mess is not a good opening gambit!) and secondly, be sure you're not wasting your time by giving free advice.

So how do you get to the right person or group in an organisation? After you select your target, simply pick up the phone and call. In our experience, you save a lot of time and money by sidestepping staff and using your phone to go directly to the person or group in charge. Email is also a great tool for getting to the right person. We have found that, in many cases, a person who won't return a phone call for days or weeks (or ever!) will reply to an email in minutes. You may have to spend a little time with the receptionist or other employees in doing some research on who's who in the organisation, but, after you find out, be deliberate and assertive in your efforts to contact the right people.

Where to meet?

You have the option of meeting at your place, the client's place, or somewhere in between. The selection depends greatly on the nature of your business, on whether you're travelling a great distance for the meeting, and on your client's time constraints. Consider the pluses and minuses of each option.

- ✔ **Your place:** Meeting at your place may make the most sense if you have a nice place to meet. Another reason to do so is that your business may require you to demonstrate a product that is not easy to carry around. For example, a firm that provides customised computer hardware and software solutions on large office servers and networks may have a difficult time lugging the appropriate equipment to a client's site for a demonstration. In such cases, bringing the client to your site, where the equipment is already installed, configured, and up and running, makes more sense.

- ✔ **Their place:** This is often the preferred choice – especially if your prospective client is too busy to get away from the office or if you need to meet more than one or two people at a time. The advantages are that your clients are on their own turf, and they are probably more comfortable meeting you there than in an unfamiliar setting. The disadvantages may be that they answer the phone every time it rings or they spend time chatting with everyone who walks through the door.

- ✔ **In between:** Think of a favourite restaurant for lunch or dinner. The location is neutral, and you get the opportunity to get away from the moment-to-moment demands of a busy office.

Most busy clients prefer for you to meet them at their office. So where you meet a particular client really depends on whether you can effectively demonstrate a solution to your client's problem at his or her site and whether the cost of getting to your customer does not exceed the expected financial benefits of doing business. When in doubt, err on the side of going out of your way to meet your client at the place of his or her choosing.

When to meet?

Should you try to set up a meeting as soon as possible, or should you take things at a slower pace? Although some people say that good things come to those who wait, this is not necessarily the case with consulting. The truth is that consulting is a very competitive field, and the more appropriate adage is: 'The early bird catches the worm.'

When you press for immediate meetings with prospective clients, you not only impress them with your obvious interest in meeting their needs, but you also help to ensure that your firm is selected before other consultants have an opportunity to get their foot in the door.

So what is the correct answer to the question of when to meet? 'Now!' Not enough time or not enough notice to meet today? Then set up a meeting for first thing tomorrow. The point is, the sooner you get your meeting scheduled, the better chance you have of getting the business.

Follow Through Is Everything!

Despite successfully making it through all the hurdles of getting to know new clients and winning their trust and confidence, many consultants ultimately lose their contracts when they fail to follow through with their clients. Though you may prefer to think of consulting as the art of performing the services in which you're expert, the one thing that makes the world of consulting go round is ultimately your ability to sell yourself to the people and organisations who can afford to pay your bills.

If you can't sell yourself, you can't sell your services. It's that simple.

After you make your sales pitch, the next step is to set up a system of follow-through with your prospective client. As a consultant, you find that many of your prospects are very busy people, and it is easy for them to lose your proposal amongst all the other priorities that they are charged with juggling. The purpose of follow-through is to keep your proposal fresh in your client's mind and make sure that he or she doesn't forget about you.

However, don't forget the number-one rule of following up with your clients: Don't be a pest. Proper follow-through walks a fine line between an occasional reminder that keeps your name in mind and irritating pressure that makes you more trouble than you're worth. Be sensitive to the needs of your clients when you decide on your follow-through strategy. Although every situation is different, you can't go wrong by applying the follow-through techniques presented in this section.

Setting a date for the next step

What is the next step in selling yourself to your client? Another meeting? A technical demonstration? Emailing a copy of an article that you authored? A phone call to check to see whether you're going to be selected to do the proposed job? Until you land your consulting contract, make sure that you always decide on what step is required next to get you closer to your goal, and set a date and time for its completion.

Whatever the next step is, no matter how trivial, make a note of it in your diary. If the event is set for a definite time, make sure that you make a point of recording the time, too. The point is, you don't want to take the chance of forgetting what you need to do to land your consulting contract. Two of the key tests that you have to pass for your clients are punctuality and reliability. If you say that you'll call to follow up at 9:00 a.m. on 30 September, then you'd better be dialling the number at 8:59 a.m. on 30 September.

Sending a thank-you note

A thank-you note can do wonders to get you planted squarely in the middle of your client's good graces. Just as a post-interview thank-you letter makes a positive impression on a company that is hiring a new employee, a sincere thank-you note makes a positive impression on the individuals who decide whether you get a contract for your services.

Writing good thank-you notes is an art. They need to be sincere and from your heart, and they should leave the reader with a positive impression of both you and your business. Whenever you write a thank-you note, make sure that it does the following three things:

- Personally thanks your client for his or her time and interest
- Firmly expresses your interest in doing the proposed work for your client
- Includes any additional information that the client may need to make a decision in your favour

So when should you take the time to thank a potential client? Consider sending a thank-you note whenever you find yourself in the following situations:

- **You want to thank a client for agreeing to meet you at some future time.** This thank-you note also serves to confirm the date and time of your meeting.

- **You want to thank a client for having taken time to meet you.** Not only do you get to express your sincere thanks to your client, but you also get to reiterate the many compelling reasons for selecting you or your consulting business.

- **You want to thank a client for the business.** After you're hired, a thank-you letter expressing your gratitude is certainly in order.

Your note can be sent via email, or posted. You don't have to write a book – all it takes is jotting down a couple of sincere sentences of thanks and then dropping your note in the post. When in doubt, send it out! And don't delay: A thank-you email the same day or a letter the next day will impress your client far more than one arriving a week or months later.

Following up via phone, email, or letter

The medium that you select to follow up with your clients is not as important as making sure that you do follow up. Each possible way of following up with clients has its pluses and minuses, and which one you choose depends on your style of doing business and on what seems to work best with a particular client. You always have the flexibility of selecting one method or a combination of methods of follow-up. Ultimately, the decision is up to you.

Consider the advantages and disadvantages of several media for client follow-up:

- **Phone:** The most personal form of follow-up besides a face-to-face meeting is a personal phone call. When you phone your clients, you demonstrate that their business is important to you and that you're very interested in winning it. On the plus side, you can make a phone call from anywhere, most any time you like. On the minus side, playing 'phone tag' over a prolonged period of time or getting lost in voicemail hell is certainly not unheard of.

- **Electronic mail:** Computer email is a bit less personal than either a letter or a phone call, but, when used properly, it can still be quite effective. On the plus side, email offers the ultimate in flexibility and convenience. On the minus side, if you get the address wrong, your message might bounce right back to you undelivered.

- **Letter:** You can easily hand-write or type up a letter any time or any place. Although a personal letter delivered by messenger, by overnight delivery, or by post is the most impressive to potential clients, you can also send it via fax. On the plus side, letters are convenient and effective. On the minus side, letters can get lost in the paper shuffle of busy executives.

However you decide to thank your clients for their time, you need to keep one key rule in mind: Be sure to thank them. Not only do you leave a positive impression in their minds that may help you get the contract, but you'll also be remembered for future opportunities even if you don't do business this time.

Moving On

In the process of selling your services to potential clients, you have to decide which ones have the greatest potential of doing business with you or your firm and which ones have the least potential. Although being able to put your all into pursuing every single lead that you get may be nice, it just isn't realistic from a cost perspective.

Following through with clients takes both time and money – and lots of it. Because both time and money are available in limited amounts for most consultants, the wise thing to do is to split your client list into two categories, active and inactive, and put most of your resources into the former. Consider the differences between active and inactive clients:

- ✔ **Active clients** are the clients who have shown a definite interest in commissioning you or your firm. Because they're the most probable source of future work, they need to get most of your attention. Make sure that you place them on a schedule of regular follow-up communication – phone calls, emails, product brochures and newsletters, and more – from your firm that keeps you and your services in their mind.

- ✔ **Inactive clients** may have once expressed an interest in your business, but your repeated attempts over a prolonged period of time (six months or more, depending on your own criteria) have failed to land a deal. You can downgrade such clients from active to inactive status and also decrease the amount of resources you devote to them. A good way to keep in touch with inactive clients is to add them to the mailing list for your firm's electronic newsletter. For little or no cost, you keep open the possibility of doing business in the future.

In our experience, considering both active clients and inactive clients as potential clients is always wise. You never know when a client who has been inactive for months or even years will suddenly spring to life and want to hire you for an important job. We have seen this happen time and time again. Never burn bridges with your clients. Always build bridges with your clients. After all, in consulting, it's not always what you know, but who you know – and what they think about you – that can make the difference between success and failure.

Part V
Taking Care of Business

'Have you dealt with consultants before,
Mr Mafielli?'

In this part . . .

Despite rumours to the contrary, becoming a consultant isn't quite as easy as simply printing a set of business cards and waiting for clients to come walking through the front door.

Consulting is a business, and there are right ways and wrong ways to set up a consulting practice.

In this part, we talk about the right ways to negotiate contracts, track your time and your money, communicate with clients – and prospective clients – and troubleshoot a variety of common business problems.

Chapter 16

Contracting for Business: It's a Deal!

*W*hy are contracts important to consultants? You'll be consulting in exchange for money and contracts define important things like exactly what you'll do and when you'll do it, how much you'll get paid and when you should be paid. If there's ever any dispute and, heaven forbid, you end up in court, the first thing a judge would want to see is the contract. For these reasons – and many more – every consultant needs to understand contracts.

Getting to Grips with Contracts

What exactly is a contract? A *contract* is nothing more than an agreement between two or more parties to do something (or not do something) in return for something of value – called *consideration* amongst those who make a habit of practising contract law. Contracts can be oral or written and range in size from simple one-page agreements to incredibly complex documents as thick as a telephone book. The details and complexities of a contract depend on the nature of the agreement and often the number of lawyers who are involved in drafting the contract.

In theory and in law, oral or spoken contracts may be just as valid as written contracts. However, in practice we strongly advise you to put everything in writing. Although some consultants run up high fees on the basis of a 'gentleman's handshake', most have learned that in the long run it is far less risky to get agreements set down in writing.

In this section we discuss the essentials of contracting as a consultant and negotiating over the terms of a contract. As a consultant you ignore this topic at your peril. Because every contracting case is different our advice is to seek competent legal advice before entering into any contract.

The key elements of a contract

Every contract must have four key elements and each of these elements has to be in place. Meat Loaf may have sung 'Two out of three ain't bad' but you need four out of four for a contract to exist. These are the elements:

- ✔ **Offer:** An *offer* in consultancy takes the form of a proposal to undertake certain actions for another party (that is, the client) in exchange for a consideration (what's a consideration? – be patient and read on). For example, you can offer to provide a website updating service to your client in return for a monthly fee. To be valid, your offer must be specific and it must contain definite terms. Consultants, including all the big firms, therefore attach *'terms of business'* as an appendix to back up the main proposal.

- ✔ **Acceptance:** You have *acceptance* when the client gives you an unqualified agreement to the terms in your offer. For example, how long you would spend, what you would deliver, for how much, and so on. It is almost always better to get this agreement in writing. In UK consultant-speak we call this an *engagement letter*. However, a client's actions can constitute agreement. For example, say you send a proposal to survey motivation levels in a local firm and there is no disagreement over terms. If the client calls and asks you to run the first focus group that afternoon and then fixes dates for further work, in law these actions can constitute agreement. However, we say again (and again) it's better to get acceptance in writing. Politely ask clients to sign the bottom of your proposal where it says they agree to your day, the work, and terms. But what if the acceptance is not qualified? What if the client writes back and says okay but we want the work done more quickly or for 10 per cent less in fees – where does that leave the contract? The qualified acceptance letter now in effect constitutes another offer. If you ignore the letter but start work anyway you can become bound by those new terms because they postdate yours and through your actions you can be deemed to have accepted them. Lawyers call such events *the battle of the forms*. A common example is where your client sends you a purchase order and it contains different terms to your proposal – if you accept it, then the client's form has won the battle.

✔ **Consideration:** *Consideration* is something of value given in exchange for performance or a promise of performance. Examples of valid consideration include money, goods, services, the promise to do something that there is no legal obligation to do (for example, build a website for a client at some future time), or the promise not to do something that there is a legal right to do (for example, take a client to small claims court for nonpayment of a bill for services rendered). Adequate consideration is generally whatever the two parties agree to, unless there is evidence of fraud or duress.

✔ **Intention to create legal relations:** In business agreements it is generally presumed that the parties intend to establish legal relations. Sometimes you might see the phrase 'subject to contract', which is used primarily to postpone the stage at which legal obligations will arise, but this is rare in consultancy. However social and domestic agreements are not presumed to be intended to have legal effect. In other words if you're consulting for a friend or family member as an individual and not as a business then you need to confirm in your proposal that you intend the contract to have legal effect (that's if you do). The pros and cons of working for family members need to be considered carefully in consulting just as in any other trade or profession!

Terms of Business

We advise you not (ever) to send proposals to your clients without attaching your terms of business (ToBs in the trade). Often for small pieces of work your client will simply accept them and therefore start to do business with you on your own preferred terms. Most consultants attach them as a small print appendix to their proposal. However you want to ensure that the terms you propose are reasonable and that you do not use the small print appendix as an opportunity to tie your client to unreasonable conditions.

When Philip started Techniques for Change he was aware of what terms the large consulting firms included in their proposals so he tried to make his terms slightly more favourable. For example, at the time, some of the larger firms charged a handling fee for expenses and charged for document production. Philip thought this a little unfair so he left these charges out to differentiate his consultancy a little. He then got a solicitor to look his draft document over. You must do this too to avoid any problems – it may cost a little but you'll use your terms of business hundreds of times and they do offer protection. Before giving you his or her advice, the solicitor will more than likely write you a letter and on the back will be his or her firm's terms of business. Seek legal advice but here are some of the points you need to consider including in your ToBs:

- ✔ **The contract.** This states that the contract will be made under these terms and states also what law governs the contracts e.g. English Law.

- ✔ **Fees.** This indicates on what basis fees are quoted and whether and when they can be increased – also included here are payment terms, that is, when and how often you'll invoice and how long your client will have to pay. You can also include a provision for interest in the event of late payment even though you may not enforce this clause.

- ✔ **Expenses and office services.** Define what expenses you'll charge for. Also state what facilities or services you generally expect the client to provide. You need to make it clear what your fee includes or excludes.

- ✔ **Confidentiality.** Gives assurances that you'll maintain strict confidentiality about the client's information but requires similar assurances from the client side to treat your information confidentially too. If there are copyright or intellectual property issues, cover these here too.

- ✔ **Limits of liability.** Most consultants use words to the effect that they undertake to carry out the work to the best of their ability. They point out that statements made and advice given are made in good faith, and on the basis of information available at the time, and statements and advice shall not be deemed in any circumstances to be undertakings, warranties, or contracts. You solicitor can help you to find the right wording for your firm.

- ✔ **Consultant recruitment.** This restricts the client seeking to recruit one of your employees or sub-contractors.

- ✔ **Termination.** This sets out under what terms the contract can be cancelled or your work can be postponed.

Avoid oral contracts

Most people are involved in an incredibly wide variety of transactions every day – both business and personal – that are conducted on the basis of oral, or verbal, agreements. The counter person at the sandwich shop down the street says that he'll make you the best ham and cheese sandwich you've ever had if you'll pay him £3 for it. You agree. He makes the sandwich, you pay him the money, and you're on your way. Think about all the other agreements that you enter into on an oral basis each and every day of your life.

In many cases, a court of law may consider an oral contract to be just as binding as a written contract. However, this doesn't mean that oral contracts are as good for your business as written contracts. Despite their ease of use, oral agreements often have a number of problems:

✔ **People forget.** Although your oral agreement may be very clear and precise at the moment you agree to it, either or both parties may soon forget the exact terms. And, even if they don't forget, whenever you've got two or more people involved it's easy for misunderstandings to occur.

For example, Peter once hired a landscaper to fell four trees at his home. As they walked around the garden, Peter pointed out exactly which trees he wanted felled, and then left for the office. When Peter returned, he was shocked to find out that his landscaper had cut down one of his favourite trees – three were right and one was wrong. A written agreement along with a detailed map of the garden might have saved this particular tree's life.

✔ **People go away.** Sometimes people get sick or die, and the terms of any oral agreements that they were party to can go away with them. You've seen how hard it can be to sort out a business disagreement when there are written contracts and agreements to guide the parties. Well, imagine how difficult it is trying to figure out who owes what to who when one of the parties isn't there to give his or her side of the story. Unfortunately, enforcing an agreement can be very difficult when there is no proof or evidence that it exists.

✔ **Complexity can lead to confusion.** If an agreement goes very far beyond the simplest terms and conditions such as who, what, when, and for how much, the complexity of the contract grows quickly. As the complexity of your contract grows, so too does the potential for confusion and mis-understandings. Clearly, oral contracts are inadequate for dealing with complex terms and conditions.

✔ **You just might end up in court some day.** You never know. You can be going along for years doing jobs simply on the word of your clients and a handshake when, suddenly – bang! – a client refuses to pay for a project that you toiled many long hours over. Now, if it's a £100 job, no big deal – you're probably not going to lose your business over it. But if it's a £3,000 job, or a £30,000 job, then you have a problem – a problem that can potentially put you out of business. Though most people never plan to end up in court, some do. And if you do, an oral contract is much more difficult to prove to a judge and enforce than a written contract.

Conducting business based on oral contracts is simply too risky. So here's our advice – don't!

Clients' contracts

For larger pieces of consultancy with larger client organisations they might send you one of *their* contracts. Think about how you would write yours and consider how they may write theirs. Exactly, you've got it: they'll write their contract to suit themselves. What you need to then decide is, do their terms suit you? The contract they send you will vary from a simple purchase order to a long contract containing scary terms like 'warranties' or 'force majeure', or intimidating clauses like 'hereby grant xyz plc a perpetual and worldwide licence' or 'no damages will be too great'. Firstly read the contract very very carefully and seek advice from a competent solicitor who understands business service contracts. Secondly, consider your two options:

- ✔ **Option 1:** If the terms aren't too bad and you can live with them then you can accept them. This makes it easy for the client to do business with you. Be careful though not to kid yourself because if the contract turns out to be a long one then you really do need to be able to live with the terms. For example, if the contract provides for 60-day payment and this would create huge cash flow issues for you, consider your position carefully.

- ✔ **Option 2:** Negotiate changes to their terms. Bear in mind that in most large organisations it may not be easy for a client to agree to changes. Whereas a smaller firm's owner or MD is empowered to accept certain terms of business, a middle manager or even very senior manager in a large organisation may not be. So if you're requesting a change, be aware that it can create a problem for the client and possibly delay the start date. The next section gives advice on negotiating terms but if you only want to change a few smaller items do suggest specific amendments and type them in red on a new contract version.

Legal and procurement departments will often agree to contract variations if you send them the specific wording you want instead of theirs. For example, if you wish to change 60-day payment terms to 30 days, send them either an electronic version with your text in red or a covering letter stating which text needs to be deleted and what you wish to replace it with.

The ABCs of Contract Negotiation

What would a chapter about contracts be without a discussion of how to negotiate them? It would simply be a chapter on contracts! Although it would be nice if all your clients would just accept everything that you propose (okay, we know – that would truly be a fantasy world), there comes a time in every consultant's career where you're required to negotiate terms and conditions with your clients. Don't worry, as you'll soon see, anyone can become a better negotiator – it just takes being prepared, and applying some easily learned skills and techniques.

Without a doubt, each one of us negotiates every day for a wide variety of reasons and purposes. *I don't think I can make a 3:00 meeting – how about 4:30? £35 to do an oil change for my car seems too high – make it £25 and you've got a deal. There's no way that I can do everything that you want for only £25,000. Now, if you can raise it to £35,000, I think we may be in the ballpark. I said, you need to be in bed by 8:00 tonight – no ifs, ands, or buts! Okay – you can stay up until 9:00, but that's it!* In fact, it may not be exaggerating to say that life is one long series of negotiations.

As you may have noticed, there is no shortage of books available on the topic of negotiating. In this section, we distill the wisdom and tips gleaned from literally thousands of years of human negotiating experience into a concise package that fits neatly into your pocket. Well, it fits if you tear this section out and fold it a couple of times before you try to stick it in your pocket.

Anticipating the negotiation

No matter how simple a negotiation seems on the surface, or how trivial or small the amount of time or money involved, it always pays to think ahead and anticipate the negotiation on which you're about to embark with your client. Even if it's only to briefly outline your goals or do a little bit of research on your client's needs, the additional insight that you gain by anticipating your negotiation puts you in a position to better achieve your personal, business, and financial goals.

Although you can do many things to get ready to negotiate, always take these four essential steps before you open a negotiation:

1. **Prepare your goals.**

   If you don't have goals, then you never know where you're going, and you won't know when you've arrived. Goals are the ultimate targets that you're going to work hard to achieve in a negotiation. Take time before you negotiate to determine your goals and how important they are to you. Would you be willing to give up certain goals in exchange for others? Decide what's more important to you – hourly rate? the number of hours allocated to the task? expenses? payment terms? size of deposit? Know exactly what you need to achieve in your negotiation, and be prepared to get it.

2. Research pertinent background information.

What do you know about your client's company? Are they in the news? Are there pressing issues for the company or the industry? What is the client's past experience with consultants? Is the company at the beginning of its financial year and anxious to start spending the money that it budgeted for consultants? Or is the company at the end of its financial year, thus trying to pinch every penny and make money stretch as far as possible? A wide range of information about the organisation you plan to negotiate with is available. (Do a few different searches on the Internet, or check the business press for starters.) Use this information to help plan your negotiation strategies for achieving your goals.

3. Evaluate your client's positions.

What do you expect your client's positions to be? Do you expect that the client may want to shorten or lengthen the period of performance? Or request that you cut your fee or increase or decrease the number of hours you've proposed for performing the project? Put yourself in your client's shoes for a moment and anticipate his or her positions. After you do that, determine how you'll counter them if and when your client introduces them.

4. Prepare your own positions.

Before you enter into any negotiation, prepare the positions that you'll present and defend. Positions are the wants that you communicate to the other party in a negotiation. They differ from goals in that they are interim stops along the way to achieving your goals. For example, your goal may be to make £50 an hour on a particular job, but your initial position may be to charge your client £60 an hour. It's likely that you'll have already prepared your initial positions and submitted them to your clients in your proposal. However, before you negotiate, also prepare back-up positions in the event that your primary positions are not acceptable to your clients and you can't get them to see the infinite wisdom of going with your suggested plan.

Figure 16-1 presents a quick and easy worksheet that you can use to prepare for any negotiation.

Basic rules of the negotiation road

In negotiation, a number of basic rules have evolved over millions of years of human existence. Master these rules, and you'll be a real pro at negotiation. You'll always get exactly what you want and your life will be full of unlimited success and happiness. Well, maybe not. However, if you ignore these basic rules, or fail to practise them effectively, we can guarantee that you'll end up with a lot less from your bargains than you hope for.

Prenegotiation Worksheet

- What are your top three goals for this particular negotiation?

    1.

    2.

    3.

- What do you expect your client's top three goals for this particular negotiation to be?

    1.

    2.

    3.

- What do you expect your client's initial positions to be?

    1.

    2.

    3.

- What do you expect your client's backup positions to be?

    1.

    2.

    3.

- What are your initial positions?

    1.

    2.

    3.

- What are your backup positions?

    1.

    2.

    3.

Figure 16-1:
Use this
worksheet
to prepare
for any
negotiation.

Anyway, here are the seven basic rules of negotiation:

- ✔ **Be prepared.** Being prepared gives you a definite advantage in every negotiating situation – so much so that the downside of not preparing for a negotiation far outweighs the small amount of time and effort that it takes to prepare. And what do you need to be prepared for? For starters, go back to the previous section titled 'Anticipating the negotiation' and do the four things that we recommend there. Back so soon? Then go on to the second basic rule of negotiation.

- ✔ **Leave plenty of room to manoeuvre.** Nobody likes to be boxed into a position with no room for compromise or for flexibility in meeting the mutual goals of both parties. When you develop your negotiation goals and positions, build in enough flexibility to allow you to modify them to better achieve both your clients' goals and your goals.

- ✔ **Have lots of options in mind.** For every possible reason that your client gives for not agreeing to one of your requests or positions, have one or more options ready to go. For example, if your client says that four weeks is not an acceptable delivery schedule, then be ready with another option that gets your client the delivery in two weeks that he or she wants, but with an increase in fee to compensate for the rush job.

- ✔ **Keep your word.** In business, as in life in general, your word must be your bond. Negotiation is built on a foundation of trust and mutual respect. If you aren't willing to keep your word, then you quickly lose both trust and respect. It's one thing to make an honest mistake – almost anyone can understand and deal with that – but if you can't keep your word, then what do you have left? (Here's a hint: not much.)

- ✔ **Listen more than you talk.** One of the most important negotiating skills is the ability to listen – really listen – to the other party. If you ask the right questions and then let your counterpart talk about the answers, you usually find out exactly what it will take to successfully negotiate and close a deal. Don't forget: When you're talking, you're not listening!

- ✔ **Don't give up too much too soon.** In our experience, it pays not to give up too much too quickly when you're dealing with a tough negotiator. Not only do you appear weak and perhaps a bit desperate (neither perceptions of which work to your favour), but you also miss out on getting any significant concessions from your client. Take your time when you're negotiating with your clients. It's better for them, rather than you, to be in a big rush to close the deal.

- ✔ **Learn to say no.** Telling a client no is a very difficult skill for many consultants to acquire. We all want to tell our clients yes to encourage positive client relations. However, when you're negotiating a deal, sometimes you have to say no if you want to achieve your own goals. For example, if your client wants you to cut your normal fee in half and you don't want to do so because you'll lose money on the deal, then just say no, but offer an alternative, such as a slight reduction in fee in exchange for payment in 10 days instead of 30.

Closing a deal

Closing your deal successfully – that is, reaching final agreement on all terms and conditions and signing all the appropriate documents on all the appropriate dotted lines – is the ultimate goal of every negotiation. Countless business deals have lost a wheel and careered out of control and into the ditches of commerce because the parties couldn't reach final agreement and close their deals.

Closing is an art. The more you do it, the better you get. However, it's never too late to learn a few new tricks or brush up on old ones. Here are a few tips to help ensure that you close your deals efficiently and with a minimum of bumps along the way:

- ✔ **Give your clients lots of reasons to say yes.** The more reasons your clients have to say yes, the greater the chance that they'll say yes. Find as many ways as you possibly can to make it easy for your clients to say yes. If you do, you'll definitely close a lot more deals.

- ✔ **Confirm your agreement.** To ensure that your understanding of the final agreement matches the other party's understanding, confirm your agreement – first verbally, and then in writing. If there's a problem, you'll undoubtedly hear about it very quickly!

- ✔ **Don't be surprised by last-minute surprises.** We have all been in many negotiations where we had reached (or at least thought we had reached) a final agreement with the other party, only to have him or her toss in a new demand or condition at the last possible moment. Be prepared for clients who use this negotiation tactic to wring additional concessions from you. If this happens to you, it's a good idea to calmly tell your counterpart, 'No, this is not what we agreed to', and demand that he or she stick to the original deal. If your counterpart refuses, then it's up to you to decide if you need the business so much that you'll take the deal anyway, or whether it may be in your interest to just walk away. Sometimes walking away from a bad deal (and a difficult client) is the wisest thing you can do.

- ✔ **Follow up with a thank-you note.** Not only is sending a thank-you note a nice way to express your personal thanks to your client for hiring you or your firm, but it is also a great way to build rapport. The best business, after all, is built on long-term relationships with your current clients and the future clients that they refer to you.

✔ **Move on if you can't close the deal.** Despite all your efforts to reach a mutually beneficial agreement, some deals are just not meant to be. If this is the case, and nothing you can do will bring negotiations to a successful close, then simply tell your client that you can't do business and move on. By breaking off negotiations, you show your clients that you're serious, and they may very well make the final concessions necessary to close the deal. If not, then you can get on with your life and direct your efforts to more fruitful pursuits – such as lining up your next clients.

Chapter 17

Keeping Track of Your Time and Money

- -

In This Chapter

▶ Tracking your time

▶ Invoicing clients and collecting money

▶ Creating and monitoring budgets

- -

*W*hen it comes right down to it, keeping track of the financial aspects of your business is really quite simple. There are really only two kinds of money that you need to focus on in your business: the money that's coming in and the money that's going out.

This chapter is all about keeping track of your time – the hours of work for which you invoice your client – and your money. We start by talking about how to keep track of your time and how to track the work you do on specific projects for specific clients. Then we briefly consider the ins and outs of budgeting and the importance of keeping to budget.

Keeping Track of Your Time

Although some consultants invoice their clients as they complete specific percentages of the project – say, every third or half – and some work on retainers where they are paid a fixed amount of money each month, many other consultants charge their services on the basis of some increment of time (usually hourly). Although you need to seriously consider keeping track of the use of your time regardless of how you invoice for it (what better way to find out that you're spending more than half of each workday playing computer games?), you absolutely must do so when you're paid based on the number of hours you work on a particular project.

Although there are many different ways to keep track of the time that you spend working on client projects (an abacus, perhaps? Post-It notes?), you'll probably find that your needs can be accommodated using just two different forms: the client activity log and the client time sheet. The following two sections examine exactly what each of these forms is all about.

The daily client activity log

If you're the kind of consultant who invoices your time hourly or on another basis related to time, then the best way to track your time is to maintain an activity log. An activity log is a daily record of everything you do for your clients, broken down into your smallest invoicing increments – say, an hour, half an hour, or quarter of an hour. By the way, some solicitors we know break their hours into six-minute increments.

Figure 17-1 represents a simple daily client activity log that is appropriate for almost any kind of consulting work that is invoiced on an hourly basis. Although it's up to you to decide the smallest increment of time that you use to invoice your clients – most consultants use 15-minute blocks – for simplicity's sake (and to keep the log from taking up two whole pages of this book), we have selected 30-minute increments for our example. You can select any portion of an hour that you like (and to which your clients agree!).

The first thing you may notice is that the client activity log looks very similar to a diary – in fact, a diary, either a desk diary or software-based, makes a great activity log – with every half-hour noted, from 7:00 a.m. until 5:00 p.m. Of course, you can tailor your client activity log to fit your exact schedule. If, for example, you start work at noon and work until midnight, you can set up your log on that basis.

As you can see from the sample client activity log in Figure 17-1, the consultant worked on projects for four different clients on 8 February. The consultant worked on the Ramsey project from 7:00 to 8:00 and worked on a draft report for Willis from 9:00 to 11:00. Just before lunch – from 12:30 to 1:00 – the consultant made phone calls for Martinelli, another client. After a satisfying break for lunch, our intrepid consultant jumped into an Internet search for Speedway Associates from 1:30 to 3:30, and then finished the workday with another phone call to Martinelli from 4:30 to 5:00.

What's the point of going through the trouble of keeping daily client activity logs – isn't that a lot of paperwork to fill out every day (and who has time for that)? Before you decide that filling out an activity log every day is too much pain for you to endure, consider these advantages:

✔ **You're going to want to invoice your clients someday.** Sure, working on all those fun consulting projects can be very satisfying in itself. However, you still have to pay your bills. And if you want to pay your bills, then your clients have to pay theirs! Keeping a client activity log makes it much easier to invoice your clients when the time comes.

✔ **One sheet of paper is a lot better than lots of little sheets of paper.** The temptation to scribble your hours on a scrap of paper or a Post-It note is often overwhelming, but you must resist this temptation at all costs! You can easily lose or forget about all those little scraps of paper, or your cat or dog can eat them. Before you know it, you've done a heck of a lot of work for nothing because you can't invoice your clients for it.

Daily Client Activity Log	
February 8, 2009	
7:00	Internet search for Ramsey project
7:30	Internet search for Ramsey project
8:00	
8:30	
9:00	Worked on draft report of recommendations for Willis
9:30	Worked on draft report of recommendations for Willis
10:00	Worked on draft report of recommendations for Willis
10:30	Worked on draft report of recommendations for Willis
11:00	
11:30	
12:00	
12:30	Phone calls on behalf of Martinelli
1:00	
1:30	Internet search for Speedway Associates
2:00	Internet search for Speedway Associates
2:30	Internet search for Speedway Associates
3:00	Internet search for Speedway Associates
3:30	
4:00	
4:30	Phone call to Martinelli
5:00	

Figure 17-1:
Sample
client
activity log.

✔ **Your log has a better memory than you do.** You may think that you can rely on your memory to keep the ten different projects that you're working on for seven different clients separate from one another and then to invoice them properly at the end of the month. Though you may be blessed with a memory that would make 'Who Wants to be a Millionaire?' fans around the world green with envy, we guarantee you that the memory in your client activity log is longer and much more precise – especially when you're considering 250+ workdays in a year filled with a variety of projects for a variety of clients. Do yourself a favour and start using a client activity log to keep track of the time you spend on your consulting projects.

So, you may be wondering if we practise what we preach. In a word: yes. Bob keeps a daily client activity log on his computer in the form of an Excel spreadsheet. While he doesn't always have a chance to update it every day, he doesn't let more than a couple of days pass before he does, picking up client time from his appointment book and notes. Peter is also a big fan of daily client activity logs, but his log is in the form of a spiral-bound notebook that he keeps on his desk to keep track of work priorities and to take notes of conversations with clients. Every time Peter starts or stops work on a client project, he notes the client name, the start and stop times, and a short description of the work done.

Philip has a team of office staff who firstly track consultants' time in a large desk diary and then cross-tally it against his accounting and invoicing software (apparently the desk diary has never crashed).

Now that we've convinced you that it's in your best interests to use daily client activity logs to record your time (we have convinced you, right?), what do you do with all the information that you have gathered? This is the best part. Now it's time to transfer all that information to your client time sheets. Coincidentally, that just happens to be the next section of this chapter.

Client time sheets

Eventually – perhaps once a month or maybe more, depending on your client invoicing arrangements – plan to send an invoice to each of your clients for the work you did for them during that invoicing period. Believe us, this task is much easier and a lot more accurate when you have been maintaining your client activity logs on a regular basis. (You are maintaining your client activity logs, aren't you?)

A client time sheet is simply a summary of the exact work that you do for a client, including how much time you spend on each task or project. Deciding what approach you want to use to present your information is up to you and your client.

Figure 17-2 is a sample client time sheet that breaks down the consultant's work into specific tasks.

As you can see from the sample client time sheet, the consultant performed a total of 90 hours of work for Speedway Associates in February. This total was further broken down into specific tasks, including client consultation (20 hours), Internet searches (45 hours), draft product marketing plans (10 hours), and focus groups (15 hours).

Where did these numbers come from? They came directly from the client activity logs that the consultant completed and maintained for each and every workday. Because the consultant invoices his clients on a monthly basis, he goes through the month's client activity logs and prepares client time sheets for each client at the end of each month. The client time sheet – which is merely a summary of the information contained in the daily client activity logs – can then be used as the basis for the consultant's monthly invoice.

Remember, you need only two things to track the time you spend on client projects: a daily client activity log and a client time sheet. With those two pieces of information, you can track your time and then invoice your clients for your services appropriately and accurately. And that is the firm foundation that will help your consulting business grow – and grow and grow.

Client Time Sheet	
Speedway Associates	
February 2009	
Client consultation	20 hours
Internet searches	45 hours
Draft product marketing plans	10 hours
Focus groups	15 hours
Total hours	90 hours

Figure 17-2:
Sample
client time
sheet.

Invoicing Your Clients and Collecting Your Money

Although the entire topic of accounting is important when it comes to ensuring the financial health of your enterprise, the effectiveness of your invoicing and collections procedures probably has the greatest impact – whether positive or negative – on the health of your consulting practice. If you invoice your clients quickly and accurately and then follow up to ensure that you collect your payments when they are due – or even sooner whenever possible – you do a lot to ensure the financial viability of your business.

Take a look at some different aspects of invoicing your clients and collecting your money when it is due.

Invoicing for your services

How you invoice your clients for the work you do for them depends on your contract or – in the absence of a written contract – any other agreements you may have made regarding invoicing and payment. If your contract is set up to pay you as you achieve specific milestones – say, completing a quarter of the project or submitting a draft report of recommendations, then you invoice your clients for the amount due upon completion of each milestone. However, if you work on an ongoing basis and invoice your clients for the number of hours that you work plus expenses (photocopying, travel, and so on), then you charge your client at the end of the agreed invoicing period, usually the end of each calendar month.

Figure 17-3 shows a sample invoice based on the Speedway Associates example used earlier in this chapter. As you can see, Speedway simply totalled the number of hours for all the work done in February and multiplied that by its contracted invoicing rate of £50 an hour for a total payment due of £4,500. If your client agreed to reimburse you for other expenses you incurred on behalf of the project – say, for example, a three-day trip to Edinburgh – then the actual cost of the airline ticket, hotel, food, and ground transport would be added to the bottom of the invoice.

Here are some tips on maximising the effectiveness of your invoicing process:

  ✔ **Front-load your invoicing.** If you invoice on a milestone basis during the course of the project, try to arrange your fees so that you charge your client the bulk of them towards the start of the project rather than the end. For example, push for an advance payment to start the project, or simply make your first couple of payments higher than those that are due later in the project. Doing so gives your project a financial head start that is very beneficial to the financial health of your practice while minimising the risk if a client moves into a late-pay status during the course of a project.

✔ **Invoice your clients often.** The more often you get paid, the better the effect on the positive flow of cash through your practice. Although monthly payments are pretty much the standard for consultants who invoice for hours and expenses, you can agree with your client to invoice them more often than that.

✔ **Invoice immediately.** Immediately after you complete a milestone or reach the end of your invoicing cycle, send an invoice to your client. The sooner you send an invoice, the sooner your clients pay their bills. And the sooner they pay their bills, the better off your practice is financially. Peter tries whenever possible to send out invoices to clients within a day or two after the end of the month.

✔ **Use email whenever possible.** In the good old days of business, invoices would typically be posted to clients, taking up to a week to arrive. However, many clients today welcome invoices sent via email, which cuts the amount of time it takes to deliver an invoice from days to seconds. The sooner your invoice gets to a client, the sooner it will get paid. Make email invoicing a regular part of the way you do business, and encourage your clients to do the same.

✔ **Offer a discount for prompt payment.** To help motivate your clients to pay early (or at least on time), offer a nominal discount (say, in the range of 0.5 to 1 per cent) for paying their invoices within 10 or 20 days. You effectively lose a small amount of money when you offer your clients this privilege, but the positive impact on your cash flow usually makes the cost a worthwhile one. If you offered to discount the work at the outset, then link the discount to prompt payment during the negotiation and confirm it in the contract.

✔ **Monitor client payments closely.** Keep an eye on the status of your invoices and make sure that your clients pay their bills on time. If certain clients don't, call them personally to see what the problem is. If it looks like you're going to have a hard time getting them to pay the amounts they owe you, act quickly to initiate your collections procedure.

What? You don't have a collections procedure? Then it's a great time for you to read the next section of this chapter.

Invoice	
Speedway Associates	
February 2009	
Client consultation	20 hours
Internet searches	45 hours
Draft product marketing plans	10 hours
Focus groups	15 hours
Total hours	90 hours
Billing rate	Ł50/hour
Total amount due	**Ł4,500**
All payments due 30 days after invoice date. A prompt payment discount of 1%	
will be granted for all payments made no later than 10 days after invoice date.	
Thank you!	

Figure 17-3:
Sample
invoice.

Collecting overdue accounts

No matter how great your clients are or how wonderful they are about paying their bills, eventually you'll encounter a client who either pays you late or doesn't pay you at all. Believe us when we tell you that we have ourselves had some of the best clients in the world. But even the best clients sometimes have not-so-great clients who don't pay them, and then they find themselves stuck in the middle when they can't afford to pay their own consultants and suppliers. What should you do? Do you ignore this behaviour and just be glad that you have the work, or do you need to take action? Our advice is to take action – immediately.

The action you need to take to collect the money owed to you can be turned into a mathematical equation with variables for many things: the size of the job, the length of the relationship with your client, the total amount of money owed to your firm, the number of days (or months) that the money is overdue, and other factors. When you decide to initiate your collections procedure, you need to weigh these factors in your decision. Whatever action you take, we recommend that you establish a clear order of precedence – starting with a simple phone call and then increasing the intensity of your actions depending on your client's response – to guide you through the process.

If you decide that it's time to start the collections procedure, consider taking these steps as a part of your efforts:

1. **Call or send an email to your client directly.**

   Politely mention that your payment is overdue, and ask if your client can check what's happened. In some cases, you find that the client has forgotten to approve the invoice or submit it for approval. In other cases, the client's accounting department may be sitting on the invoice, waiting for some additional bit of information from your client. Regardless of the cause, the first part of your collections procedure must be to deal directly with your client. Your client most likely has much more leverage than you do from outside the organisation and, therefore, probably will have more success getting your bills paid than you will if you call the payments department yourself. You can often solve the payment problem in only a few minutes with a call to your client.

2. **Send an overdue notice.**

   If the call to your client doesn't resolve the payment problem within a reasonable amount of time, say, a few days or a week, then send a written overdue notice to your client along with another copy of your invoice. Send these letters by normal post – weekly or monthly – until you receive your payment. If the amounts are serious, and it appears that your client is trying to get out of paying you, then be sure to send the letters by Recorded or Special Delivery, which have to be signed for. Follow up your letters with phone calls to your client and to your client's payments department, asking for help in solving the problem.

3. **Escalate.**

   Write to the Company Secretary, the Finance Director, even the Chairman explaining that the invoice is fair and hasn't been disputed. Include a copy of the contract and records of what you've delivered to back up your claim. For sums under £100,000, you can initiate a claim at the HM Court Service (HMCS) Money Claim online website. Claims of up to £5,000 are dealt with by the small claims track of your local county court, which means you don't need to get a solicitor. In Scotland, claims are handled by the Sheriff court. Visit the Adviceguide website at www. adviceguide.org.uk to find out how. Claims below £15,000 must be issued in a county court while claims over £15,000 can be issued in the High Court. We strongly suggest you take legal advice before contemplating claiming through the High Court.

4. **Stop work.**

   If you aren't being paid, consider suspending your work until you're paid. Your work may be the only leverage – short of legal action – that you have to get your client to pay you. Of course, when you stop work, you risk angering your client and destroying your relationship, so be sure you take this step only after careful deliberation.

5. **Call in a collections agency.**

   If the client continues to ignore your requests for payment, you can turn your overdue account over to a collections agency. The agency will pursue the collections process for you for a part of the money that is ultimately collected, usually around 8 to 12.5 per cent. However, if a claim is two to three years old that fee can rise to 20 per cent. Older debts can warrant up to 35 per cent. You take this step only when you're convinced that your client isn't going to pay you, and the relationship you've built is effectively defunct.

6. **Mediate.**

   In lieu of going to court, both parties can submit to mediation, in which an independent third party helps you resolve your differences, or to arbitration. If both parties submit to arbitration, an independent arbitrator listens to both sides of the story and then makes a decision in favour of one party or the other. Check your contract to see if it has an arbitration clause.

7. **Take the client to court.**

   Taking your delinquent client to court is the last remedy that you have. Ideally, you'll never have to go to court to get your clients to pay you. The good news is that most clients will pay what they owe well before you get to that point. By monitoring your payments closely and contacting your clients at the first hint of trouble, you minimise your risk of exposure due to late payments or payments that are never made.

Building Better Budgets

A budget is an estimate of the amount of money that you expect to bring into your organisation or pay out of your organisation for whatever business activities you undertake. For example, you may estimate (and budget) that you'll bring in £25,000 worth of business in October. Or you may estimate (and budget) that you'll spend £300 in telephone charges in January.

Why must you consider developing budgets for your consulting business? You must do so because budgets provide you with a baseline of expected performance against which you can measure the actual performance of your consulting enterprise. With this information, you can diagnose and assess the current financial health of your business.

You can also use budgets to fulfil another important purpose: to provide a baseline against which you can measure your progress towards the successful completion of client projects. For example, if you're 50 per cent of the way through a project but have spent 75 per cent of the amount you budgeted, then you have an immediate indication that you may run out of money before you complete the project. This is not a good situation for any consultant. Either you've underbudgeted your expenses for the project, or you're over-spending. Whenever budgeted performance and actual performance disagree, your job is to find out why.

Budgeting for different parts of the business

Depending on the size of your business, the budgeting process may be quite simple or, alternatively, very complex. Regardless of the size of your business, you can budget for almost anything within it. While many home-based or small consulting firms get by with few or no budgets at all, larger companies will be likely to use a greater variety of budgets.

For example, although Philip and his team of consultants work on a wide variety of projects every year and his business does well financially, the two budgets he uses day in, day out are a sales budget and marketing budget. Philip's sales budget is on a huge whiteboard and at a glance, Philip can see his anticipated revenues – on a month-by-month basis – and where they are coming from, and identify shortfalls in future months that need to be addressed with additional marketing attention. Philip's team constantly updates the budget with new information as soon as it is available, including orders as they are received from clients, contracts when they are signed, and the addition of new proposals – and the deletion of failed proposals. Here are some examples of commonly used budgets:

- ✔ **Project budget:** A project budget is an estimate of all the different potential expenses that you will incur during the course of a project against the amount of money that your client intends to pay you.

- ✔ **Staff budget:** Staff budgets show the number and names of all the various positions in a company (if there are various positions in the company), along with the salary or wages budgeted for each position.

- ✔ **Sales budget:** The sales budget is an estimate of the total number of products or services that will be sold in a given period. Most consultants determine total revenue by multiplying the number of units (hours or days) by the price per unit.

- ✔ **Overheads budget:** Overheads budgets cover all the different expenses that you may incur during the normal course of operations. You can budget for travel, training, office supplies, and other similar costs to your business within your overheads budget.

- ✔ **Capital budget:** This budget is your plan to acquire fixed assets (those with a long useful life), such as furniture, computers, facilities, physical plant, and so forth, to support your business operations.

Creating a budget

There's a right way and a wrong way to create budgets. The wrong way is simply to take a copy of your last budget and stick a new title on it. The right way is to gather information from as many sources as possible, review and check the information for accuracy, and then use your good judgement to anticipate what the future may bring. A budget is only as good as the data that goes into it and the good judgement that you bring to the process.

Here are a few tips to help you put together your budgets:

- ✔ **Gather data.** Retrieve copies of your previous budgets from your filing cabinets and then compare the figures in your budget against your actual experience. Look at this historical data to determine whether you overestimated or underestimated figures in any of your previous budgets and to see what previous years or similar projects cost your company. Take time to consider whether you need to recruit more people, lease new facilities, or buy equipment or supplies. Finally, consider what effect possible large increases or decreases in sales or expenses may have on your budget.

- ✔ **Meet your clients.** When you start the budgeting process, meet your key clients to get a firm idea of the fees that you can expect your work for them to generate. You also want to get some idea of when the money will hit your system.

- ✔ **Apply your judgement.** Hard data and cold facts are an important source of information in the budgeting process, but they aren't everything. Budgeting is one part science and one part art. Your job is to take the data and facts and then apply your own judgement to them to determine the most likely outcomes.

- ✔ **Run the numbers.** Put your estimates of money coming into your business and money going out of your business into a budget spreadsheet and hit the calculate button on your computer. Review and modify this draft of your budget before you finalise it. Don't worry if the draft is rough or is missing information. You always have the opportunity to fine-tune it later on.

- ✔ **Check results and run the budget again as necessary.** Closely review your draft budget and see whether it still makes sense to you. Are you missing any anticipated sources of revenue or expenses? Are the numbers realistic? Do they make sense in a historical perspective? Are they too high or too low? When you're finally satisfied with the results, finalise your budget and print it. Congratulations! You did it!

Staying on budget

After you start your consulting business and after you begin each client project, you need to closely monitor your various budgets to make sure that you don't exceed them. If your actual expenditures start to exceed the amounts that you budgeted, you need to take quick and decisive action before you dig a financial black hole that quickly sucks up all your financial resources.

Here are some things that you can do to get back on track if the money you pay out of your business starts to significantly exceed the amount of money that you bring into it:

- ✔ **Freeze discretionary expenses.** Some expenses, such as computer repairs, telephones, and electricity, are essential to your business and cannot be stopped without jeopardising it. You can curtail discretionary expenses, such as purchasing new carpeting, upgrading computer monitors, or travelling first-class, without jeopardising your ability to complete client projects. Freezing discretionary expenses is the quickest and least painful way to get your actual expenditures back in line with your budgeted expenditures.

- ✔ **Freeze recruiting.** Of course, you can cease recruiting new employees only if your business is large enough to recruit employees in the first place. By delaying the recruiting of new employees, you save not only on the cost of hourly pay or salaries but also on the costs of any fringe benefits that you provide, such as medical care, and overheads expenses like water, electricity, and cleaning services.

- ✔ **Increase your rates.** Part of the problem may be that you aren't charging a high enough rate for your services to cover your reasonable and necessary expenses. If this is the case, consider raising your rates for new business that you bring in.

When it comes to keeping track of your money, budgeting is really just the tip of the iceberg. Whether you like it or not, as the owner of your own business, you need to have a basic understanding of the process that your business goes through in order to account for the money it makes and the money it spends. Check out *Understanding Business Accounting For Dummies* by Colin Barrow and John Tracy (published by Wiley) for all the information you need to know about the wonderful world of accounting.

Chapter 18

Communicating Your Way to Success

*I*f your goal is to be a successful consultant (and how could you wish for anything less?), you first have to be a successful communicator. Relationships are the foundation upon which you build your business with clients, and you can help build and strengthen your client relationships by becoming an effective communicator. If you communicate well with your clients, not only do they have more confidence in your abilities, but they also enjoy working with you more and are more likely to consider you for other jobs later.

Of course, some people are better communicators than others. Some people just have a knack for presenting their thoughts in speech or in writing. Others just ooze the kind of charisma that makes everything they say seem to be accompanied by the voices of angels. Fortunately, for those of you who still have a way to go before angels start providing backup to your words of wisdom, there's good news. You can learn to become a better communicator. How? All you need to do is follow some very simple advice and then practise, practise, practise. And when you've finished practising, practise some more.

The more you communicate with others – whether in speech or in writing – the better communicator you become. And the better communicator you are, the more confident you feel communicating, the more you enjoy it, and the more effective you are with your clients.

One thing about communication and your clients: Make sure that the way you communicate with your clients is based on their preferences – not your own. If your client prefers a personal phone call over an email message, then pick up the phone and call. If your client prefers to have one point of contact within your business instead of several, then provide that single point of contact. If your client prefers long meetings over lunch for project briefings, then do it that way – even if you hate lunch meetings. Be sensitive to your clients' communication needs and your clients will have one more reason to send more business your way. Of course, you still have to do a good job on your projects!

This chapter is about communicating with others and, in particular, the way in which you communicate. We find out how to sharpen those rusty writing skills, and address the importance of communicating in person with your clients and asking the right questions at the right time. Finally, we explore how best to use the telephone to reach out and touch your clients. For detailed information on another important aspect of communicating with your clients – making presentations – see Chapter 10.

Putting It in Writing

Technology offers us a glut of ways to communicate with clients, including mobile and land-line phones, email, fax, voice over IP, instant messaging, and many more. We suppose that you could still use semaphore or morse code if you were so inclined (but then again few of your clients will be). As a result of all these new-fangled ways to communicate, you may think that good old-fashioned writing is obsolete and soon to be replaced with something better. If that's what you think, you couldn't be further away from the truth.

The simple fact is, writing is more important than ever. Whether you're writing a proposal for new business, sending a thank-you note to a client, or responding to an associate's email message, good writing never goes out of fashion; it's also an essential element of your success as a consultant.

What to put in writing

Although it looks like writing has many happy and healthy years ahead before it becomes obsolete (witness this book and its many yellow-and-black-covered brothers and sisters, for example), it has turned into a bit of a lost art. And although voice mail, email, and the like have generally supplanted the need for a large amount of business correspondence that traditionally used to flow between consultants and clients, writing still has a vital role to play in the world of business communication. In fact, because of its increasing scarcity, well-written business correspondence can set you apart from the rest of the pack.

So now that you may be thinking that writing is worth considering, what things do you need to write? Here are a few forms of communication that can help you foster good relationships with your clients:

- ✔ **Business letters:** Business letters – printed out and delivered by the Royal Mail, by an overnight courier, or by fax or as an attachment to an email message – are the traditional backbone of all business correspondence between consultants and their clients. Consultants write business letters to their clients for many reasons, including persuading, thanking, selling, apologising, communicating good news, communicating bad news, asking questions, and seeking information. Crafting a good one- to three-page business letter takes more work than a two-sentence email message, and the extra effort is usually worth it.

- ✔ **Notes:** Writing and sending notes to your clients and prospective clients should be a central part of your writing campaign. Today, notes most often take the form of email messages. You can send your prospects thank-you notes after you meet them or after you complete a project for them.

- ✔ **Proposals:** Very few clients will hire you without some form of written proposal of what you plan to do for them. Proposals require a very precise and organised style of writing that conveys not only the fact that you can do what you say you can do, but that you can do it well and cost-effectively. A well-written proposal can make the difference between winning the contract and being rejected. See Chapter 7 for detailed information on how to write winning proposals.

- ✔ **Reports:** For many consultants, reports – and the presentations that go along with them – are the only products that they deliver to their clients. Because of this, the contents of reports – and the way that reports are written – are critically important in the acceptance of consultants' recommendations by their clients. The next section addresses the important issues involved in writing good reports.

Two basic consulting reports

No matter what kind of consulting you're doing, in most cases you use two different kinds of written reports to communicate with your clients: progress reports and the final report. In some cases – particularly in complex projects of long duration – your consulting projects will use both types of reports. In others – particularly projects that are relatively simple and short in duration – you may need to submit only a final report.

Although you can choose to employ many different formats to get your information across to your client, perhaps the most important consideration of all is your client's expectation. If your client expects a short report, make sure that you deliver a short report. If your client expects a long, detailed report, make sure that you tailor your format to meet that need. And while you're at it, make sure that you price your consulting proposal appropriately.

Progress reports

Progress reports – also known as milestone reports or project status reports – do just what they say: They report your progress at different stages on the way to completing a project. A progress report can be anything from a short, one-page update to a full-length, multipage extravaganza. Regardless of the length of your progress reports, make sure that they are concise and to the point.

The exact length and format of your progress reports are up to you and your client, but make sure that they contain at least the following information:

- ✔ **Executive summary:** Write a brief but complete summary of the progress of the project during the reporting period, highlighting accomplishments and recommendations. This summary gives your busy clients a chance to get a quick overview of your progress without having to read the entire report.

- ✔ **Key accomplishments:** Your clients will be particularly interested in any notable accomplishments that you've achieved on the project. If you had any key accomplishments during the reporting period (and make sure that you do), make them known to your clients in the progress report.

- ✔ **Work completed during the reporting period:** Summarise the exact work that you completed during the reporting period and discuss how it relates to the overall project. Your progress report is a snapshot of your activity during the period of time that you're covering in the report.

- ✔ **Percentage of completion:** This information is simply an estimate of the percentage of completion of your project during the period of the report. If, for example, you're approximately one-third of the way through the project, simply note your percentage of completion as 33 per cent.

- ✔ **Work to be completed:** Briefly discuss the work to be completed during the next reporting period and how it relates to the rest of the project. If you anticipate any particularly notable accomplishments – or particularly problematic issues – highlight them to your clients in this section of the progress report.

- ✔ **Issues:** If you've encountered any problems or other issues that need to be brought to your clients' attention, list them here. Make sure that you follow up this written presentation of project issues with personal,

> face-to-face discussions with your clients. You absolutely do not want to surprise your clients with project issues or problems. Bring up challenging issues as soon as you encounter them and ensure that they are promptly acknowledged and addressed.

How often do you need to produce progress reports? The specific answer to that question depends upon the exact nature of the project, how long the project is scheduled to last, the expectations of your clients, and the terms of your contract. If the project is a short one – say, only a few weeks' duration, you may not need to do a progress report at all. However, if your project runs for a month or more, then progress reports are clearly in order. Although monthly progress reports are the norm for most consultants and their clients, no rule exists that says you can't do your progress reports on a weekly, quarterly, or any other basis that suits your needs and the needs of your clients.

Final reports

Your final report presents the results of your project and, as such, is the culmination and central focus of the efforts you've undertaken on behalf of your client. Depending on the exact nature of your work, your final report may be the showcase of the project, and it may form the basis for company-wide changes or restructuring.

In many cases, your final report will be the only product that your client will receive from you; its importance cannot be underestimated.

Final reports are different from progress reports in many ways. Here are the key ingredients that you always include in your final reports:

- ✔ **Executive summary:** Your clients are busy, busy people, and they don't have lots of time to wade through long reports. Briefly summarise the information you're presenting in your final report and highlight key project accomplishments and problems.

- ✔ **Project background and scope:** Some of the people who read your report may not know much about your project and why you were selected to do it. Use this part of the final report as an opportunity to discuss the nature and scope of the project, how it came to be, and your role in it.

- ✔ **Methodology:** How did you approach the problem? Did you conduct a market survey? A statistical analysis? A review of the literature? Your readers want to know how you came up with the results and conclusions that form the basis of your report. The right answers to those questions add to your credibility and strongly support your recommendations.

The wrong answers detract from your credibility and possibly create doubt about your recommendations.

✔ **Findings and conclusions:** This section of your report contains the results of your work and any conclusions you can draw from what you found out in your investigation. All your good news – and your bad news – goes into this section of your final report.

✔ **Recommendations:** Even more than your findings and conclusions, your recommendations are probably what your clients are most interested in reading. In this section of your report, you apply all your experience to develop and present your prescription to cure your clients' ills. Make sure that your recommendations are concise and easy to understand and that they can realistically be acted upon.

✔ **Implementation guidelines:** Although your clients may not have asked you for specific guidance on implementing your recommendations, use this option to show your clients how your expertise can be of particular benefit to them. Do them a big favour by spelling out a step-by-step approach for putting your recommendations into place and include scheduling milestones and budgetary information. While you're at it, take the opportunity to propose your role in the implementation, along with a price and timetable for it. Don't be shy – many consultants win a lot of business this way!

✔ **Summary of benefits:** Although your findings, conclusions, and recommendations may make perfect sense, most organisations need some sort of incentive to make any change to the status quo. Summarise the benefits of your recommendations in a way that shows your clients why they must implement them. Increasing sales, decreasing expenses, avoiding litigation, improving customer satisfaction, and decreasing employee turnover are just a few of the possible benefits of your recommendations.

Seven steps to better writing

Like anything else, the more you write, the better you get. So how can you write better? Dust off that old pen and paper or boot up your laptop and get to work! Here are seven steps for improving your writing that you can start using right now:

✔ **Know your point.** Before you write a single word, think about the point that you want to make. What's your point, and what kind of reaction do you want from those who read what you write? Keep your thoughts tightly focused and sharp.

✔ **Get organised.** Writing is difficult when your thoughts are a disorganised mess. The solution is to organise your thoughts before you start writing. One of the best approaches is to create an outline of what you want to say. An outline – or even a few notes – can help you pull your thoughts together into a coherent written product. As an additional aid to getting your thoughts organised, bounce the logical flow of your ideas off clients, business associates, or significant others.

✔ **Write in the way that you speak.** The best writing is natural, like everyday speech. Write the way that you speak. Don't be artificially formal or too businesslike and sterile when that's not your style. Not only does that make your writing less accessible, but you end up masking your individuality and personality.

✔ **Be concise.** Don't write just to fill up a sheet of paper with your words – every word needs to have a purpose. Avoid fluff and filler at all costs. When you write, make your point, support it, and then move on to the next point.

✔ **Make it simple.** In writing, as in life, simple is better. Why waste your time writing a 300-word memo or letter when a 50-word note is sufficient? Why use jargon and indecipherable acronyms when plain English works just as well or even better? Make it your life's purpose to simplify, simplify, simplify.

✔ **Write and then rewrite.** There's no writer, amateur or professional, on the face of this green earth who doesn't need to rework much of what he or she has written until it's just right. We have lots of experience in this regard – just ask the editors of this book. When you write, first create a draft of what you want to say and then edit it for content, flow, grammar, and readability. You may need to write a few drafts before your work really shines, but the effort will be worth it.

✔ **Convey a positive attitude.** People naturally prefer upbeat, positive writing over writing that is negative and a drag to read. Falling into the negativity trap is easy, but don't let yourself become a victim! Even when you have to communicate bad news, be active, committed, and positive in the words that you choose and the way that you write. Your readers will really appreciate your approach!

If you want to learn more about how to develop your writing skills , you can find plenty of books and classes to help you. Check your local library or bookshop or contact your local community college or private training companies. People who write for a living and are quite good at are often the teachers of classes offered by such organisations.

Harnessing the Power of the Spoken Word

Communicating occupies a large portion of every consultant's day. Whether you're trying to persuade a prospective client of the infinite wisdom of hiring you to appraise her collection of Barbie dolls, or asking an accounts payable clerk about how he processes payments to suppliers as part of your audit of his firm, or presenting your recommendations to a company's management team, your success depends heavily on your ability to speak and be understood.

Understanding the power of the personal touch

In an increasingly impersonal world, filled with email, voicemail, and text messages, faxes, and other technology-driven forms of communication, communicating in person – face to face – has become a rare commodity. And it is exactly because of its rarity that communicating in person is perceived to be more valuable – and is therefore more powerful – than most other forms of communication that you may choose.

In a face-to-face meeting with a client, you rely on your ability to speak clearly and effectively. And, if there's anything that most people think they do pretty well, it's probably speaking effectively with others. However, even if you have a great deal of practice talking to clients, you can do several things to become an even better communicator:

- **Think before you leap.** Whether you're responding to your clients' questions or preparing to ask some questions of your own, you need to stop for a moment to get your bearings before you leap into the breach. Reacting rather than reflecting can be tempting, but your first reaction may very well not be your best reaction.

- **Keep it simple and brief.** When presenting information to your clients, keep the information as simple as possible so that your clients understand it clearly and easily. Also make your statements as brief as possible while still conveying the information you need to convey so that you hold your clients' attention as you speak. Complexity begets confusion, and confusion makes it more difficult for you to control the outcome of your discussion.

✔ **Ask lots of questions – and listen to the answers.** Not only does asking lots of questions show that you're genuinely interested in what your clients have to say, but it also is a great way to obtain information about your clients' needs and expectations. Vary the number of questions you ask, depending on the exact purpose of your contact and the amount of time available.

✔ **Be enthusiastic.** If you're excited by the prospect of doing a project for a client or providing an update of your progress, make sure that your client knows it. The more enthusiastic you are about doing your client's project, the more enthusiastic your client will be about getting you to do it (and about paying your invoices when they become due!).

✔ **Be empathetic.** Your client will receive your message more favourably if you tailor it to his or her individual needs. As the old saying goes, you must 'walk a mile in their shoes'. For example, your approach with a client who is too busy to spend more than a few minutes at a time with you needs to be quite different from the one you adopt if he or she seems to have all the time in the world and likes to philosophise for hours and hours.

✔ **Get personal.** A key component of consulting is building relationships with your clients. The best way to do so is to get personal with them. Although you must maintain a certain amount of professional decorum in your business relationships, you need to get to know your clients as people, not just as customers. Get to know their likes and dislikes, whether they have children, and what kinds of hobbies or other non-job interests they have that you may share (anyone for tennis?). Do business over lunch or dinner. Play a round of golf or squash together. However, before you dive in too deep, be sensitive to where you draw the line between your personal relationships and your business relationships with your clients. Although some clients may prefer to develop friendly, personal relationships with their consultants, others may prefer to keep some distance. Regardless, keep in mind that the rapport that you develop with your clients helps you cement long-term relationships with them. And that's good for you and for your clients.

As you can see, you can do many things right now to increase the power of your personal touch. Give them a try. We guarantee that you'll see a marked difference in your client relationships almost immediately.

And don't forget: you can't always be there in person. When you find yourself on the telephone with a client instead of there with him or her, then these same tips for face-to-face interactions apply. Speak a little more clearly, a little more slowly, and a little louder so that your client has a better chance of understanding you.

Asking the right questions at the right time

If consultants need to do one thing well, it's ask questions. Lots of questions. How much can you afford to spend to redecorate your house? When do you need this marketing survey completed? Not a day goes by when consultants don't ask clients – or clients-to-be – questions about something.

Because asking questions is such a big part of your job as a consultant, how do you make sure that you ask the right question at the right time? Before we answer that question, first consider exactly why consultants ask questions.

The reasons for asking questions

If you stop and think about it, consultants ask questions for many different reasons. Although you may at first think that the number one reason to ask questions, such as why, what, when, and where, is to find out simple answers, in fact you ask questions to get far more than those simple kinds of responses.

When asked the right way and at the right time, questions can give you direct insight into the heart and soul of your clients and provide you with a road map of where you need to take your discussion. Here are some of the many different reasons that consultants ask their clients questions:

- **To obtain information:** You can solicit information from your clients by asking them questions along the lines of, 'Exactly what results are you hoping to achieve?' or 'How soon do you plan to select a consultant for this project?'

- **To provide information:** You can use questions to inform your client about the capabilities of your consulting business and any number of other things. Try asking questions like, 'Did you know that, in addition to providing graphic design services, our consultants also produce press kits and other publicity tools?' or 'Would you believe it if I told you that our largest customer is Apple Computers?'

- **To check comprehension:** Although your clients may be nodding their heads up and down throughout your presentations, do they really understand what you're talking about? You can check by asking questions like, 'Does this make sense?' or 'Do I need to clarify anything we've discussed?'

- **To measure interest:** Of course, you want to quickly get a sense of whether your clients are interested in what you have to say or what you have to sell. Do so by asking your clients questions such as, 'Are you interested in contracting to have this work done?' or 'Are you ready to make a commitment to this project right now?'

✔ **To encourage client participation:** Engaging your clients in your discussion is in your interest. You can encourage client participation by asking questions like, 'What do you think about our approach?' or 'What is the biggest problem that you're having with your current system of production scheduling?'

You have many more reasons to ask your clients questions than to simply find out when they plan to issue a contract or how much money they have to spend. Now that you know why consultants ask questions, read about the two kinds of questions they ask.

How to ask questions

Although you can ask your clients an infinite number of questions, there are only two key kinds of questions – open and closed. Just like you can open or close a door, you can either open up communication with your clients or close it down just by the kind of questions you ask.

There's a right time and place to ask open questions and a right time and place to ask closed questions. The type of question to ask all depends on the particular goals that you've set for your question-and-answer session. Following is a description of open and closed questions, including when you need to use (and not use, as may be the case!) each kind.

✔ **Open:** Open questions expect some amount of explanation in the answers. When you want to explore what your client thinks about a particular topic, you use open questions. However, if you need a simple yes or no response, then open questions are definitely out. Open questions, such as 'What suggestions do you have that can help make our proposal fit your needs?' or 'How should we approach obtaining that particular information?' encourage your clients to go beyond simple yes or no answers and to open up and reveal their personal opinions and beliefs to you.

✔ **Closed:** Closed questions can be answered with a simple yes or no or another such specific response. Closed questions, such as 'How many years have you been in business?' or 'Do you like our proposal?' are great for getting specific responses and information, but they are lousy for getting your clients to open up and offer you any sort of insight into what they are really thinking. When you merely want to get specific answers to specific questions – and to avoid wasting time with a lot of needless discussion, you use closed questions.

We've delved deep enough into the whys and wherefores of asking questions. It's now time to stop all this beating about the bush and find out the right questions to ask your clients. Determine the goals of your question-and-answer session before you start it and then apply the following rules when you ask your questions. Know where you want to go – and map out your route – before you start your journey, and you'll probably get there!

✔ **Do your research ahead of time.** Before you launch into your question-and-answer sessions, spend some time learning about your clients and the kinds of issues they face and may need you to help them with. Don't waste your time or your clients' time going through a list of issues that you can easily obtain the answers to in advance.

✔ **Ask straightforward questions.** Don't beat about the bush or try to trick your clients. Ask your questions in a straightforward manner, and you're most likely to get straightforward responses.

✔ **Move from the big picture to the little picture.** Start with broad questions that give you a general sense of what your clients are thinking. As your clients answer your broad questions, use their responses to ask more precise questions that take you to the heart of the information you need to know.

✔ **Use answers as a foundation for more questions.** You may frequently have absolutely no idea where your questions will lead. Use the answer to each question as a bridge to your next question. Tailor your questions to the responses that you receive from your clients.

✔ **Try different angles.** If one approach doesn't work, don't be afraid to try another. You may have to ask your question many different ways before you find the one that gets the response you need.

Making in-person meetings efficient: Five tips

As you may have long suspected, meetings are a notoriously inefficient way of getting business done. Years ago, researchers determined that approximately 53 per cent of time spent in meetings is unproductive, worthless, and of little consequence. And today – with the added distractions of Blackberrys and mobile phones competing for everyone's attention – our suspicion is that things are even worse.

But meetings don't have to be that way. By working the following five tips into your in-person meeting plans, you can become a meeting hero, instead of a meeting zero.

✔ **Be prepared.** Countless hours are wasted each and every day in meetings for which the participants were unprepared. The good news is that you can choose to be prepared for your meetings, and you can help ensure that your clients are prepared, too. If your clients need some material for them to be knowledgable in the meeting, be sure to send it to them in plenty of time for the meeting. And be sure to let them know they need to look through it!

✔ **Have an agenda.** Another big time-waster is meetings without specific direction. An agenda sets the topics you'll discuss, so it provides a framework on which participants can focus. Again, send it to your clients before the meeting so you can get their input and commitment before you show up, and not during the course of the meeting.

✔ **Start on time and end on time.** As a top-notch, highly professional consultant, always strive to be on time in all your client interactions. If you say you'll call at 3:00 p.m., then call at 3:00 p.m. This same philosophy extends to meetings. If you've ever waited for someone to show up for a meeting so that it can start – and waited, and waited – you know how much time can be wasted when this practice is not adhered to.

✔ **Maintain focus.** It's easy to drift off onto topics that have nothing to do with the purpose for your meeting – especially when the topics that you end up discussing are more interesting or entertaining than the business matters at hand. In most cases, topic drift is bad for meetings. When you're not focusing on moving the meeting agenda forward, then it's going to start taking a step or two or three backwards.

✔ **Capture action items.** Be sure you've got a system in place for noting and keeping track of action items as they are discussed during the course of the meeting. You can have a great meeting, but if no one follows up and does what they promised to do, then maybe you didn't actually accomplish as much as you thought you did. Write down the action items, summarise them, and send copies to all attendees within a day or two after the meeting.

Become a better communicator and you become a better consultant. Whenever you pick up the telephone, or jot down a short note, or compose an email message to a client, be conscious of what you're saying – and how you're saying it. First impressions count, so be sure it – and any subsequent messages – give positive ones.

Chapter 19

Troubleshooting Issues and Problems

*W*hen you're a consultant, either: (a) you work for a consulting business, or (b) you own and operate your own consulting business. Either way, you find that – just as with any other business – you encounter issues, problems, and challenges that you need to address and solve. Sure, you can choose to ignore them, but in our experience, most issues, problems, and challenges don't go away when ignored – they often only get bigger, meaner, and harder to solve.

It's therefore in your interest – and in the long-term interest of your consulting firm, whether you own it or work for someone else – to identify problems as they arise, and address them quickly. In this chapter, we explore some very common consulting issues and problems, and provide you with the kind of advice that helps you identify them in your own organisation and solve them.

Poor Cash Flow

The old saying that money makes the world go round is nowhere more true than in your consulting business. The presence of cash can make it thrive, while the lack of cash will eventually break it. Every business needs cash to cover payroll, pay suppliers, and more. It's easy to recognise the signs of poor cash flow: the balance in your business account is getting lower and lower, and you're getting anxious about when the next payment from a client is going to arrive. When it gets really bad, you find yourself making payments to your suppliers late because you don't have the cash to pay them.

Improving your cash flow is a quick and relatively easy way to improve the overall financial health of your consulting business – both in the short and long term. There are three main ways of improving cash flow: speeding up cash receipts from customers, slowing down cash payments to suppliers, and reducing expenses. Each of the following suggestions accomplishes at least one of those three things.

Require immediate payment (Or sooner!)

Wouldn't it be nice to run a cash business, one in which your customers paid you in cash when they purchased their merchandise or services? While relatively few businesses today run solely on a cash basis – even McDonald's and Starbucks take credit and debit cards now – many do require immediate payment by way of cash, cheque, or credit or debit card when an item or service is purchased. This is a near-ideal situation from the standpoint of cash flow. Instead of waiting 30 days (or more) after you send a customer an invoice to get your money, you have it in hand – right *now*!

Only one other situation is better: getting paid in advance. Many businesses require deposits, retainers, and other forms of advance payment as a normal part of doing business. Building contractors take deposits before they start work, authors receive advances before they start writing, and consultants may be paid a portion of their fee before they set foot in their client's building.

 If you don't already do so, it will definitely be worth your while to require payment on delivery, or even advance payment. Don't forget: Happiness is a positive cash flow. If one of your suppliers wants to negotiate a fee increase (and if you can't avoid giving in), link any increase to payment on more favourable terms, such as 45 or 60 days for example.

Don't pay sooner than you have to

Every invoice has a due date. Though some businesses may require payment 30 days after delivering an invoice, others may require payment in only 15 days or less. *Always* pay your bills on time, but don't pay your bills sooner than you have to. If your supplier has agreed to finance your purchase for 30 days for *free* (which is exactly what is happening when you're sent an invoice with payment required in 30 days), then take full advantage of this free loan. By waiting to pay until payment is due, you have the benefit of your cash for longer, and this has a positive impact on your cash flow.

Make sure your invoices are right

A lot of companies simply reject invoices that have mistakes in them. And if an invoice is rejected, it won't be paid, and it may not even be returned to you for correction. After all, the company you invoiced is also taking advantage of the preceding tip (don't pay sooner than you have to). And by sending an invoice with a mistake on it, you're giving them an easy and semi-ethical way to extend the payment time.

Be sure that your invoices are absolutely correct before you send them out. And while you're at it, make sure they are addressed to the right place *and* the right person. When invoices go to the wrong place or to the wrong person, they tend to sit around unpaid or, worse, eventually find their way into the rubbish bin. If you want to get paid sooner rather than later, double-check all your invoices before they are posted, and make sure they're going to the right person at the right place.

Invoice upon delivery

Some companies invoice all their customers on a set schedule, perhaps once a month. The trouble is, if an item is delivered on the first of the month but an invoice doesn't go out to the customer until the end of the month, you've built 30 days of nonpayment into your cash flow equation – automatically. Then, if it takes your customer 30 more days to pay your invoice after he or she receives it, you've gone 60 days between the time you delivered the item and were paid for it. Unfortunately, this is an easy recipe for cash flow disaster!

When you deliver a contracted item to a client, invoice your client that same day, or no more than a day or two later. Check your contract for the method of invoicing, but always push for the method that is quickest – usually via email or fax. The goal is to start the payment clock ticking as soon as you can. You get your money more quickly, and your cash flow is better for it.

Invoice more often

If you provide a service under contract over a long period of time, you may send out invoices after particular services have been delivered, or after a set period of time – say, a month – has elapsed. If you're in this specific situation, an easy way to improve your cash flow is to increase your invoicing frequency. So, for example, if your current agreement requires you to invoice monthly, you can renegotiate it to allow for invoicing twice a month, or perhaps even weekly.

The more often you invoice your clients, the better the impact on your cash flow. The payments are smaller, but you get your money sooner. And sooner is better when it comes to cash!

Manage your expenses

Cash flow is nothing more than the net result of the money that comes into your organisation minus the money that goes out. The less money that goes out, the better your cash flow. Every business has to spend money for things it needs in order to operate, but the timing of this spending can have a major impact on your cash flow. One way to reduce the amount of money that flows out of your organisation – and to improve cash flow at the time – is to manage your expenses.

Only spend money when you absolutely need to. Need a new computer? Why not try to get another year out of your old one? Your courier has raised its rates? Why not check to see what UPS, DHL, or the Royal Mail charges? It pays to project your cash inflows (payments from clients) and to try to match them with your cash outflows (payments to suppliers). For example, if you expect a big payment from a customer two months from now, you must defer all possible expenses until you have the cash in hand. That way you avoid the dreaded cash crunch that can occur when you spend more money than you have available to you.

Remember that Her Majesty's Revenue and Customs (HMRC) generally collect VAT quarterly, income tax six-monthly or annually, and corporation tax annually. Be sure that your cash flow forecast takes account of these hefty amounts of money leaving your business, otherwise one month you may be feeling happy but the next month be in tears. Philip reviews his cash flow forecast at least weekly, especially around Christmas time when large PAYE, VAT, corporation tax, and personal income tax cheques all go out within a few weeks and customers' cheques slow to a dribble during the Christmas to New Year shutdown. Remember that cash flow is MITYM: More Important Than Your Mother (okay, perhaps not *that* important but you get the point don't you?).

Clients Who Want Free Advice

Doctors have long known that once someone finds out the nature of their profession – say at a cocktail party or other social event. it won't be long before they are asked their advice about some physical ailment or pain. 'Doctor, I've had this pain in my back for years now – do you have any idea what it might be?' We're sure that many doctors avoid parties for this very reason.

Consultants often find themselves in the same boat when someone they meet or know finds out what they do for a living. Peter often experiences this when someone finds out that he is a professional writer. Many such new acquaintances instantly tell him about the book that they've long wanted to write, asking questions about the merits of the idea, what it would take to get the book published, and if Peter has any interest in co-writing it. While Peter always enjoys talking books with people, there's a fine line between simply talking books, and providing advice that Peter should be charging consulting fees to dispense. This line is not always clear-cut, and it's easy to give too much information away for free – removing the incentive for a client-to-be to pay for your services.

So, what must you do when someone asks you for free advice?

We've heard lots of good arguments on both sides of the issue. Some consultants argue quite convincingly that you should never, *ever* give out freebies. According to their way of thinking, to do so sets a dangerous precedent that will lead your client to expect further freebies in the future. But other experienced consultants argue just as convincingly that it can make perfect sense to give out freebies – especially if it will help you get your foot in the door for more business (or help ensure you keep it there once you've got it firmly planted).

So, which approach is best?

Actually, giving free advice can be a good thing – especially when it leads to new business. For example, you might meet someone while you're networking who – based on the limited information you give him – decides to offer you a full-on consulting job. And it can definitely be a good thing when a current client wants to explore other areas of business that you can help with.

Our advice is to weigh up the pros and cons of giving free advice in each and every case before you give it. Many consultants don't advertise their services, instead relying on referrals from happy clients to bring in new business. And if, for whatever reason, your clients aren't happy, then you're not going to get a lot of referrals to potential new clients. Giving some free advice is a kind of advertisement for your business, a marketing cost that must be anticipated, budgeted, built into your rates, and then happily extended when you feel the time is right.

Of course, you can't do *all* of your work for free – that's a one-way ticket to negative cash flow and bankruptcy. And, unfortunately, there are more than a few unscrupulous clients out there who would love nothing more than to have you do lots of work and never pay a penny for it – we've experienced that for ourselves more than once or twice. But for every bad client like that, there are many more for whom an occasional freebie will work wonders – making it well worth taking a chance to give it. It all comes down to balancing your cost of doing the work for free against your assessment of the long-term potential of the relationship.

Can't Get That First Sale

If you've just started up your consulting business, you'll soon realise that you're not really *in business* until you have completed your first sale to a real, live client. Setting aside a bedroom as your consulting world headquarters doesn't mean you're in business, nor does printing new consulting business cards or setting up a website for your firm. Until you have your first client, and until you actually start performing work for him or her, you're just getting ready to do business.

Breaking the ice with a first sale, however, can be difficult for new consultants. While some consultants already have clients lined up before they make preparations to start up their businesses, others find that they put up their nice shiny, new consulting sign and wait . . . and wait . . . and wait. So, what can you do if you're having a hard time getting that first sale? Here are a few tips to help you get out of the car park of consulting and into the fast lane:

- ✔ **Check your marketing.** Let's say that you've got the right product or service, and you've got it for the right price. But, even so, you've yet to land your first client – what could be wrong? In this situation, it's likely that the news about your product or service is not getting to your target audience of potential clients, which means that your marketing efforts are falling short – *way* short. Take a close look at your marketing – what are you doing (or not doing) to publicise your consulting firm and the services that you offer? Do you have a website? Do you use Google adwords advertising? Are you networking with potential clients in your community or industry? Are you seeking opportunities to publicise your business through the local media or blogs? Do you have a marketing plan? If your marketing needs work, then plan to spend some quality time reading Part IV of this book – Sales and Marketing.

- ✔ **Check your pricing.** Okay. So you've got a great product or service, and you're getting the word out to a wide audience of potential clients who very much need what you've got to offer. All systems are ' go', but you're still not getting that critical first client – now what? Take a close look at your pricing. How much do you charge for your services, and how do these rates compare to your competitors? (If you don't know what your competitors charge, then find out.) Are your prices significantly higher? If you're new to the market, you may find it difficult to get people to pay the same for your services as for those of consulting firms that have been around longer and have long-established reputations. Are you trying to compete on price alone, and neglecting to convince your prospective clients of the value that you'll bring to their organisations, above and beyond the money that they spend? Consider dropping your price for your first few clients to break the ice and to begin to develop a stable of happy clients who will refer others to you and your firm.

✔ **Check your product or service.** You may have a great price, and you may have great publicity and marketing, but you may simply have the wrong product or service for your target market. For example, you might have identified a great local target market populated with fast-growing, small technology firms. Only one problem – the consulting service you offer is of no interest to these fast-growing small businesses. Be sure that your products and services are relevant to the market you want to enter. It they're not, then you can either change your target market, or change the products and services you offer.

✔ **Check your competition.** Your competition can teach you a lot – especially when it comes to landing your first sale. Before you offer your products or services to the public, take some time to survey your competition to see exactly what they offer, at what prices and in what time frames, and what your prospective clients like – and dislike – about working with them.

✔ **Check your expectations.** One more thing you need to check out if you're having problems landing your first client: your expectations. Have you quit your career and launched yourself headlong into a new consulting venture? If so, you may have put a lot of pressure on yourself, and your clients-to-be may sense that pressure, deciding to steer clear of you for now. Or, alternatively, have you kept your day job, and are you just dipping your little toe into the consulting water? Again, your clients-to-be may sense that you're not fully committed to your business – and to their satisfaction – and so they may be reluctant to take up your offer to provide the services they need. Are you hoping that becoming a self-employed consultant will rescue you from a life of quiet desperation working for someone else? (It might, but then again, it might not.) Are you expecting your consulting business to be a moneymaker that will solve all your financial problems and keep the debt collector at bay? (It might, but probably not for months, or even years.) In short, be sure you understand your own motivations and expectations for becoming a consultant, and then check to see how they are colouring your interactions with prospective clients. They can sense desperation a mile away, and they'll probably run – not walk – to your competitors when they sense it in you.

Clients Who Are Slow (Or Refuse) to Pay

Every consultant eventually comes across a customer who either habitually pays late ('I'm expecting a big cheque this week – as soon as I get it I'll pay you!') or not at all. This is a problem for any consultant, but especially for those who own their own firms. You need a steady supply of cash coming into your business to enable you to keep it afloat.

When is the last time that you took a close look at who owes you money, how much they owe you, and how far overdue their payments are? If you aren't keeping a close eye on your accounts receivable (the money that your clients owe you), you're potentially leaving your business exposed to a financial disaster.

No matter how much we love our customers, some of them invariably don't understand how important it is to us that they pay their bills on time. A day or two late isn't a big deal. A month or two late *is* a big deal. Once your customers get in the habit of paying late, it can be almost impossible to get them to start paying on time.

Managing the money coming into your business is an important part of any self-employed consultant's job. (Even consultants who work for someone else must keep an eye on the money coming into their company – if their clients aren't paying, these consultants may soon be out of a job.) When your clients don't pay you for your work when you deliver it, then you're in effect granting them a loan. In accounting-speak, you're creating a *debtor* – a client with an obligation to pay you at some point in the future. While the generally accepted time for payment is 28 or 30 days after delivery of an invoice, that date can vary widely depending on the terms and conditions of your contract or agreement.

Unfortunately, trying to get all your clients to pay their obligations on time – the full amounts they owe – can often make you feel like you're herding cats. While most clients will pay you on time, there'll always be a few who'll wander away from the pack and decide to do their own thing. The reasons are many – perhaps their clients are paying *them* late, or maybe their business has declined, or it could be that they haven't been managing their own business expenses as well as they should. Whatever the reason, before you can collect on those late payments, you first need to know that they're late. You can do this by managing your debtors – the money owed you by your clients.

Here are a few tips for keeping on top of your debtors, and for helping to keep your late payers on track:

✔ **Create a system for tracking your debtors.** This system needs to list all outstanding client invoices, when and for how much each invoice was issued, and the date by which payment is due. If your consulting firm is large and you have many invoices outstanding at any given time, you may want to focus the majority of your efforts on invoices for more than a certain amount of money, say £5,000. Or you may decide to focus on payments that are more than 30 or 45 days late.

✔ **Call or email your tardy customers when invoices are issued**. Let them know that an invoice is on the way, and be sure to ask them to let you know if it hasn't been received by a certain date, or if there are problems or questions that need to be resolved before they'll approve payment. Now is also a good time to ask your client when the invoice will be paid.

✔ **Call your customers a week before payments are due.** The idea is to ensure that your invoices are set up for payment on the date promised. If they aren't, ask what you can do to help ensure payment is made on time. Be sure to address any problems now, before they threaten to delay your receipt of funds.

✔ **When a payment is late by even a day, call your customer immediately.** Ask why the payment is late and determine what can be done to expedite payment.

None of us enjoy calling clients to encourage them to pay their bills. However, if you extend payment terms to your clients rather than requiring them to pay you at the time you deliver your products or services, you'll eventually be faced with doing just that. And, when times get tough, this task is more important than ever.

Part of the overall job of managing your cash flow is the task of monitoring receivables, the money owed to your company by your clients and customers. A number of very capable business accounting software programs – including Sage and others – have built-in aged debtors' reports (essentially a listing of unpaid invoices showing how long they've been unpaid) that make the task easy.

Okay, so you've sent the invoices out to your client, and confirmed that that they are correct and acceptable for payment. You've been promised a date of payment, but that date comes and goes – as do many more. Now what? Now you need to get very serious about collecting the money that your client owes you.

Here are a few tips for collecting your money:

✔ **Make a call directly to your customer asking for his or her help.** Don't simply mark a copy of the invoice with one of those handy rubber stamps from an office supply store that says something like, 'We value your business – we hope you'll pay soon', or 'Second notice – we would really like to be paid now' and post it to your customer's accounting department. Ask your client to help you. Your payment will get a much higher level of attention if your client acts as your advocate inside the company than if you try to go it alone.

✔ **Ask what's holding up payment and find out what you can do to free it up.** Sometimes a payment gets held up because a client's accounting department has lost an invoice, doesn't have proof of delivery, or can't find a signed copy of the purchase order or contract that authorised your work in the first place. Find out what's holding up payment and offer to provide it – as quickly as you possibly can.

✔ **As a last resort – and this is only if you aren't concerned about getting any future business from your client – turn the payment over to a debt collection agency or take them to court.** If your client hasn't paid you what he or she owes on a timely basis – and is ignoring or avoiding your phone calls and email messages – then you have little choice but to take action quickly. This means either turning your client over to a debt collection agency (which will keep a hefty portion of any collected fees as a commission) or taking him or her to court. If the amount is relatively small (up to about £15,000), you may be able to take your client to the small claims court. Keep in mind that once you take one of these actions, you can kiss this client goodbye, but in cases like this, that might not be such a bad outcome.

Whatever you do, when a payment is late, get onto it right away – don't wait for days or weeks (or months!) hoping it will come in. Chances are, something is wrong, so it needs your immediate attention.

Can't Get Clients to Pay You What You're Worth

We'll venture a guess that you probably think you're worth a lot to your clients. Indeed, you may very well be worth a lot. However, if you can't get your clients – or your prospective clients – to agree with this self-assessment of your worth, then you've got a problem. The problem is that you end up either accepting jobs that are paying you less than you're worth, or not landing any jobs at all. Getting your clients to look beyond the fees that you charge and to see the value that you bring to the table is a fine art – and it's an art that you need to master if you hope to gain long-term success in the wonderful world of consulting.

When you find yourself in a situation where your client is more focused on the fee that you charge than on the value that you create for their organisation, one of two things may have happened:

✔ You haven't done a good enough job linking the price you propose to charge to a strategic value proposition of the organisation's overall business case.

✔ You're dealing with somebody who's not responsible for the organisation's overall performance.

In the first case, you need to clearly make the case for the value that your consulting organisation provides to your prospective client. How much will your client save each week, month, or year by giving you the job? How many times is his or her investment in you multiplied because of the more effective organisation that you have created? You can find more about the topic of value-based pricing in Chapter 21.

In the second case, be sure that you're talking to somebody who sees or is responsible for the big picture, instead of someone – perhaps a department manager – who is just looking at what you're going to cost. Your job is to move up your client's chain of command until you reach the person who can see that your organisation will provide far more value than the fees that you charge.

In either of these cases, avoid doing consulting work on an hourly fee basis. Once you set an hourly rate, it can become a trap that will hamstring your efforts to build a value proposition for your clients. It is far better to charge a flat fee for the work you do, which will help your client avoid getting hung up on hourly or daily charges. You can develop this approach by consistently producing value and building solid relationships with your clients. Become an essential partner for your client, and your value will be easy to see – and easy to sell.

Part VI
Taking Your Consulting Business to the Next Level

'Ah — here's the consultant on ethics.'

Part V

Taking Your

Consulting Business

to the Next Level

In this part . . .

One day – it may be weeks, months, or years after you get your consulting business off the ground – you're going to realise that you're ready to take your business to the next level.

In this part, we consider a variety of strategies to do just that, including how to use your current success to move into new areas, advanced pricing strategies that can make your business even more profitable, and a variety of approaches for enhancing your image and reputation.

Chapter 20

Building on Your Success

In This Chapter

▶ Growing your consulting firm

▶ Understanding what makes you successful

▶ Building partnerships

▶ Giving back to the community

*E*very business goes through phases. In the initial start-up phase, you're focused on the nuts and bolts of getting your business off the ground – setting up your office, establishing accounting and other administrative systems and procedures, creating a limited company, landing your first clients. A growth phase often comes next, during which happy clients start referring their colleagues to you, and your own marketing efforts begin to pay off with new business. How much – and how fast – you grow is pretty much up to you. There are a number of things you can do to expand your business if you like. Alternatively, you may be happy with things just the way they are, and see no need to grow. That's fine – it's your business, so you get to decide.

In this chapter, we consider a variety of different approaches for building on your success. Some of these approaches include consciously growing your business, understanding the keys to success, building partnerships, and giving back to your community. Even if you decide that you're happy with the status quo, keep in mind that you've always got the option to grow your business whenever you want. If you do good work – and you do it on time and on budget – you're almost guaranteed to have a very long line of clients clamouring for your services.

Tuning Up Your Growth Engine

To grow or not to grow? That is the question. If you own your own consulting business, at some time you'll have to address this question by answering it. Of course, you can choose to ignore it, but by doing so you're actually making a decision. While some consulting firms may rocket into the stratosphere with little or no planning or action on the part of those in charge, the majority won't grow unless *you* take action to bring in a steady stream of new business.

To grow – or not

So we're back to our original question: To grow or not to grow?

To decide on the path to take with your consulting business, consider reviewing the following checklist:

- ✔ **What does your heart say?** Are you a driven, thrusting entrepreneurial spirit who will stop at nothing to get to the top of the consulting heap, or are you a bit more laid-back? If your heart is telling you to go slow, then perhaps you need to listen – and proceed accordingly.

- ✔ **What kind of lifestyle do you prefer?** Many consultants find themselves on the road a lot, looking after clients the other side of town, in different cities, or even around the world. This means many long days and nights away from home. If you've got a family or have obligations back home, then a high-growth consulting business may be in direct conflict. Assess your lifestyle, and use the result to help you determine how much growth to pursue.

- ✔ **How are your finances?** Pushing a business into a high-growth mode usually requires a sizeable investment of both time and money. It takes a lot of cash to market your services, to travel here and there, and to recruit the extra employees you need to deal with all the new clients you get as a result of the growth process. If your finances are healthy and strong, then growth is a very real option. If your finances are weak and anaemic, then you may be putting your entire business at risk by pushing for growth too aggressively.

- ✔ **What's the state of the market?** Some consultants assume that an unlimited supply of clients are just waiting to buy whatever it is that they have to sell. While there may indeed be many clients who would be interested in buying these consultants' services, the pool of prospects certainly has a limit – and this limit varies depending on the market. Before you decide whether or not to fire up your growth engine, take a good look at your market and decide if it can support your anticipated growth. If so, then you've got the option. If not, then you may want to defer your growth plans until the market conditions are more favourable.

Remember: only you can decide whether you want to turn your consulting company into a high-growth operation – with all the good things and bad that growth entails – or whether you'd like to do something a bit more relaxed. Whatever choice you make, the good news is that you can always change your mind. If you decide that growth is now your number one priority, you can start up your growth engine any time you like. And if you decide you want to step off the high-growth merry-go-round, you can also do that – any time you like. The choice is yours.

Stages of growth

Your consulting business is a living, breathing thing. It reacts to the environment around it, and is always moving and changing – sometimes for the better, and sometimes not so much. According to Jana Matthews – founder and CEO of The Jana Matthews Group (www.janamatthewsgroup.com), a management consulting firm that specialises in working with growing businesses – most companies typically go through a start-up stage, and then three distinct growth stages. These stages are:

- ✔ **Start-up.** At this stage, you're trying to figure out what product or service to offer that will meet the needs of the market, and ways in which your company can provide value to its customers. If you're the head of a consulting business in the start-up stage, your role is to act as a doer and decision-maker.

- ✔ **Initial growth.** In this first stage of growth, your company is very sales-driven as it tries to launch a new or different product, capture market share, and increase revenue. Company operations are fast-paced, highly flexible, even chaotic. People do whatever is necessary to be successful. If you're the head of a consulting business in the initial growth stage, your role is to be a delegator and direction setter.

- ✔ **Rapid growth.** In the second stage of growth, your company is trying to achieve widespread use of its products or services, gain a significant share of its chosen markets, ward off advances from competitors, and move into a market leadership position. Lots of new people need to be recruited and integrating them and aligning their efforts can be a daunting, never-ending task. If you're head of a consulting business in this stage of growth, your role is to act as a team builder, coach, planner, and communicator.

✔ **Continuous growth.** This final stage of growth comprises successive rounds of turbulence and periodic 'reinventions' of the company. Rapid growth has led to many more customers and market opportunities, a much larger employee base, a more complex organisation, and the potential to dominate the industry. But more of everything also includes more potential to go out of control. If you're the head of a consulting business in the continuous growth stage, your role shifts to acting as a change catalyst, organisation builder, strategic innovator, and controller of the company's culture.

In what stage is *your* consulting business right now – in start-up, or in one of the three stages of growth? Does your company culture match up with the descriptions of the different stages above? If not, what can you do to get them in sync?

Growth strategies

There are a variety of specific strategies you can pursue to grow your consulting business, either alone, or in combination with one another. Some of the most common strategies include:

✔ **Develop new products or services.** This strategy can be made easier by developing new products and services that are related to existing products and services.

✔ **Expand into new markets.** Many consulting firms find that by expanding their geographical markets (including onto the Internet), they can grow beyond local markets, which may be saturated. In addition, expanding into entirely new industries (for example, an information technology consulting firm expanding from its base in the aerospace industry and into the car industry) offers even more growth opportunities.

✔ **Go international.** Why limit your company to just one country, when you've got an entire world of them out there?

✔ **Recruit more employees.** When you recruit more employees, you are by default growing (unless you're firing even more employees than you're hiring). However, when you you're staffing up your organisation, you've got to have work for them to do, otherwise these employees will quickly become an expensive burden.

✔ **Create strategic alliances.** It's true – one plus one can equal three. By finding the right organisations to align with – perhaps other consulting firms, or companies in a related industry – you can dramatically increase the reach and power of your firm. The key is to find the right allies – firms that aren't competing with you and that multiply your effectiveness rather than detract from it.

✔ **Pursue corporate partnerships.** Putting together a corporate partnership is similar to creating a strategic alliance, but it is an even more formal (with written agreements) and potentially longer-term relationship between firms. We cover such partnerships in detail later in this chapter.

✔ **Pursue acquisitions and mergers.** Companies have long pursued acquisitions and mergers as a relatively quick way to grow. And while they can indeed help a consulting firm grow and lead to great success, they often fail as a result of mismatches between the cultures and values of the firms.

✔ **Float your company on the Alternative Investment Market (AIM).** There's nothing like a little bit of cash (okay, a lot of cash) from investors to fuel your growth engine. With an AIM flotation, you raise money by selling shares in your company to the public. If your consulting firm happens to be the next big thing, then the amount of money you can raise – and the growth that money will support – can be substantial. AIM flotations take massive amounts of effort and are very expensive, so think carefully before taking this route.

Whatever combination of growth strategies you decide to pursue, be sure to take the time required to plan your moves in sufficient detail before you execute them. The more planning you do (up to a point – you can 'over-plan', after all), the greater your chances of success.

Nine Keys to Success

Many business owners – including the owners of consulting firms – wonder if a secret of success exists, some set of rules that will ensure their company is built to last. As it turns out, researchers have done a lot of work in this area and they've found that there are certain characteristics that successful businesses share in common with one another.

One such researcher – Professor William Bygrave, one of the top experts on entrepreneurship, found that there are nine keys to success for an profit-making enterprise. Bygrave named these keys *The Nine Fs*:

✔ **Founders:** Every start-up must have a first-class entrepreneur. (If you're the owner of your consulting firm, that means *you*.)

✔ **Focused:** Entrepreneurial companies focus on niche markets. They specialise. (To be a successful consultant, you need to realise that you'll be much more valuable to your clients – and in demand – if you're an expert in some specific field, rather than a generalist in a wide range of fields.)

✔ **Fast:** They make decisions quickly and implement them swiftly. (But don't make decisions so quickly that you don't have time to appreciate the alternatives before you take the steps required to implement them.)

- **Flexible:** Entrepreneurial companies keep an open mind. They respond to change. (If you run your own consulting firm and keep it small and nimble, you can respond much more quickly to changes in your business environment than much larger consulting firms.)

- **Forever innovating:** They are tireless innovators. (Successful consultants are always looking for new ways to bring value to their clients – while providing their own firms with advantages over the competition.)

- **Flat:** Entrepreneurial organisations have as few layers of management as possible. (When you're in charge, *you* decide how your consulting firm will be structured.)

- **Frugal:** By keeping overheads low and productivity high, entrepreneurial organisations keep costs down. (And when you keep costs down, your profits go up.)

- **Friendly:** Entrepreneurial companies are friendly to their customers, suppliers, and workers. (This builds tremendous client goodwill and loyalty.)

- **Fun:** It's fun to be associated with an entrepreneurial company. (There are few things more fun and satisfying in the world of business than being part of a growing company that is solving important problems for its clients.)

While there are no guarantees (sorry about that), we think that Professor Bygrave is on to something here. It's a good idea to take a close look at your own consulting firm – whether you're an owner, or an employee – and see how many of The Nine Fs you can tick off. As the old saying goes, the more the merrier.

Using Partnerships to Build on Your Success

Forming partnerships with other individuals – and other consulting firms – can be an excellent way to build on your success. How? Because forming a partnership can give you access to additional resources, expertise, and markets that you don't currently have access to. Not only that, but bringing an outsider into your organisation can give you a fresh perspective on your consulting firm – and its own opportunities and challenges – that you may not see for yourself.

Partnerships can be informal – just a handshake or meeting of the minds – or formal, complete with legally binding partnership agreements. Whichever approach you decide to take with your partnerships, it's always a good idea to get the understandings of who will do what – and how the resulting rewards will be divided – in writing. Believe us: More than a few partnerships have crashed and burned as a result of misunderstandings of these kinds of business issues.

To keep your own partnerships from crashing and burning, here are a few tips for you to consider:

- ✔ **Make sure you have trust.** Sharing your consulting business with someone else requires a lot of trust. Without trust, it's unlikely that your partnership will be at the level that is required to make it successful. Become partners only with those you trust, and if that trust is lost, then don't hesitate to cancel the partnership.

- ✔ **Be sure that your business can stand on its own.** The idea of forming a partnership is not to shore up a weak business; it's to build on the strengths of each business and then multiply them for the benefit of all. If your business is weak, strengthen it before you think about creating partnerships with others.

- ✔ **Focus on becoming partners with firms that bring value to your business.** While you don't want to form a partnership from a position of weakness, you do want to find partners who will add value to your consulting firm by providing skills, knowledge, expertise, and resources that may be missing in your own firm. This, ultimately, is one of the key reasons for forming a partnership in the first place.

- ✔ **Share wealth – and the risk.** Partners must share both the rewards of their success – in proportion to their participation – and the risk. Although it can sometimes be difficult to gauge just how much each partner contributed to a consulting firm's success, it's important to get close. If one partner is stuck shouldering the majority of the risk – for little reward – then he or she will not be happy with the partnership.

- ✔ **Put it in writing.** Even if you decide not to enter into a formal partnership, it's important for you and your partner to spell out your key understandings in writing. These understandings must include a summary of each party's responsibilities and a clearly spelled out division of the partnership's revenues and income.

- ✔ **Consider a trial relationship first.** Just as most couples date for a while before they get engaged and eventually married, you and your prospective partner must consider a trial relationship before you enter into a formal partnership. Before long you'll know whether or not a longer-term relationship is in your future.

If you take time to find a good partner, and you spell out your key understandings – preferably in writing – before you enter into your partnership, then it's likely that it will be successful. Of course, not every partnership is destined for success, no matter how great your consulting firm is, or how wonderful your partner's business is. If it works, great. If not, then you've always got the option of dissolving this partnership and moving forward without partners, or finding another one. If you own your consulting firm, the choice is all yours.

Giving Back

There will come a time in your business life when you'll achieve a certain amount of success, and you'll start to feel the urge to have an impact in your community, or to change the world. While each of us finds our own level, true success is not measured in pounds and pence, but in the satisfaction you feel in helping your clients, and in the respect and reputation you develop over time for your good work. And true success can also be measured by the extent of the difference you make in the lives of others.

For many business people, making a difference is most effectively accomplished by giving back – getting out into their communities and participating in non-profit organisations as a volunteer, leader, board member, or contributor. As with anything else, some approaches work better than others. The US-based Institute for Educational Leadership (www.iel.org) published the following list of recommendations for business people who plan to volunteer to lead community efforts:

- ✔ **Stay focused.** Identify an area that best suits your interests and abilities – affordable housing or improving workforce skills, for example – and focus on it. Avoid grand, all-encompassing approaches. Don't lose patience if your ideas don't instantly resonate with the people you're trying to help – remember that their previous experiences with 'outsiders' may have been dismal.

- ✔ **Avoid magic solutions.** Management systems such as total quality management, re-engineering, or virtual organisations that work in corporate settings may not work for a government agency or a community. Be practical. Be clear about objectives and expected results.

✔ **Don't act like a 'typical' corporate leader.** Top-down leadership will not work in community settings. Collaborative, collective leadership is more likely to succeed. Other pointers:

- You can't fire people, so don't try.

- Avoid self-promotion.

- Respect communities' realities, but make sure that the information you get stands up to tough criteria.

- Try to work within and around restrictive regulations instead of trying to change them, at least at first.

✔ **Use your best people.** Community activists can easily spot unqualified newcomers. Direct participation from the leader, a top aide, or any other well-qualified member of the business is best. Whatever the approach, it's important that company representatives have strong, public backing from senior management.

✔ **Hang in there.** This work isn't easy. Expect the unexpected, because life in poor neighbourhoods can be politically messy. Business leaders working with these communities will encounter problems of a magnitude and a complexity beyond anything they've dealt with before. Resist the temptation to bail out when things get tough. Don't spread yourself too thin, and be flexible.

As we have seen in this chapter, there are many ways to build on your s uccess. Some involve growing your business and bringing in more money, and some involve helping others – from your clients, to your neighbours, to the world as a whole. Remember: You don't have to be Bill Gates or Warren Buffett to make a difference. There are countless community-based organisations that would greatly benefit from your business experience and network of connections. By helping others, you find the kind of success that is especially precious – and particularly needed.

Chapter 21

Advanced Pricing Strategies

. . . .

. . . .

*I*n Chapter 6, we discuss the basics of pricing, including such topics as establishing your value to clients, different ways to structure your consulting fees, changing your pricing, and knowing when to say 'no.' Depending on what kind of consulting you do and the nature and complexity of your projects, you may find that the material in Chapter 6 will be all you need to set your prices and negotiate deals that are profitable to you, and fair to your clients.

However, you may find that the basic information in Chapter 6 is not enough. Perhaps you provide services in a field that is narrowly based on a particular commodity – for example, home inspection – for which clients make their buying decisions primarily on price, and you're trying to figure out a way to increase your fees without losing business. Or maybe the projects you do are very expensive and specialised, and you need to find a way to help your clients look beyond your fee to see the value that they'll receive as a result of the work that you'll do for them.

As it turns out, there are many different ways of pricing your consulting services that clients may not find as objectionable as the good-old-fashioned hourly rate or fixed price – and that may actually encourage them to choose your consulting firm over the competition. In this chapter, we consider a variety of topics related to advanced pricing strategies, including the philosophy of pricing, value-based pricing, and contingent fee and performance-based pricing.

The Zen of Pricing

The psychology of sales – why people buy what they buy, when, and for what price – has fascinated researchers and salespeople (and the managers of salespeople) alike for centuries. It's no accident that there are countless books, seminars, workshops, online courses, and other teaching tools available for those who want to learn how to work the psychology of sales for their own advantage. And, truth be told, the gallons of potions these people are peddling do have some validity. Why? Because people often make purchasing decisions based on their emotions – justifying their purchases intellectually later on.

When you set a price, you don't do so in a vacuum. Sure, you need to cover your expenses – your salary, your electricity bill, the cost of acquiring computers and office space, and much more – and you need to make a profit to grow your consulting firm, but setting a price involves much more than your side of the equation. You've got your client's side of the equation to deal with, which includes his or her emotions, attitudes, previous experiences with consultants, pressures from management, upbringing, personal values, available budget, level of authority, and much more.

In this section, we'll dive a bit deeper into the Zen – the basic philosophical underpinnings – of pricing for your consulting business. Whether you own your own consulting firm – or simply work for one – this section applies to you.

Who sets your price?

You may think that the answer to the question that forms this section's title is obvious and straightforward. Who sets your price? Well, you do – don't you? Actually, the answer is not quite as obvious as you may think. While you may be the one who puts a price in a proposal to a prospective client, or who publishes a price list for your consulting services, you have to be responsive to your client's needs and expectations.

So, who really sets your price? Your *client* does.

Here are some of the factors that will enter into the psychology of your buyer, helping to determine how much he or she will be willing to pay for your consulting services:

> ✔ **Demand.** If your service is in high demand – for whatever reason – then it will be more valuable to your prospective clients. This is especially so in the case of a shortage of talented consultants working in your particular area of expertise. For example, every four years in the United States

a presidential election takes place. You can bet that in the months – and even years – leading up to the actual election, talented political and election consultants with proven results are in great demand. And you can also bet that the cream of the crop can demand almost any price they like.

✔ **Competition.** When you've got a lot of competition, your buyers usually realise that they have many buying options, and they are therefore less willing to pay you a premium for your consulting services. Taken to its extreme, this can lead to your service being considered a commodity where potential clients use lowest price as their primary buying consideration.

✔ **Features.** Does your consulting service or products have unique features that other consultants don't offer? For example, perhaps you have a money-back guarantee if your services don't bring about the promised results. If your competition doesn't offer a similar policy, then your firm may be perceived as offering more value than they do – potentially allowing you to demand a higher price.

✔ **Technology.** Some consultants ride on the leading edge of technology, and their clients are willing to pay them a premium for this.

✔ **Positioning.** Your positioning in the market can dramatically impact clients' expectations of your value, and thus the price they are willing to pay for your services. For example, if you're a branding consultant who specialises in working with high-profile household name corporations, you can command a much higher price than someone who specialises in working with small local businesses.

While these are some of the key psychological factors that enter into your clients' perception of your value, and therefore what price they should pay for your services, there are no doubt others. Be alert and aware of the signals that you send to your prospective clients, and what those signals say about the price they should pay you. It's not a coincidence that up-market estate agents often drive luxury cars and not clapped-out old Ford Escorts – they are sending prospective clients a message of value.

Common pricing strategies

In Chapter 6, we considered a variety of basic consultant pricing methods, including the hourly rate approach, the rule of thirds, the per-item or per-project approach, and retainers. However, when considering the actual philosophy behind your approach to pricing your products or services, it is instructive to take a close look at the most common pricing strategies used by all sorts of businesses, not just consulting firms.

✔ **Cost-based pricing.** When you use this pricing strategy, you simply add up all of your costs to provide a specific consulting product or service, tack on an additional amount for profit, and use the resultant number as your price. While this pricing strategy ensures that you'll be compensated for all of your expenses, it does not take into account that other consultants may be able to trim their costs – enabling them to significantly undercut your own price.

✔ **Demand-based pricing.** Your prospective clients are very likely to have expectations of how much they should pay for a given product or service, perhaps gained from previous experience or from talking to colleagues who have previously enlisted the services of consultants. By doing some market research, you can find out what prices your prospects will be willing to pay, and price your consulting products and services accordingly.

✔ **Competition-based pricing.** In applying a competition-based pricing strategy, you look at the prices your competition is charging to determine your own pricing. You can actually proceed in any of three different directions with the information you gain by looking at your competitors' prices. You can simply match their prices, pound for pound. Or you can undercut them to become a more attractive option yourself. Or you can intentionally price your products and services higher than the competition to achieve a premium aura of exclusivity.

✔ **Loss-leader pricing.** You've seen this strategy at work when a supermarket sells milk, eggs, or some other basic food commodity at a very low price, hoping to bring people into their shops where they'll inevitably buy other – more profitable – products. Consultants often use loss-leader pricing when they offer some of their products or services at a particularly low price (sometimes free) to get their foot in the door with a client, hoping it will lead to additional business. A management consultant might offer to perform an initial assessment of an organisation's recruitment process, for example, for a nominal fee – say £500 – with the actual consulting services that will be required to develop and implement solutions costing the prospective client much more.

✔ **Demand-curve pricing.** This pricing approach generally applies to manufacturers of products. Demand-curve pricing is offering a new product at a relatively high price when demand is high. As demand eventually lags – and manufacturing costs are decreased due to economies of scale and other manufacturing efficiencies – the price is gradually decreased to generate ongoing buyer interest and additional incremental sales.

✔ **Skimming.** Imagine being a consultant who offers a service or product that no one else has, but that your clients – once they learn about it – really want. Believe it or not, it does happen. And when it happens, you can price your consulting products very high – at least until competitors enter the market and start driving your prices down.

✔ **Penetration.** Let's say you want to enter a crowded market, and you want to capture a lot of business as quickly as you can. To do this, you need to dramatically undercut the competition while getting the word out far and wide that potential clients have a great opportunity to obtain your services at a great price. As you build your business – and land a solid base of clients – you can then gradually increase your prices in line with the rest of your competitors.

✔ **Psychological pricing.** Why is it that the price £19.99 looks significantly less expensive than £20.00 to many consumers? Researchers have found that such 'odd/even pricing' results in a higher sales volume – buyers perceive they are getting a bargain with odd prices. Whatever the cause, such pricing seems to work. For a consultant, this may mean pricing a particular service at £499 instead of £500, or £9,999 instead of £10,000.

We're not suggesting that you need to go through all of these pricing strategies each time you set a price for your consulting products or services. However, we are suggesting that you need to consider them as you develop the pricing philosophy to apply in your business. As we have seen, there are lots of different approaches. Your job is to decide which approach will work best for your firm – and for your clients.

Value-Based Pricing

Value-based pricing has taken the world of consulting by storm over the past decade. *Value-based pricing* simply means basing your prices on the value that clients believe they get from your services and products rather than on your costs in providing them. A client's perception of value is related to three factors:

✔ **The supply of consultants available to do the necessary work.** The more consultants available to deliver a particular service or product, the lower the client's perceived value.

✔ **The intensity of demand.** The greater the client need, the higher the perceived value of consultants who can do the necessary work.

✔ **The level of trust.** The more a client can trust a consultant to follow through on his or her promises, the higher the perceived value.

We explore these factors in the following examples.

Example 1: Cost-based pricing

Let's say that you're an industrial energy efficiency consultant, someone who specialises in helping manufacturers discover and implement new, more efficient ways to use energy within their operations. You can do this through the application of on-site energy generation facilities (combining heat and power generation), improved and more efficient space heating and lighting, process heat recovery, measurement and control systems, and so on.

As a consultant, you may choose to use a cost-based pricing approach, working up a fixed-price proposal to first do an assessment, and then make recommendations and help with implementation of the resulting plan. In this example, the first phase of the project – which covers your costs plus a healthy profit – is priced at £25,000, and the second phase is priced at £50,000.

Example 2: Value-based pricing

In this example, you're still an industrial energy efficiency consultant, but instead of pricing your services using a cost-based approach, you have instead decided to use a value-based approach. Now, let's say that you've studied your potential client's operation, and you're certain you can wring significant cost savings out of the manufacturing plant – to the tune of £1.5 million a year for the next decade.

While a client's perception of consultant value includes more than just the money he or she can save, the prediction of £1.5 million in annual savings – £15 million over the next 10 years – will certainly get his or her attention straightaway, and it provides you with the opportunity to use a value-based pricing approach. Instead of charging just £75,000 for the two phases of your consulting job as in Example 1, you may be able to charge £500,000 or more based on the tremendous value that you bring to your client.

Now, which approach would you rather take – the cost-based approach for £75,000, or the value-based approach for £500,000?

Of course, the problem is to convince your client that he or she needs to pay the higher, value-based price of £500,000. This can become particularly challenging if your client has also received proposals from other consultants with cost-based pricing closer to Example 1's £75,000 for the entire job. So, what can you do to help convince your clients that they need to focus on value instead of cost? Here are a few tips:

> ✔ **Be ready to help your clients see the value of your work.** Your clients may not be aware of just how much value you can potentially bring to them – it's your job to tell them. Be specific, and point out the advantages

in terms of time and money saved, processes streamlined, efficiencies gained, expenditures deferred, and so on. Contrast these savings with the alternative scenario: that they do nothing at all. Take time to create clear and compelling ways – in writing, over the phone, in person – to express your firm's value proposition.

✔ **Focus on the performance of your client's business, not yours.** If you're running a business, sure, it's important to keep an eye on the bottom line. But if you're a consultant who hopes to convince your clients of the value that you bring to them, then you've absolutely got to focus on your client's business, not your own. What are the key challenges for your clients – and what can you do to help solve them?

✔ **Point out the advantages of a value-based approach.** When you charge by the hour, there really is no limit to the total bill, except, ultimately, your client's budget. The number of hours you expect to work for him or her is an estimate at best, and you may actually put in more or less to complete the project. When you apply value-based pricing, you're most likely to quote a fixed price which caps the investment your client will have to make. Unlike the possible situation with a project that exceeds the estimated number of consultant hours, there will be no surprises – your client will know exactly how much he or she will spend for your consulting services.

✔ **Create incentives for clients to make the leap.** Many clients are used to the tried and trusted cost-based pricing approach of hourly rates, and they may be reluctant – in fact, *very* reluctant – to accept a contract using value-based pricing. If you've been focusing throughout the selling process on the value that you'll bring to your clients, then it shouldn't be too difficult for your client to make the leap. However, you may still need to provide your clients with incentives to switch from an hourly rate to a value price. One such incentive is a guarantee. Using Example 2 above, you might guarantee that, as long as your recommendations are followed, your client will experience at least £1.5 million in energy savings a year or no fee will be payable. Chances are, given a guarantee like that, your client will be very willing to give your value-based proposition a try.

Alan Weiss, author of the popular book *Million Dollar Consulting* (McGraw-Hill), pioneered the idea of value-based pricing for consultants. At his Summit Consulting Group website (www.summitconsulting.com), Weiss offers a list of 40 methods to increase and/or protect fees. Here is a selection of some of Weiss's suggestions:

✔ Establish value collaboratively with the client.

✔ Base fees on value, not on task.

✔ Never use time as the basis of your value.

✔ Don't stop with what the client wants. Find out what the client needs.

✔ Never voluntarily offer options to reduce fees.

✔ If you must lower fees, seek a *quid pro quo* from the buyer.

✔ As early as possible, ask the key scope question: 'What are your objectives?'

✔ Psychologically, higher fees create higher value in the buyer's mind.

✔ Always be prepared to walk away from business.

Is there a value-based price in your future? Maybe. According to researchers, both time-and-materials and project-based pricing dominate in consulting but are on the decline, while value-based pricing is increasing in popularity. Whatever approach you decide to take, value-based pricing is another tool for differentiating yourself from the competition while potentially boosting your bottom line. Not too shabby.

Contingent Fee and Performance-Based Pricing

Are you willing to put some or all of your fees at risk in the event that you can't deliver what you promise? If the answer to that question is 'yes', then consider using contingency or performance-based pricing. While both require you to put some amount of your fees at risk, the upside potential if you're able to perform as promised can be considerable. Here is additional information for you to take into account as you consider these options.

Contingent fee

Commonly used by law firms, a *contingent fee* is one that is paid only if you provide the results that are promised by your firm. Using the example of a law firm that is defending someone on a drink-driving charge, in a contingent fee situation, the client pays only if he or she is acquitted of the crime. If the client is convicted, then no money is owed to the law firm.

Before you consider agreeing to contingent fees, be fairly certain that you'll be able to provide the desired results. Obviously, if you don't have enough clients paying their fees, then it won't be long before you go out of business. Carefully consider whether your firm would be better off adopting a more traditional approach to doing business.

Performance-based pricing

Here's an idea: Why not base your price on some measure of improved client performance? For example, if your client is able to double the number of widgets he produces after your recommendations are implemented, then why not double the amount paid to you? Or, how about charging a flat rate regardless of performance, with an additional 'fee as a reward fo improved performance? Or what about taking 15 per cent of your client's net profits as your fee?

Each of these situations is an example of performance-based pricing, where some portion of your fee is based on the extent of your success. Here are some examples of common ways to gauge your success – or lack thereof:

- ✔ Number of items produced per hour.
- ✔ Weekly sales.
- ✔ Monthly expenses.
- ✔ On-the-job injuries.
- ✔ Number of working customer installations.
- ✔ Employee turnover rate.

As with contingent fees, you need to be fairly certain you can deliver on your promises when you propose the idea of performance-based pricing to your clients (or when they propose it to you). If you're new to consulting and have not yet developed a steady track record on which to base your decision, then you may want to avoid it. However, if your performance is steady and predictable, and you can minimise the potential risk, then performance-based pricing may be a viable option for you and your consulting firm.

Chapter 22

Enhancing Your Image and Reputation

. . . .

In This Chapter

▶ Creating a professional image

▶ Putting together a winning website

▶ Building your reputation

. . . .

A big part of finding success as a consultant is your ability to convince prospective clients that you and your consulting firm are the best choice for the job. Certainly, price and technical skill are both key factors when clients weigh the pros and cons of hiring various consultants. No one (at least no one in his or her right mind) is going to choose a consultant who is technically incompetent just because that person happens to offer the lowest price or dresses well or has a firm handshake. However, beyond price and technical expertise, something less tangible and significantly more subjective weighs very heavily in the decision to approach a particular consultant.

This additional factor is image.

Image is the overall impression that others have of you. Many different things go into the mix that, when blended together, becomes your image. And make no mistake about it – image and reputation are very important factors in the impression that you make on your clients and they weigh heavily in their decision to give you the job.

A favourable image and reputation are important to most clients, and clients are generally more willing to hire (and to pay more for) consultants who possess these attributes. If you had the choice between choosing a consultant with good technical skills but a so-so reputation and image and choosing one with equally good technical skills but an excellent reputation and image, wouldn't you be willing to spend more for the consultant with the much better reputation and image? Most clients probably would.

The good news is that image, reputation, and ethics are all things that you can work on and improve. This chapter is about creating a positive image with your clients and prospective clients, creating a winning website, and building your professional reputation.

Creating a Professional Image

Though image isn't everything for a consultant, it is a big part of the selection process when clients go shopping. Many things add up to make your image. The way you dress, the way you speak, the way you carry yourself, the kind of office you work in, the brand and model of the car you drive – all these things influence the way others perceive you and the impression you make.

Fortunately, you can always change your image. Although the adage that you have only one chance to make a first impression is true, the impression that others have of you can change over time. Some things, like the style of your business cards and the look of your office, are easy to change. Other things, such as converting your negative personality traits into positive personality traits, may take a bit longer.

Anyway, here are a few things you can do to enhance your professional image:

✔ **Get real.** The first rule of creating a professional image is to be yourself. Don't try to be someone you aren't. Take advantage of your best personal attributes – perhaps your ingenuity, or your persistence, or your ability to perform under pressure – and amplify them. If you have any negative characteristics, whatever they may be, work hard to minimise them.

✔ **Look after your appearance.** If you look professional, your clients and prospective clients will perceive you to be professional. Despite the old saying that you can't judge a book by its cover, clients do so all the time. If you're asking someone to entrust his or her multimillion-pound company to your care – a company that your client spent a significant part of his or her life building up from nothing, then you're going to find it difficult to get the contract if you look like you just came in from your morning jog. You must appear serious about your work and the way that you do it.

✔ **Build trust through action.** Actions speak louder than words. Although your proposal may wax lyrical about your commitment to quality, if you don't follow up these words with action, then your clients will think otherwise. Believe us: If you follow up your words with action, your clients will love you forever, and you'll soon have more business than you know what to do with.

✔ **Create an environment that matches the work you do.** If you're an investment adviser, your environment should be one that exudes an atmosphere of quiet success, conservatism, and stability. However, if you're a graphic artist or an interior decorator, your environment needs to be energetic, creative, bright, and full of life. The point is that when your clients come to visit your office, you want your environment to send the kind of message that matches their expectations for a high-quality consultant.

✔ **Make your media your message.** Your business cards, your report covers, your website, and other forms of business communication speak volumes about your professionalism and your commitment to quality. High-quality paper and printing; professional-looking brochures, newsletters, and mailshots; and a well-done website send a message that you're the kind of consultant that your clients will want to hire – and retain far into the future.

Creating and maintaining a professional image can play a very important role in your ability to achieve the kind of success you're aiming for. Be aware that you're constantly being judged and assessed by your clients and your prospective clients. With a little work, you can make your good image even better. And doing so translates not only into more business but also into better, higher-paying business to boot.

Building a First-Class Website

When deciding to put together a first-class website, perhaps the first decision you have to make is whether to do it yourself or to hire someone to do it for you. Each approach, of course, has its pluses and minuses.

If you decide to build your own site, you have ultimate control over the site and most likely spend less than if you pay someone to do it for you. Unfortunately, unless you're pretty savvy at building websites, the results may look amateurish at best and reflect poorly on your business. Not only that, but while you're building the site, you're distracted from doing the things you normally do to make money – like consulting. On the other hand, while paying a professional to create and maintain your website will most likely get you a better-looking and functioning site, it may also cost a lot of money. Not only that, but you may have to wait a while for your web designer to make site updates for you.

Building your own website

All it takes is a basic knowledge of the Internet to create your own website and have a lot of fun in the process. There are a number of very capable website development programs available to you that are relatively simple and easy to use. In addition, some web-hosting services offer templates that make putting together your own website a breeze.

If you decide to build your own website, here are three steps to making it happen:

1. **Select a web-hosting service.**

   You need a web-hosting service to set up your website address (or URL), something like yourname.co.uk. The hosting service then hosts your site on its computers where anyone with access to the Web can view it. You'll quickly find that there are many, many web -hosting services, and they vary considerably in price and level of service, and it definitely pays to shop around. Before you select a web-hosting service, check with your friends and colleagues to see who they use, and read up on the reviews posted on Internet sites such as `www.hostfinder.co.uk`.

2. **Build your website.**

   Some website hosting services offer simple, built-in website creation software and templates as a part of their hosting packages. This is probably the best option if you're new to all this Internet stuff and you don't have a lot of time to waste learning. If your needs go beyond these basic templates, consider buying software specifically designed for creating websites such as Microsoft FrontPage, Macromedia Dreamweaver, or NetObjects Fusion. Also, Microsoft Word has the ability to save regular text pages as HTML (hypertext markup language, the language of the Web) documents.

3. **Maintain your own website.**

   One good thing about creating and maintaining your own website is that you have full control over the content and when and how it is updated or modified. It takes just minutes to update your own site yourself, while it can take days or even weeks for someone else to get round to making even minor updates for you.

For more information on this approach, take a look at *Marketing Online For Dummies* by Bud Smith and Frank Catalano (Wiley).

Paying someone to build and maintain your website

If you've got better things to do with your time than creating and maintaining your own website – or if you'd simply like to get the most professional-looking site possible – there are plenty of website design companies (many of them consulting businesses) that would love to design it for you. You can end up spending anywhere from a couple of hundred pounds for a simple site to thousands for a much more complex one, but if it helps you enhance your image while providing clients with the information they need, then the investment will be well made. The UK Web Design Association website will help you to find a web designer near you.

Be careful who you choose to build your website for you. Some web consultants tell a good story, but deliver far less than they promise. Here are a few tips for finding a great website designer:

✔ The very first thing to do is to ask your business colleagues if they know someone they can recommend. Put these recommendations on your shortlist.

✔ After you've got your shortlist of candidates, conduct interviews, get references, and thoroughly check out the sites they've built for other firms.

✔ Be sure to compare the work of several different designers before deciding – don't just go with the first one that walks through the door.

✔ If you're wandering around the Internet and see a website that's just what you would like for your own business, find out who designed it and contact them. The designer's name is usually posted at the bottom of the home page, although sometimes you need to ask the site owner who they used.

Optimising your site

Once you've got a good-looking, professional website – then what? The next step is to get people to visit it – preferably the people who are your best prospects for future clients. There are lots of ways to attract and hold your clients' attention, including the following:

✔ **Make it easy to find.** If it's hard for your clients to find you, they probably won't waste much time trying. If your company's name is the Susan Griffin Group, make your URL www.susangriffin.co.uk or www.sgriffingroup.co.uk. Clients (and prospective clients) who don't have your address at their fingertips may easily guess it, and it will show up at or near the top of most Internet search engine results. And set aside some time to register your website with the most visited Internet search engines and directories, including Google and Yahoo!.

✔ **Promote your new address.** Plaster your website address everywhere you possibly can, including on your business cards, letterhead stationery, invoices, marketing brochures, your car, the side of your house – anywhere you can possibly fit it.

Don't waste your time with firms that promise to increase the traffic to your website by submitting your name to hundreds of search engines. Truth be told, most people use only the top few most popular search engines, and according to the information company Experian, Google has a staggering 90 per cent market share in the UK, so you might waste your time and money by submitting your site to the also-rans.

✔ **Give your visitors a reason to visit.** If your site is boring, or if it takes too long to load, your client or prospect will click right back out of the site. One of the best ways to see how you compare is to take a look at your competitors' sites. What have they done to make their sites *sticky*, that is, keeping visitors there once they arrive? Be sure to provide lots of fresh, value-added content in the form of news, reports, articles, surveys, industry trends, networking forums, and the like that will keep your clients and prospects coming back for more.

✔ **Capture contact information.** Once your visitors arrive on your site, encourage them to provide you with contact information so you can add them to your mailing list. One way to do this is by offering a complementary subscription to your client newsletter to anyone who is willing to give you his or her contact information. You can also encourage visitors to provide their contact information by way of competitions, special offers, and surveys.

✔ **Keep close tabs on your site.** Make your website the home page for your Internet browser so that you visit it frequently. Have a look around and make sure all the pages are loading as they should and that all the links work. And check your site statistics regularly – the number of visitors each day, where they're from, how long they stayed, which pages they viewed, and which search engine (if any) referred them to your site – to get a feel for who is dropping by your site, and what they're doing once they get there. You can quickly identify which parts of your site attract the most (and the least) visitors and test visitor response to site changes on a real-time basis.

The ten best ways to promote your website

While there are many ways to promote your website, some ways work better than others. Here are ten of the best ways to promote your website:

✔ Send announcements for your website (including a picture of your home page) to all your customers and clients, as well as to the media and targeted mailing lists of potential clients.

✔ Include your website address on all external materials, including letterheads, business cards, catalogues, invoices, newsletters, packaging, and so on.

✔ Incorporate your website address into your standard fax cover sheet.

✔ Include your website address in your voice-mail system and in your on-hold message.

✔ Include your website address in all advertising.

✔ Visit Internet newsgroups and message boards, leave messages, and participate in relevant discussions.

✔ Seek out specialist websites where you can volunteer to host online chats and conferences.

✔ Register your site with the most popular Internet search engine (Google) and be sure it is optimised to rank high in the search results (by incorporating meta tags and other tricks of the trade).

✔ Set up reciprocal links with your customers and clients and with other relevant websites.

✔ Create an email signature for yourself and your employees that includes your website address. A *signature* is a short paragraph that's automatically included at the bottom of every email message you send out. It usually contains a plug for your business, along with your address, phone or fax number, and a website address that your clients can simply click on to enter your site.

Enhancing Your Reputation

Just as a good reputation can enhance your image in the eyes of your clients, a bad reputation can tarnish it. And just as many different factors add up to your professional image, many different factors make up your reputation. The quality of the work you do, the time you spend in the public eye, the work you do for charity, and much more play a part in determining your professional reputation.

One thing about reputation: Enhancing and maintaining a good reputation is much easier than trying to rehabilitate a bad one. Once you develop a bad reputation, many clients won't bother to consider you for any sort of work, no matter how great your proposal or how low your price. And after your reputation has become tarnished, many clients will never believe that you have turned things around in your firm and changed for the better – even if you have. Turning around a bad reputation can take years. Therefore, doing whatever you can to enhance your reputation is clearly in your best interests. Your current clients will be proud to tell their associates that they are affiliated with you, and future clients will be more likely to seek you out.

With that point in mind, here are a few tips for enhancing your reputation or for helping to repair your reputation if you've fallen on hard times:

✔ **Do consistently great work.** Of course, one of the best ways to enhance your reputation is to do great work. And if you do great work consistently, that's even better. Your clients want and deserve the best you have to offer. Give it to them. Consistently deliver more than you promise.

✔ **Be easy to work with.** What's one of the most effective ways to get a bad reputation – quickly and easily? By being difficult to work with. You can be a brilliant consultant and your price can be right, but if you're an incredible pain in the neck to work with, clients will avoid you like the plague. Be someone your clients look forward to talking to, and certainly don't get your assistants to say that you're in a meeting – even when you're not.

✔ **Keep your clients informed of your successes.** A great way to enhance your reputation is to keep your clients well informed about your doings. If you land a big new contract with a high-profile client, let all your other clients know about it! If you successfully complete a highly visible project, get the word out! (But be sure to get a client's prior approval before you publicise your work for that client.) If your business has been featured in a newspaper or you've appeared on television, get copies to your clients. Newsletters, emails, voicemail, brochures, newspaper and magazine articles, podcasts, videos of television appearances – use all these methods to spread the word and raise your standing in the eyes of your clients and your prospective clients.

✔ **Get in the public eye.** Give speeches to community groups or groups of your peers. Write articles for trade magazines or submit pieces to your local newspaper or national publications, such as *The Financial Times*. Become an expert resource for your local newspaper or radio and television stations. Develop a press kit and a regular newsletter and distribute them to a wide variety of national media.

✔ **Teach.** Teaching at a local college or university can be a very effective way for you to enhance your reputation, broaden your skills, and expand your professional network. You may learn a few new things from your students, too!

✔ **Write a book.** Many consultants find their professional reputations greatly enhanced after writing and publishing a book. Not only can you enhance your reputation by writing a book, but organisations may invite you to present the ideas from your book to their employees. You may eventually find yourself making more money from activities related to your book than you do from consulting.

✔ **Work for free.** Many worthy non profit organisations – youth clubs, environmental groups, churches, and others – could really use your expertise and skill but can't afford to pay for it. By offering to work for free for a few organisations that you really believe in, you're not only doing something good for your community but also building your reputation and network at the same time. Be sure to publicise your support for these organisations via your website and newsletters.

✔ **Work ethically and honestly.** It goes without saying that engaging in unethical and dishonest behaviour is a sure way to destroy your reputation and lose all you've worked for. Because some of the work you do for clients may be of a sensitive or confidential nature, any hint of dishonesty or lack of ethical fortitude can be the death knell of a consulting relationship. Always work honestly and ethically. This topic is so important that we devote an entire section of Chapter 5 to it.

Work hard at developing and enhancing your good reputation and, at all costs, avoid doing the kinds of things that could tarnish it and destroy the client relationships that you've worked so hard to establish and nurture.

Part VII
The Part of Tens

'I think it's the Consultant of the Lake, sire.'

In this part . . .

These short chapters are packed with quick ideas that can help you become a better consultant and build a more profitable and more effective consulting business. Read them whenever you have an extra minute or two.

Chapter 23

Ten Ways to Improve Your Cash Flow

- -

In This Chapter

▶ Managing your debtors

▶ Holding onto your money

▶ Calling in a professional

- -

*F*or businesses, cash makes the world go round. Without a constant inflow of cash, you can't afford to pay for the things you need to run your business. Anything you can do to improve your cash flow – the difference between the money coming into your business, and the money going out – is guaranteed to have a positive impact on your business.

Manage Your Debtors List

One of the most important things you can do to improve your cash flow is to keep a close eye on your debtors list – the money owed to your firm by your clients – and to be sure that clients are making their payments to you the moment they are due, or sooner.

Unfortunately, some clients invariably don't understand how important it is to us that they pay their bills on time. A day or two late isn't usually a big problem – but a month or two late will wreck your cash flow. And it can have devastating, long-term consequences for your firm. Once your customers get in the habit of paying late, it can be almost impossible to get them to start paying on time. By managing your debtors, you identify your late payers as soon as you can, and then take steps to get them to pay.

Forecast Your Cash Flow

How can you run a healthy consulting business (or even sleep well at night) if you don't know when money will be received from clients, and when major expenditure will be necessary to support your business. Frankly, you can't. The solution is to budget. A *cash flow forecast* is a detailed budget of cash inflows and outflows that takes into account payments you receive from clients and expenses you'll need to make to run your business. The result is a statement that clearly shows the forecast cash balance of your business at specific points in time (usually weekly). As the owner or manager of a consulting firm, a cash flow forecast is perhaps your most important planning tool. By studying your forecast, you're able to determine if you have enough money to run and grow your business, or if you need to push harder for new work – or squeeze your current customers to pay the money they owe you sooner. You can also figure out if you'll be able to withstand major expenditure on capital equipment or to recruit new employees at some future time.

Ask for Advance Payment

When you run your own business, you get to decide the terms and conditions under which you accept work from clients. When considering payment, you could decide to do all your work for free. However, you probably wouldn't be in business very long if you tried that approach. You could perhaps try letting your clients pay whenever they like, but some clients might not pay at all, and your business would certainly suffer. And you could invoice as you do your work, and give clients 30 days to pay. That's not a bad approach, but there's something better yet: having your clients pay you in advance – before you actually start work. By getting a large payment or deposit up front, you jumpstart your cash flow, putting your business in a very positive financial position.

Hold on to Your Money for as Long as You Can

There are two fundamental ways to improve your cash flow: increase the speed and size of cash inflows, and decrease the speed and size of cash outflows. Holding onto your money as long as you can – by slowing down the speed at which you pay the money that you owe others – will definitely improve your cash flow. But, don't get us wrong. We're not saying that you should pay your bills late. What we're saying is don't get into the habit of paying your bills sooner than you have to. Some business owners as a matter of course pay their bills as soon as they receive them – regardless of the payment terms. So, if your supplier has agreed to finance your purchase for 30 days for free (which is exactly what is happening when you're sent an invoice with payment required in 30 days), you must take full advantage of this free loan. By waiting to pay until the bill is due, you have the benefit of your cash for longer. If your supplier offers a prompt payment discount, be sure to consider whether the savings for paying early outweigh the value of hanging onto your cash for the full 30 days. Better still, negotiate hard with your supplier to get more than 30 days. If you have a good credit rating and the supplier is hungry for business you may be able to get 60 or even 90 days, which helps your cash flow considerably.

Make Sure Your Invoices Are Right

Some companies have a very simple approach to paying invoices with mistakes in them: they don't. They don't pass Go, and they won't send you £200. They won't even call to find out why you made the mistake. They just won't pay it. And if you're not managing your debtors list (see the first item in this chapter), you may not even notice that you haven't been paid yet.

Be absolutely sure that your invoices are correct before you send them to your clients. Make sure that the numbers are right, and that they are addressed to the right place and the right person. When invoices go to the wrong place or to the wrong person, they tend to sit around in someone's in-tray – unpaid. Don't give your clients an excuse to pay you late – make sure your invoices are right.

Invoice More Often

While some consulting engagements are short – perhaps just a week or two – many others run for months or even years. If your services are provided over a long period of time, then an easy way to improve your cash flow is to invoice more often. For example, instead of sending your client a bill for £2,000 at the end of each month, you can invoice your client for £1,000 halfway through the month, and then another £1,000 at the end of the month. Or – even better – how about charging your client £1,000 at the beginning of the month, and then another £1,000 halfway through the month? While your individual payments are smaller, you get your money sooner, which has a positive impact on your cash flow. Believe us: Sooner is better when it comes to cash.

Give Prompt-Payment Discounts

A quick and easy way to encourage your clients to pay their invoices sooner, improving your cash flow at the same time, is the prompt-payment discount. A prompt-payment discount is when you allow a customer to decrease a payment by some set percentage – say 1 per cent – for paying an invoice within a specific period of time, usually 10 or 20 days. We can already anticipate your question: Doesn't giving a payment discount decrease the money you receive, resulting in a negative impact on cash flow? Actually, in many cases, the positive impact on cash flow that you experience by getting your money sooner exceeds the small amount of money that's lost in extending the discount. You've got to assess the impact yourself, and then decide if it makes sense for you.

Start with the standard 30 days net payment terms and analyse the average time your clients take to pay their invoices. Next, offer a minimal prompt-payment discount to your clients, perhaps a half of 1 per cent for payment in 20 days, and see what happens. Do payments come in sooner? How much sooner? Enough to make it worthwhile?

When your clients push you for discounts try to link the discounts to a prompt payment clause.

Manage Your Costs

Your business's cash flow is impacted by two different things: the money coming into your business, and the money going out. Just as you can have an impact on the money coming in, you can impact the money going out. In fact, we would venture to guess that most business owners have a much greater impact on the cost side of the equation than on the revenue side. You're the one who decides whether or not to hire that new employee, or buy those new computers, or pay for first-class air travel instead of economy. Before you spend any money on behalf of your business, stop and ask the following question: Is this expense necessary? If the answer to that question is 'Yes', then ask one more question: Is this expense necessary right now? Don't spend money just because you can.

Only spend money if and when you absolutely have to. Want a pretty new desk or chair? Why not try to get another year out of your old one? Or find inexpensive used – but more up-to-date – office furniture on eBay (www.ebay.co.uk).

Don't Be Afraid to Push for Payment

It's a rare consultant who doesn't occasionally have a client who pays late. Of course, an occasional late payment is usually not a problem for most consulting firms. However, when late payments become common or habitual, you've got a choice to make: Do you put your clients on notice that they are late and demand payment, or do you just ignore it. The choice you make will depend on a number of factors: the state of your consulting firm's financial health (a healthy firm can afford to wait longer for payment than one that is on its way to intensive care), how important the customer is to you and your business (you don't want to make a key customer angry), and the size and age of the invoice itself (the larger the size and the older the invoice, the more urgent payment becomes).

As soon as you decide that you've waited long enough for payment, then don't be afraid to push your client to pay. In our experience, the most effective way is to personally pick up the phone and call your client directly. Point out that payment is overdue, and ask if he or she has a problem that you can help with. You can send an email message or a letter instead of making a personal call, but we have found that a one-to-one phone conversation can get action when other methods fail. Be respectful of your client and be polite, but be firm when you ask for payment. The sooner you follow up on a late payment, the sooner you get paid.

Call in a Professional

As much as we'd prefer to avoid having to bring a debt collections agency or a solicitor into client relationships, sometimes there's no choice. When a client refuses to pay a late invoice, then you've got to take action. Unfortunately, if you can't get it done yourself, then you need to call in a professional. The first choice for most outstanding invoices is a debt collections agency that will use its powers of persuasion to try to get your client to pay. For the privilege of helping you out, the agency will be paid a significant portion of the money they collect, probably between 8 to 35 per cent depending on the age and quality of the debt. Of course, if you get any money out of a client who refuses to pay, then you're doing a lot better than nothing, and the high fee is worth paying. If the invoice is particularly large, or if there are legal issues involved (such as whether or not the consulting contract was complied with, or client fraud), then you probably need to call on the services of a solicitor who has experience working with consulting firms.

To find the professional who's right for you, we suggest first asking around for a referral. Ask other consultants or colleagues if they have anyone they can recommend. Alternatively, you can do an Internet search, which will provide you with enough names to keep you busy for months.

Chapter 24

Ten Effective Marketing Strategies for New Business

. . . .

In This Chapter

▶ Trying different approaches

▶ Getting the word out

. . . .

Marketing is a wonderful thing. Really. As you can probably guess, part of your job as a consultant is to do great work for your current clients. However, attracting and winning future work with new clients is equally important. Without a steady stream of new work coming in – from new clients, your business is always at risk of failure if and when key current clients decide that you're no longer needed. Although you can approach your marketing in a haphazard, hit-or-miss fashion, the best marketing comes from identifying your target clients and then planning exactly how best to reach them. What do they read? Where are they? What do they like to do? Before you develop your marketing plan, review the following marketing strategies.

Choose Your Targets

Before you do anything else, your first task when developing your marketing plan is to identify your target clients. As you choose your targets, always have two questions in mind:

✔ Who are your best clients?

✔ How best can you contact them?

The answers to these questions help you select the most effective ways to get the message to your targeted audience. If you're involved in executive coaching, then you know that your target clients are people who are running organisations. You know therefore that sticking an advertisement on the noticeboard at your local supermarket is unlikely to generate any new clients. However, getting interviewed in a business newspaper or a national publication, such as *Management Today*, may lead to lots of business.

 And notice that the question is, 'Who are your *best* clients?' Some clients are better than others – some pay their bills on time, and others don't; some will appreciate the hard work you do, and others won't; some make being a consultant a pleasurable challenge, while others make it a living hell. Focus on attracting the best clients for your business, not the worst.

Discover What Works

Good marketing is a state of constant experimentation to discover what works and what doesn't work. Your goal is to learn from your experimentation, build on what works, and discard the strategies that don't work. When you develop plans for marketing your business, firstly identify every possible way to get your message out to your targeted audience; then start trying them out. You can try one approach at a time or several at once – it all depends on your budget and how much time you can devote to tracking the results. What is the response from your direct mailing campaign? Good? Then try it again with a somewhat wider distribution. How did the newspaper advertisement fare? Not well? Then drop it. Keep fine-tuning your marketing campaign and trying new things. To determine what works, you must set up criteria in advance to judge the effectiveness of the technique. For example, you decide that each newspaper advertisement needs to generate ten prospects, of which two can be converted into clients. If you find that a newspaper advertisement is generating only two prospects, then you know that your approach needs more work. If, on the other hand, it generates 50 prospects, then you know you've picked the right strategy.

Use Client Success Stories

Nothing breeds success like success. As you successfully complete jobs for your clients, you automatically create a pool of client success stories that you can draw from to publicise your firm. And the more work you do, the larger the pool grows. The beauty of using success stories for publicity is that potential clients get an idea of the kind of work you do; at the same time, the success stories build a positive impression of your abilities and expertise. Use client success stories whenever you can: in proposals, advertisements, newsletters, websites, speeches, seminars, and so on. Even better, ask your clients if you can get an endorsement or testimonial from their organisation for use in your publicity materials. Whichever way you decide to use client success stories, be sure to get your clients' permission first if you plan to use their names.

Encourage Word-of-Mouth Referrals

Some of the best marketing you can get is from your satisfied clients. And it's free! Encourage your clients to tell their friends and business associates about your business. You can encourage this word-of-mouth advertising by meeting or exceeding your commitments, being reliable, doing great work, and asking for referrals. Give your clients extra business cards, brochures, and other promotional materials to pass on to potential clients. You can thank them for referring you to others by sending a thank-you note or by giving them a nominal reward, such as a free subscription to your newsletter or a copy of a report on industry trends – or an agreed fee, subject or course to their organisation's policies.

Peter does no advertising at all, instead relying on referrals from his many happy clients to bring in a steady stream of new business. He has a website – www.petereconomy.com – specifically designed to serve as a high-tech business card and exhibit his many successful projects and relationships with clients.

Become a Media Animal

If you want to get prospective clients' attention, you have to be relentless in your campaign to get it. Depending on the nature of your consulting business, you have to select the media outlets that are most effective in broadcasting your message to your clients, and then bombard them with newsworthy materials. If you're serious about getting publicity, get on the phone, write letters, send emails, make personal visits – in short, do whatever it takes to land an interview, place an article, or end up on the evening news. Don't take no for an answer. Keep pushing until you get the attention you want. Of course, positive media is the best media. You certainly don't want to find a BBC *Watchdog* team in your office waiting to interview you!

When Philip launched Techniques for Change he sent press releases to a wide range of publications and followed up by calling them. He secured an article in the *Independent on Sunday* and immediately picked up large contracts off the back of this absolutely free publicity. He then quoted the article in subsequent promotional materials to maximise the benefit gained from national press coverage.

Hire a Good Public Relations Person

Good public relations people are definitely worth their weight in gold. If you're a media novice and you try to approach the media on your own, you can waste a lot of time (and don't forget: for consultants, time equals money). Public relations experts already know how the system works, which media outlets are best for telling your story, and the most effective ways to convince the people in power to take time to listen. And the good ones have already developed personal relationships with editors, producers, and the other people who can get your message in front of the widest possible audience. Not only can public relations specialists line up media opportunities, but many are happy to create your press kits, press releases, biographies, brochures, and other marketing materials. Be sure you know what your PR person can do for you. Get referrals from friends and colleagues whose opinions you trust. To keep things affordable, you can pay the person by the hour and authorise specific tasks as the need arises, or you can specify a retainer arrangement that provides you with a constant level of service for a set fee every month. The choice is up to you and your budget.

Start a Newsletter

Newsletters are great publicity tools for every kind of consulting business. Not only are they an inexpensive (especially when you choose the emailed variety instead of the printed and posted variety) and practical way to target potential clients, but they are also effective for retaining and developing new business with current clients, who typically want to be on the inside track about what you're doing. Newsletters also add to your credibility. The heart and soul of most consulting newsletters are stories describing the numerous successful projects that the firm has undertaken. These success stories make terrific publicity – both for your firm and for the firms that you serve. Typical newsletters also contain statements of the owner's vision for the firm and its clients, letters to the editor, tips on how to improve a certain aspect of your business, and general industry news. And although subscriptions to some newsletters are free, others – particularly those produced by popular management consultants – can cost hundreds of pounds per year. And if you email your newsletters, the money you earn is all profit!

Offer Free Samples

Countless businesses have found offering free samples to be a highly effective way to secure new clients. What better way to show your potential clients the value of your service than to let them try it at no risk and no obligation? Depending on the exact nature of your business, you can offer a free needs analysis, inspection, initial use, product sample, or other such avenue for letting your clients get a taste of what you offer. Some consultants offer free public information sessions. For example, a financial adviser may present a short programme of investment advice and an overview of the services that his or her firm provides, sometimes accompanied by a free meal. A freelance advertising copywriter can send prospective clients samples of his or her work taken from the local newspaper. What do you have to offer to your clients to get their future business?

Be Responsive to the Media

Newspapers, television, radio, magazines – and, increasingly, blogs – are among the quickest and most effective ways to reach a wide audience of potential clients. Whenever the media wants to talk to you, you must always drop everything and run, don't walk, to the phone or to your computer keyboard. Unless you just gave birth to quintuplets, you usually can't get media attention without spending a lot of time, money, and effort; therefore, when the media is ready for you, you need to be ready for it. Go out of your way to be responsive to the needs, deadlines, and opportunities of media outlets.

Help Clients Even If You Can't Do the Work

From time to time, you'll get requests from clients to do work that is outside your firm's focus or experience, or that exceeds your current capacity to fulfil it. Instead of just telling your clients that they need to go elsewhere, do everything you can to help connect them to someone who can get the work done. Why pass on perfectly good clients to someone else? Firstly, because what goes around comes around, and the firms to which you pass your clients just may return the favour someday. Secondly, because the client may need your services in the future, and he or she will be grateful that you helped out in his or her time of need. This is an opportunity to begin to build a long-term relationship with a prospective client. And you establish a network of future partners – both on the delivery side and on the client side.

Keep a list of consultants in your industry who you trust to do good work. Not only will such a list be of benefit to your clients when you're unable to fulfil a request, but the list can benefit you when you need an extra hand completing a project because you're overwhelmed with work.

Chapter 25

Ten Ways to Build Business with a Client

In This Chapter

▶ Delighting your clients

▶ Asking your clients to help you build your business

*H*ere's Consulting Rule Number 1: Your current clients are your best friends. Love, honour, and cherish them until death do you part. Why the drama? Because your current clients are the source of the revenue that keeps your lights on, your computer humming, and the finance company from repossessing your car. In addition, if you're successful at building long-term relationships, your clients are your absolute best source of future business – both through additional business and through referrals. You can significantly improve your odds of building business with your current clients by heeding the advice in this chapter.

Always Be on Time and Within Budget

In our experience, dependability is a particularly important quality for consultants to possess. It only takes getting burned once or twice by an undependable consultant for most clients to realise that getting what you're paying for – done right, and on time – is ultimately more important than finding the least expensive consultant for the job. Being dependable means doing what you promised to do, when you promised to do it, and for the price you agreed to. A lot of people make a lot of promises, but few actually live up to the standards they set for themselves. Being on time and within budget sets you apart from the individuals who promise the moon but then deliver too little too late. If your clients can't depend on you to do what you promised to do, then before long, they'll start looking for someone they can depend on. Set realistic time and budget goals when you negotiate your contract, and then do whatever it takes to achieve them. Better still, deliver more than you promise! When you deliver more than the client expects and than you promised, you create client delight. And client delight gives you a client for life.

Anticipate Your Clients' Needs (And Suggest Ways to Address Them)

When you're working on a job for a particular client, you often see other things that need fixing, too. This situation is like taking your car to a garage to get a tune-up, only to find that the tyres and catalytic converter also need to be replaced. So how can you anticipate your clients' needs? One of the best ways is to keep up on emerging industry trends – by reading business magazines, newspapers, and industry journals; visiting appropriate websites and blogs; by attending conferences; and by learning through your experience with your other clients. By anticipating your clients' needs, you can bring solutions to your clients before they even know that they need them.

As a consultant, you're in the enviable position of having a clear view of the inner workings of the organisation, as well as having the ear of the organisation's management. As you work, keep your eyes and ears open to other needs that your client may have. After you identify these needs, talk to your client about them and submit a proposal with your suggested solution. Your client will appreciate your advice, and you'll appreciate the additional business that your attention to your client's needs generates.

But, two notes of caution: Firstly, make good headway with delivering the solution you're working on (after all, that's why the client hired you) before scouting and touting for lots of other work. The client wants to know you're fully committed to that task. Secondly, don't create work where there really is none. Consultants who find problems where they do not exist – simply to churn up new business with an existing client – risk damaging the trust and credibility they've worked hard to develop. And if your client can't trust you, why should they hire you?

Be Easy to Work With

Who would you rather hire: an individual who complains every time you give him or her an assignment to do, or one who is excited by the challenge and eager to please? Your clients will ask themselves the same question when they decide whether to send more business your way. As a consultant, you're selling more than your products or services – you're selling yourself. You have to offer more than great work; you also have to be easy to work with. Displaying arrogance and throwing temper tantrums are not the ways to turn your clients into long-term partners. Go out of your way to please your clients: Take their phone calls immediately, be responsive to their requests, meet them at their offices whenever possible, and maintain the pleasant and agreeable personality of someone you would want to work with. This way, when your clients have a problem that needs to be solved, your name will be the first one they think of when they start looking for someone to help.

Keep in Touch

What's the old saying – 'Out of sight, out of mind'? If you let your clients forget about you, you're going to be an awfully lonely consultant. After you establish working relationships with your clients, keep in touch with them. Make a phone call, or send a letter or email message, or drop in on your clients from time to time. How about lunch? Keep them abreast of your latest successes and up to date on new services that you add to your repertoire. Offer to help them solve a difficult organisational or technical problem. Above all, don't let your clients fall off your active list of contacts. Schedule regular contacts with both active and inactive (the ones you want to re-establish) clients into your time-management system. Keeping established communication channels open is much easier than establishing new communication channels with new customers.

Be Honest and Ethical

It almost goes without saying (we say *almost* because we're going to say it anyway): Always maintain the highest standards of honesty and ethics in all your business practices. Doing so not only makes it easier for you to sleep at night, but it also builds a strong foundation of trust between you and your clients upon which to build future business. Ethical lapses and breaches of confidentiality can spell disaster for your client relationships, and in some cases they can get you into legal hot water. Make a point of setting the highest standards of conduct – both for yourself and for your employees. You have only one reputation, and it is worth its weight in gold; build and enhance it.

Give More than You Promise

In life, finding people – whether friends, colleagues, or business associates – who do exactly what they say they'll do, when they say they'll do it, can sometimes be difficult. This is certainly no different when it comes to consultants – many talk a big story about all the great things they're going to do for you, but then fall short when it comes time to deliver the goods. It's simple: When you keep your promises, you have a happy client.

But, what if you want to elevate your client to a new plateau of excitement – the kind of excitement that generates unsolicited testimonials and referrals? Give a little more. Deliver your report a few days early or include an extra set of data for no extra charge. We can guarantee that if you give more than you promise, your clients will come back for more.

A brother of one of our business associates was in the painting contracting business, with many elderly customers. He was very patient with his clients in selecting colours and would stop to socialise with them as his painters worked. About three weeks after the end of a job, he would return unasked to do any touch-up work that was required. About two months later, he would stop by to do another touch-up, and frequently he would bring a small bouquet of flowers, a bottle of wine, or fresh preserves. His clients understandably loved him – and they overwhelmed him with work and with referrals to new clients.

Ask for Testimonials and Referrals

Clients like being bragged about! If you can find a showcase in which to show them as a positive example, such a testimonial can not only bring you additional business with new clients but also strengthen the bond you have with your existing clients. Testimonials are a critical ingredient in your new client proposals: Not only do they lend credibility to your words, but they also give your proposals life. Some consultants have found success by featuring their clients in their advertising. For example, if you're a make-up consultant, before-and-after photographs of your most successful clients are an important way for you to show new clients what results they can expect.

Referrals are one of the most important ways for you to get new business from your current clients. Don't be shy; give your clients extra business cards and brochures to give out to their friends and business associates. And don't forget to thank them – a personal note or spoken word of thanks is usually sufficient – whenever you get a new client as a result.

Offer Incentives

As you develop a long-term relationship with a client, offering financial incentives to help develop more business can often pay off. For example, you can offer a standing discount of 10 per cent to your best customers, or you can give them an occasional free offer.

To thank their clients for their business over the previous year, both Bob and Peter often send clients free autographed copies of their latest books or other tokens of their appreciation. It's not always the cost of the incentive that matters so much as the thought behind it. Do be sure though not to compromise clients and their own ethical policies. For example, Philip can't give small gifts to his UK public sector clients because of their tight rules on gifts and entertainment.

Educate Your Clients

Are your clients aware of all the different services that your business offers? Probably not. For example, perhaps you specialise in conducting home inspections for clients who are buying flats or houses, and you place an advertisement in the Yellow Pages for that business. When a client hires you to do a home inspection, he or she may not be aware that you also do quality carpentry work at very reasonable rates. And, how can they know unless you tell them? Your job is to educate your clients about the full range of services that you offer. And after you educate your clients, remind them from time to time about the other kinds of work you can do for them. With repeat customers, your marketing materials are the number-one focus of interactions with you and your staff. Your goal is to make them more intelligent consumers of your products and services so as to effectively manage their expectations.

Do Great Work

We shouldn't have to tell you that doing great work is what consulting is all about. Your clients choose you because they expect great work, and you went into business for yourself because you were convinced that you could deliver great work. Always do the best job you possibly can, even if you occasionally have to spend more time on a job than you anticipated. Great work creates, maintains, and enhances your reputation as a professional consultant. And delivering great work is one of the best ways to build future business with your current clients.

But, what if you can't do great work on a particular job – what if you're in too deep and can't deliver what you promised? You have a couple of choices: Either bring in someone (perhaps another consultant) to help you, or inform your client that you can't do the work. In either case, you need to act fast. Bringing in someone to help should be your first approach – that way you'll be able to preserve your client relationship. However, if you're stuck with no way out, then it's better to tell a client in advance that you can't fulfil your contract by the delivery date – and then help them find other solutions – than to deliver a poor product or service, or to deliver nothing at all.

Index

• W •

Notes

Notes

Notes

Notes

FOR DUMMIES®

Do Anything. Just Add Dummies

UK editions

BUSINESS

978-0-470-51806-9

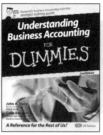

978-0-470-99245-6

978-0-470-75626-3

FINANCE

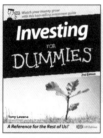

978-0-470-99280-7

978-0-470-99811-3

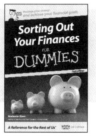

978-0-470-69515-9

PROPERTY

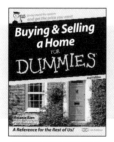

978-0-470-99448-1

978-0-470-75872-4

978-0-7645-7054-4

Backgammon For Dummies
978-0-470-77085-6

Body Language For Dummies
978-0-470-51291-3

British Sign Language
For Dummies
978-0-470-69477-0

Business NLP For Dummies
978-0-470-69757-3

Children's Health For Dummies
978-0-470-02735-6

Cognitive Behavioural Coaching
For Dummies
978-0-470-71379-2

Counselling Skills For Dummies
978-0-470-51190-9

Digital Marketing For Dummies
978-0-470-05793-3

eBay.co.uk For Dummies,
2nd Edition
978-0-470-51807-6

English Grammar For Dummies
978-0-470-05752-0

Fertility & Infertility For Dummies
978-0-470-05750-6

Genealogy Online For Dummies
978-0-7645-7061-2

Golf For Dummies
978-0-470-01811-8

Green Living For Dummies
978-0-470-06038-4

Hypnotherapy For Dummies
978-0-470-01930-6

FOR DUMMIES®

A world of resources to help you grow

UK editions

SELF-HELP

978-0-470-01838-5

978-0-7645-7028-5

978-0-470-75876-2

HEALTH

978-0-470-69430-5

978-0-470-51737-6

978-0-470-71401-0

HISTORY

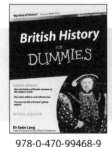
978-0-470-99468-9

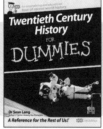
978-0-470-51015-5

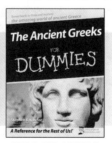
978-0-470-98787-2

Inventing For Dummies
978-0-470-51996-7

Job Hunting and Career Change
All-In-One For Dummies
978-0-470-51611-9

Motivation For Dummies
978-0-470-76035-2

Origami Kit For Dummies
978-0-470-75857-1

Personal Development All-In-One
For Dummies
978-0-470-51501-3

PRINCE2 For Dummies
978-0-470-51919-6

Psychometric Tests For Dummies
978-0-470-75366-8

Raising Happy Children For
Dummies
978-0-470-05978-4

Starting and Running a Business
All-in-One For Dummies
978-0-470-51648-5

Sudoku for Dummies
978-0-470-01892-7

The British Citizenship Test
For Dummies, 2nd Edition
978-0-470-72339-5

Time Management For Dummies
978-0-470-77765-7

Wills, Probate, & Inheritance Tax
For Dummies, 2nd Edition
978-0-470-75629-4

Winning on Betfair For Dummies,
2nd Edition
978-0-470-72336-4

FOR DUMMIES®

The easy way to get more done and have more fun

LANGUAGES

978-0-7645-5194-9

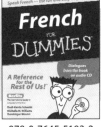
978-0-7645-5193-2

978-0-471-77270-5

MUSIC

978-0-7645-9904-0

978-0-470-03275-6
UK Edition

978-0-7645-5105-5

SCIENCE & MATHS

978-0-7645-5326-4

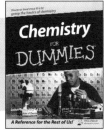
978-0-7645-5430-8

978-0-7645-5325-7

Art For Dummies
978-0-7645-5104-8

Baby & Toddler Sleep Solutions For Dummies
978-0-470-11794-1

Bass Guitar For Dummies
978-0-7645-2487-5

Brain Games For Dummies
978-0-470-37378-1

Christ For Dummies
978-0- 4482-8

Filmm for Dummies, 2nd Edition
978-0-4 4-1

Forensic mmies
978-0-76 -0

German nies
978-0-76

Hobby Fa nmies
978-0-470

Jewelry Mak Reading For Dummies
978-0-7645-2571-1

Knitting for Dummies, 2nd Edition
978-0-470-28747-7

Music Composition For Dummies
978-0-470-22421-2

Physics For Dummies
978-0-7645-5433-9

Sex For Dummies, 3rd Edition
978-0-470-04523-7

Solar Power Your Home For Dummies
978-0-470-17569-9

Tennis For Dummies
978-0-7645-5087-4

The Koran For Dummies
978-0-7645-5581-7

U.S. History For Dummies
978-0-7645-5249-6

Wine For Dummies, 4th Edition
978-0-470-04579-4

13902_p3

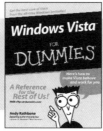

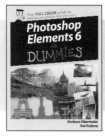